D0854959

DATE DUE

NEW BOOK	
DEC 0 4 1997	
MAR 0 4 1998	
1-3-08 OCLC	
5-19-14	

BRODART, CO. Cat. No. 23-221-003

Dust Bowl

Migrants in

the American

Imagination

Rural America

Hal S. Barron
David L. Brown
Kathleen Neils Conzen
Carville Earle
Cornelia Butler Flora
Donald Worster

SERIES EDITORS

Dust Bowl

Migrants in

the American

Imagination

Charles J. Shindo

University Press of Kansas

Published by the University
Press of Kansas (Lawrence,
Kansas 66049), which was
organized by the Kansas
Board of Regents and is
operated and funded by
Emporia State University,
Fort Hays State University,
Kansas State University,
Pittsburg State University,
the University of Kansas,
and Wichita State University

British Library Cataloguing
in Publication Data is
available.

Library of Congress
Cataloging-in-Publication Data
Shindo, Charles J.
    Dust bowl migrants in the American
imagination / Charles J. Shindo.
        p.   cm. — (Rural America)
    Includes bibliographical references and index.
    ISBN 0-7006-0810-9 (alk. paper)
    1. Migrant agricultural laborers in art.
2. Arts, American.   3. Arts, Modern—20th
century—United States.   4. Migrant
agricultural laborers—United States—History.
5. Depressions—1929—United States.
6. Great Plains—Rural conditions.
7. California—Rural conditions.   8. Dust
storms—Great Plains.   9. Labor
camps—California.   10. Droughts—Great
Plains.   I. Title.   II. Series.
NX650.L32S53   1996
700′.1′030973—dc20   96-32301

Printed in the United States
of America

10 9 8 7 6 5 4 3 2 1

The paper used in this
publication meets the
minimum requirements of
the American National
Standard for Permanence of
Paper for Printed Library
Materials Z39.48-1984.

Text design by Melinda Wirkus

TO MY PARENTS

George and May Shindo

Every fury on earth has been absorbed in time, as art, or as religion, or as authority in one form or another.

—James Agee

CONTENTS

ACKNOWLEDGMENTS

This project began years ago as a seminar paper, and through the guidance of skilled teachers and the assistance of helpful archivists and librarians, patient friends, knowledgeable colleagues, and kind editors, I can now present this imperfect work with few regrets. I would like to thank the following people and institutions for their financial, intellectual, and moral support throughout this project.

The Department of History at the University of Rochester, the Faculty Research Fund at Hampshire College, and the Council on Research at Louisiana State University provided financial support for the various stages of research necessary to complete the project. The Five College Fellowship for Minority Scholars Program, Hampshire College, the Frank Stanley Beveridge Foundation, and the University of Rochester provided funding during the writing stages of the manuscript.

Many institutions provided the research resources necessary for this project; I especially would like to thank the Bancroft Library at the University of California, Berkeley; the National Archives and Records Administration Center in San Bruno, California; the Oakland Museum Art Library; the Margaret Herrick Library of the Academy of Motion Picture Arts and Sciences; the Woody Guthrie Archives; and the Archive of Folk Culture at the Library of Congress.

Intellectual assistance has come in many forms from many people. At the University of Rochester, with the help of the participants in History 482: Topics in American Cultural History, I developed this project and presented it for the critique of the class. Chris Lehmann carefully read and commented on the first rendering of this work. In Amherst, the Five Colleges staff (especially Lorna Petersen and Carol Angus), committee (especially Robert Rakoff), fellows (especially Gerard Fergerson), and the Hampshire College community (especially Sue Darlington, Julie Weiss, Aaron Berman, Susan Tracy, and Mitziko Sawada) provided me with a perfect environment of intellectual stimulation and support. In addition, I would like to thank Catherine Stock for her valuable insights.

My classmates at Rochester have consistently provided me with support and friendship. Dean Kernan, Elyse Small, Monte Bohna, Ben and Marilyn Woelk, Rosemary Finn, and Jim Perkins provided encouragement, as did Mary Chalmers, who read and commented on my dissertation. Rex Palmer read, commented on, and discussed at length with me the merits and faults of each chapter. Ian Gordon proved to be not only a fine sounding board and editor throughout the process but also the best "friendly competitor" one could have.

My colleagues in the Department of History at Louisiana State University, where I have had the good fortune to land, have given me their encouragement and support. In particular, Paul Paskoff, Victor Stater, and Christine Kooi have provided the moral support and diversionary company necessary to complete this project. Gaines Foster provided much-needed advice on revisions, as did Randy Rogers for the introduction. I am especially indebted to all who assisted me in the search for a proper title to this manuscript and to Tony Gaughan for his assistance in securing photographs. Burl Noggle not only lent his vast knowledge and advice but provided enough enthusiam to support a small army.

I have also had the good fortune to find my way to the University Press of Kansas, where everyone I have encountered has been pleasant, helpful, encouraging, and concerned for my work. I am particularly grateful to Michael Briggs for enthusiastically guiding me through the world of publishing and for sharing my concerns and interests.

The late Christopher Lasch provided a much-needed stylistic scrutiny of my dissertation, in addition to his usual incisive observations and his well-timed words of encouragement. My greatest regret is that I never adequately thanked him for the support and knowledge he gave to me.

For the last nine years Robert Westbrook has provided me with the direction and guidance necessary to undertake and complete this project while allowing me to find my own particular niche in life. His delight in my triumphs is matched only by the role he played in their making. He has taught me what I know, shown me what to do with that knowledge, and supported my attempts to add to that knowledge. Any success I may encounter, I owe to him.

Most important, my family has, without questioning, given their time, financial support, encouragement, and love to me. It is because of them that I have accomplished anything.

ILLUSTRATIONS

The Grapes of Wrath, 118

Woody Guthrie, 132

The Okies were not the cause, but the focus, of a number of problems confronting the state, problems over which they had little or no control. They intruded upon an agricultural system that contravened every myth in the Jeffersonian pantheon, and they served as unwitting publicists for those who found California's agriculture and its social effects unsound. They aggravated social and economic dislocations evoked by the depression and became pawns in deadly conflicts that arose from hard times.—Walter J. Stein

DISPLACED VOICES

The Migrants as

American Victims

In *California and the Dust Bowl Migration,* Walter J. Stein[1] argues that a small minority of the migrants to California during the depression became the center of political controversy because they best represented the underlying problems of California agriculture, the need for a steady supply of migrant farm labor. The situation in which the dust bowl migrants found themselves was not of their making, nor a situation they entered into by choice; rather, the migrants left their respective states with few options other than following the crops of California in hopes of finding some future stability.

The "dust bowl migration" not only refers to those Americans leaving the dust bowl of the Great Plains for California but includes many who were outside the region affected by the dust storms. This migration included those who left farms or agricultural jobs as well as urban dwellers who came to California during the depression. The group commonly referred to as "migrants," "Okies," "migrant agricultural laborer/farmworkers," "dust bowl refugees," and various combinations thereof, does not refer to all migrants entering California during the Great Depression; it denotes those migrants from the southwestern United States—especially the states of Oklahoma, Arkansas, Missouri, and Texas—who became migratory farm laborers in California. Migrant has the dual meaning of migrant to California and migrant within California. Only about one-third of the over one million migrants to California during the 1930s could be considered "dust bowl migrants."[2]

As white, Christian, native-born Americans, the migrants presented to California agriculture a more threatening image of the inequality and injustice of the agricultural economy than had previous Asian or Hispanic migrant labor populations. Challenged by the presence of these white migrants, the political debate over the structure of California agriculture and the need for government-sponsored relief efforts found federal support in the national agricultural programs of Franklin Roosevelt's New Deal.

The migrants served as catalysts of political debate and, through a process of cultural appropriation by well-meaning reformers, also became symbols—"unwitting publicists" of the problems of the Great Depression. They were also unwilling publicists in that the reformers, photographers, writers, filmmakers, songwriters, and folklorists who presented the migrants' story did so to further their own agendas rather than the goals of the migrants.

The appropriation of the migrant experience by government reformers and various artists created a public image of the migrant that remains pervasive today. The haunting despair of Dorothea Lange's photograph *Migrant Mother* (1936), the powerful story of Tom Joad and family presented by John Steinbeck in the novel *The Grapes of Wrath* (1939) and by John Ford in the film *The Grapes of Wrath* (1940), and the lyrical demands of Woody Guthrie's *Dust Bowl Ballads* (1940) have combined to present a portrait of dust bowl migrants as the quintessential depression victims and, as such, the key to solving the problems of the depression. Themselves displaced by circumstances, the dust bowl migrants found their voices displaced by the voices of these artists and reformers.

How is it that the events of a few years during the Great Depression, involving only a small portion of the region's population, could have had such a lasting impact on the American imagination? Images and descriptions of the dust bowl migrants proliferated in literature, music, newspapers, magazines, photo collections, films, and onstage. The dust bowl migration to California evokes the Great Depression perhaps more than any other event of the 1930s, not only because of its pervasiveness but because of its representational possibilities. Written portraits of the dust bowl migrants, worried and harassed, have come to symbolize the emotional loss, as well as the political and economic turmoil, created by the Great Depression. A description of the migrants in the April 1939 issue of *Fortune* magazine is typical in presenting the migrants and their sense of loss:

The migrants are familiar enough to anyone who has traveled much through California's interior. On the roads, where you can see them in numbers, they take on a kind of patchwork pattern. They come along in wheezy old cars with the father or one of the older boys driving. The mother and the younger children sit in back; and around them, crammed inside and overflowing to the running boards, the front and rear bumpers, the top and sides, they carry along everything they own. A galvanized iron washtub is tied to the rear, a dirty, patched tent is lashed to a fender. . . . You notice the faces of the people in these cars. There is worry, but also something more: they are the faces of people afraid of hunger; completely dispossessed, certain only of being harried along when their immediate usefulness is over.[3]

Written descriptions of the migrant experience were powerfully reinforced by the visual images presented by such photographers as Dorothea Lange in photographs like *Migrant Mother.* Lange and her husband, University of California economist Paul Taylor, collaborated on a study of the dust bowl migration entitled *An American Exodus: A Record of Human Erosion* (1939), in which Taylor added economic and academic clout to Lange's evocative photographs. Books such as Carey McWilliams's *Factories in the Field* (1939) gave further notoriety to the "migrant problem." The publication of John Steinbeck's *Grapes of Wrath* in 1939 sparked a national controversy over the causes of the migrant situation, prompting a March 1940 edition of the radio program *America's Town Meeting of the Air* to pose the question "What Should America Do for the Joads?" That same year John Ford's film version of *The Grapes of Wrath* brought to the screen many of the prevalent stories and images. Woody Guthrie featured a song used in the film, "Going Down the Road Feeling Bad," on his *Dust Bowl Ballads,* a record album consisting of folk songs about the dust bowl migration.

In each of these documents, the writer or artist placed the migrants in the position of victim, presenting an image filled with sympathy toward the displaced and oppressed. The degree to which characters reacted to their circumstances varies with each document, but the idea of victimization is constant. This collective image is based on the irony of a democratic society filled with victims. Each of these documents tells of the inhuman treatment and exploitation of Americans and their families. Poverty amid wealth, want amid plenty, and hope amid despair unite these dust bowl–era documents and create the pervasive image of the migrants that persists today. Each of the documents universalized the migrant experience, each in its own way, leading to the appropriation of the populist values, traditions, and concerns of the Okie migrants by well-meaning reformers and artists. These documents collectively created a lasting impression of the dust bowl migrants as victims of circumstance and victors against hardship.

These cultural representations of the dust bowl migrants are grounded in the belief that they were perhaps California's last great hope for social, political, and economic equality. Assuming that the migrants' plight, as an expression of industrial capitalism's inherent inequality, required a radical social democratic response, these documents seek to foster or describe the inherent democratic nature of the migrant. A preliminary look into Okie culture shows that the migrants sought and achieved ends that were far from radical. What they sought was not the social democratic ideal presented by these representations; instead, they tried to recreate an idealized past as expressed in their staunch defense of traditional values.

These migrants distinguished themselves through the formation of a subculture in California. James Gregory, in his book *American Exodus: The Dust Bowl Migration and Okie Culture in California,* defines Okie culture as a set of traits shared by white migratory agricultural workers from the Southwest. Gregory gave the name "plain-folk Americanism" to the traditional ideas maintained by the migrants in their move to California that set them apart from the dominant California culture they encountered.

> Southwestern plain folk claimed a set of social and political commitments that had once flourished widely in nineteenth-century America. Heirs to antimonopoly and citizen-producer ideas that in earlier periods had guided both agrarian and working-class radicalism, they stood also in the shadow of generations of white Protestants who had fought to preserve the Republic's ethnic and religious integrity.[4]

The migrants' belief that landownership fostered a desirable morality based on the traditional ideas of independence, family, and God clashed with reformers' efforts to proletarianize the migrants.

The migrants never became a rural proletariat. Instead they became part of the conservative movement that elected Ronald Reagan governor of California in 1966 and 1970.[5] In *Rising in the West* Dan Morgan illustrates this continuum by following the Tatham family from depression-era eastern Oklahoma to California's central valley in the 1980s. Morgan relates the story of a family who traveled the same roads as Steinbeck's fictional Joads, but the similarities between the two families seem to end with geography. Like Gregory, Morgan found the migrants to be fiercely independent, religious, and conservative, more often on the side of employers (as strikebreakers) than workers.[6] For Morgan, the dust bowl migration was the link between the Old South and the New West—not the

New West of Upton Sinclair and radical politics but the New West of conservative Republicanism and fundamental televangelism.

This image of the migrants as conservative guardians of traditional values conflicts with the image presented in *The Grapes of Wrath* (both the novel and the film), in Farm Security Administration (FSA) photographs, and Woody Guthrie's *Dust Bowl Ballads*. This conflict leads to an examination of the differences between the migrants' own expressions of their situation and cultural representations of the migrant experience, in which a mix of conflicting yet mutually reinforcing voices each seeks authenticity and authority. Lange, Steinbeck, Ford, and Guthrie could each claim some measure of authenticity or expertise in representing the migrants. Lange sought reinforcement through her fieldwork and government affiliation; Steinbeck did so through his observation of the migrants and as a native Californian; Ford identified himself with the migrants, who seemed similar to his Irish ancestors; Guthrie was an Okie migrant himself, though not a migrant laborer. Each developed a different view of the migrants' situation and ways of remedying it based on their beliefs about American democracy.

The basic conflict in beliefs is seen in the difference between the democratic aims of the government reformers and the democratic ideals of the migrants, a difference expressed in the clashes between the migrants and the camp managers at several of the government-operated migrant camps. The reformers' goal of a social democratic migrant workforce required the transformation of the migrants' position in the political economy from independent producer to rural proletariat. This transformation meant the destruction of the migrants' culture, firmly embedded in a politically conservative and economically liberal ideology based on the idea of landownership, and even though the migrants' conditions did not allow the maintenance of their culture materially, it persisted ideologically. The "plain-folk Americanism" of the migrants ran counter to the paternalistic reforms of the New Deal.

Dorothea Lange, herself one of these reformers working for the government, used her skill in and approach to documentary photography to further the goals of the government. Lange's belief that photography, used humanely and with passion, could help ameliorate the devastating effects of agricultural mechanization led her to develop a new form of documentary presentation in collaboration with her husband, economist Paul Taylor, also a government reformer. The result of their efforts, *An American Exodus: A Record of Human Erosion*, describes the ill effects of mechanization on American rural life. Lange's desire to show the migrants as victims worthy of government assistance and political support is best represented in the photograph *Migrant Mother,* in which a nameless mother tries to protect her children from the uncertainty of life in depression America.

John Steinbeck also aligned himself with the goals of the government reformers and depended on them to authenticate his identification as an Okie spokesman. Steinbeck's beliefs in the perfectibility of man, and literature's role in attaining this perfectibility, informed his representation of the migrant experience in *The Grapes of Wrath.* The elitist nature of literature, combined with Steinbeck's view of the migrants as backward and uneducated, resulted in a book that distanced itself from the migrants and supported reforms inconsistent with the migrants' own desires. For Steinbeck, as for Lange and Taylor, the migrants needed to be educated into a democratic America.

John Ford's film version of *The Grapes of Wrath* differed from Steinbeck's interpretation because of Ford's peculiar notions of a democratic America and the film industry's function as a business. Ford's faith in traditional values, evident in his other films, led him to favor the familial and spiritual aspects of Steinbeck's narrative, while the Hollywood tendency toward happy endings reinforced Ford's notions about the persistence of traditional values. The generalizing nature of film (its ability to communicate through images) and Ford's own tendency to simplify events for the sake of a good story made it possible for the migrants to understand and accept the film as other Americans understood and accepted it. As such, the film version of *The Grapes of Wrath* best represents the migrants, despite criticisms that it is the least authentic of the dust bowl documents. The desires and aspirations of the film's characters, however, were the common concerns of American people and not the specific concerns of the migrants. For Ford, the migrants were at the center of "the people" and therefore the foundation for his democratic America.

Woody Guthrie also placed the migrants at the center of his vision of a democratic America, but, unlike Ford, his vision lay in the future and not in the past. Guthrie sought to sustain the traditional morality of Okie culture by transforming the migrants' political and economic condition. Through the office of folksinger, Guthrie spoke on behalf of the Okie migrants, yet his unique rendering of the political economy distanced him from the migrants' self-expressed desires. Guthrie's *Dust Bowl Ballads* illustrate his attempts to seek reform and to politically educate the migrants through the traditional form of the folk song. Exhibiting the most direct relationship to the migrants' culture of any "expert," Guthrie nonetheless failed to realize the degree to which the migrants' culture contained a political and economic ideology different from his own.

Closely aligned with Guthrie, such folklorists as John and Alan Lomax, Charles

Todd, and Robert Sonkin sought to demonstrate the democratic nature of the migrants by placing them in an American folk tradition reinforced by Frederick Jackson Turner's frontier thesis. Todd and Sonkin collected folk songs in the California migrant camps and used these recordings to publicize the migrants' plight. In representing the migrants, Todd and Sonkin focused on the traditional aspects of the folk song form as an indication of the migrants' inherent American character. Yet, in so doing, they obscured the traditional and populist elements of Okie culture in favor of a liberal and progressive interpretation of the migrants' aspirations. Failing to see the place of the folk song and the newly emerging country music in the migrants' life, Todd and Sonkin ridiculed and rejected those aspects of Okie culture that were most important in the migrants' adjustment to their new surroundings and situation. Like the government reformers, the folklorists sought to represent a migrant that did not exist.

The appropriation of the dust bowl migrant experience by Lange, Steinbeck, Ford, and Guthrie, as well as by government reformers and folklorists, speaks more directly about the specific intentions of each of these people—intentions based on the various intellectual and ethical beliefs of each artist and reformer—than about the actual needs and desires of the migrant population itself. These beliefs are evident in ideas about the migrants' place in the democratic society held by each expert. The migrants' relationship to the envisioned democracy, the degree to which they are included or excluded, depended on the artist's attitude toward the migrants' culture. An understanding of and respect for the migrants' culture placed the migrants and their values prominently in the ideal democratic society, while a view of the migrants' culture as "underdeveloped" positioned the migrant far away from the center and sought to "develop" the cultural values of the migrants toward the ideal.

Lange's belief that increased mechanization needed to be tempered with humanity and passion led her to view the migrants as victims of technological progress and worthy of institutional assistance. In attempting to remedy the dislocating effects of agribusiness and mechanized farming, Lange discounted the migrants' own concerns of independence and desire for economic self-sufficiency. For Lange the rational, yet humane, solution to the migrants' situation was in the creation of an empowered agricultural proletariat. Viewing social processes in mechanical terms, Lange believed that passionate assistance would effectively transform the migrants into proletarians, yet she ultimately failed to perceive the migrants' humanity.

Steinbeck's belief in human perfection led him to seek a democracy based in the rational (equal) distribution of material wealth and civil rights. His belief in the perfectibility of man led him to characterize the migrants as underdeveloped, not aware of their democratic potential. By viewing elements in Okie culture such as religion and tradition as signs of Okie irrationality, Steinbeck treated these elements as detrimental and expendable through education. His disregard for Okie culture led him to advocate a series of reforms created to educate the migrant into a rational democratic order.

John Ford's belief that an inherent democratic character resided within "the people" led him to advocate a democratic America based on many of the same traditional values prevalent in Okie culture: God, family, and liberty. Ford respected these elements of Okie culture because they were not unique to the migrant experience. For Ford the struggles of dust bowl migrants represented his mythic ideal: the education of one man's family into the family of man or, in political terms, the development of frontier democracy. He spoke on behalf of the migrants not in the name of political and economic reform, as Lange and Steinbeck did, but in the name of cultural preservation.

Like Lange and Steinbeck, Woody Guthrie spoke on behalf of the migrants in the name of political and economic reform, but unlike Lange or Steinbeck, Guthrie spoke in the language of cultural tradition. Separating the culture of the migrants from their place in the political economy, Guthrie's belief in radical political change led to a characterization of the migrants as proud workers in a class struggle. In separating the cultural conservatism of the migrants from their political and economic conservatism, in the name of political and economic reform, Guthrie failed to see the migrants' desire not to eliminate the struggle between the classes but simply to switch to the winning side.

While each of the documents examined here sought a different solution to the migrants' problems, they each described the migrants' plight in the same way. Each saw the migrant as a victim—of advanced industrial capitalism, natural disaster, and the machinations of heartless businessmen. It is this representation of the migrant as downtrodden and forgotten that is at the center of their persistent image. Each of these documents sought to awaken sympathy for the migrants' challenge to their victimization. Though each document assessed the migrants' ability to overcome their victimization differently, each saw the migrants achieving some measure of success. Ironically, the success of the migrants in escaping their victimization was the result of historical circumstance (the growth of California's war production industries during World War II) and not the reforms advocated by these documents. The migrant camp program did alleviate some of the symptoms of the migrants' situation but ultimately did not relieve the causes of the problem. Once the migrants became economically assimilated into California through the war industries, concern for migrant agricultural laborers decreased, and even though the adverse conditions of migrant labor persist to this day, efforts at relief have never equaled the efforts of the FSA and the New Deal.

The dust bowl migrants, as white, rural Americans, illustrated most effectively the disparities of wealth and power in depression America. The irony of white, native-born, Christian farm families being discriminated against and ridiculed, made homeless and penniless, spoke most directly to the tensions felt by the world's richest nation in the midst of the Great Depression. Because each of these documents celebrated the ability of the migrants to persevere through hardship, the migrants have become, in essence, ideal representative victims battling against injustice. In other words, the migrants (as helpless, yet persistent, Americans) fought injustice wherever they found it. In each of the documents the determination of what was just and unjust was made not by the migrants themselves but by the artist who used the migrants as his or her protagonists in search of justice. In each of these representations the migrants became representatives of each artists' specific concerns while maintaining the image of the American victim. The religious element of Okie culture evoked by Lange's *Migrant Mother* mirrored Ford and Guthrie's view that religious faith was instrumental in remedying the problems of migrant labor, while Steinbeck saw the migrants' religious faith as detrimental to their situation. These conflicting views of religion in Okie culture do not detract from the fact that in all these documents the migrants were American victims deserving of justice. The nonspecific nature of this theme has made it possible for the story of the dust bowl migrants to represent different interpretations of American social, political, economic, and cultural life while at the same time representing the enduring, justice-seeking nature of Americans.

Despite the pervasiveness of the idea of victimization in the popular imagination, the dust bowl migrants were not the "voiceless" victims of uncontrollable forces. The migrants described by James Gregory in his study of Okie culture created their own subculture in California "based on values and institutions brought from their region of birth."[7] The creation of this subculture by the migrants expressed their individualistic nature and their desire to retain those values and customs they did not find in modern California society. By distinguishing themselves in their religion, political beliefs, and even their music, the migrants rejected the role of depression victims in need of leadership and guidance; therefore, they did not passively accept the direction of government reformers, nor did they neatly fit the characterizations of them by Lange, Steinbeck, Ford, and Guthrie, who sympathized with and supported the government's efforts to assist the migrants.

These reformers and artists also relied on the authority of one another to bring authenticity to their representation of the migrant as victim. By claiming the authority of expert or authentic witness, these reformers and artists excluded the migrants' own voice from being heard; therefore, they were able to create an image of the migrants that represented all the problems of depression America and not just the problems of dust bowl migrants. A migrant as victim is a migrant out of context. Describing how the creation of a migrant as victim came into being is the aim of this study.

Exploring fully the historical context and the individual artistic contexts of each of these documents and figures provides the basis for analysis. A critical examination of Lange's photographs (within the context of a developing documentary tradition and New Deal reform programs), of Steinbeck's writings (within the context of his intellectual development and philosophy), of Ford's films (within the context of Hollywood filmmaking and the development of Ford's own personal style), and of Guthrie's music (within the context of Okie culture and radical political activism) as cultural documents is crucial in understanding the United States during the Great Depression. The voices surrounding the dust bowl migration did not all speak about the same thing, nor did they speak in the same language; indeed, some of the voices have persisted longer and have had a greater impact on our view of American history. To understand why the voices of Dorothea Lange, John Steinbeck, John Ford, and Woody Guthrie have dominated our understanding of the Okie migrant, we must listen to each voice in turn.

1

Soon after the community had attracted sufficient families it became evident to them, as to our forefathers, that to survive machinery would have to be set up to govern and guide the lives of the community residents. A meeting was called. That first meeting was reminiscent of our early Town Hall gatherings. A committee was elected to go into deliberation, to consider what type of government machinery would work best and to draft a constitution. Do you think it strange that these American Citizens drafted and adopted a Constitution, patterning the governmental machinery after that of the United States?—M. P. Bruick, community manager, Tulare Farm Workers' Community

In the old days of our republic, patriotism was unanimous among our forefathers. Today, the mass of Americans had rather mind their own business. Can you feature why? In those days the people were bound together by a common bond: Love of God, love of family, love of liberty.

... Let is [*sic*] hold to the ideals of Democracy set up by the constitution of the U.S.A. Patriotism of this sort is advocated by all true *Americans*.—S. K. Blackmon, migrant laborer, Tulare Farm Workers' Community

THE IDEALS OF

AMERICAN DEMOCRACY

New Deal Reformers

and the Migrant

Each of these quotes from *The Hub,* the weekly newsletter of the Tulare Farm Workers' Community, illustrates its author's concern for the ideals of the Constitution of the United States and the ideals of American democracy.[1] But are they talking about the same thing? The community manager looked forward to the democratic potential of the Okies, which he saw as continuous with the past. But many of the migrants, like Mr. Blackmon, looked back at the traditional elements of a democracy lost, if it had existed at all. They saw their present situation as discontinuous with what they perceived their past to be. It is this basic opposition of "forward"-looking reformers and "backward"-looking migrants that was at the heart of the unsuccessful efforts of the government to create, in the words of Carey McWilliams, "a new rural social order in California."[2]

The idea of creating this new social order had its genesis prior to the dust bowl migration of the Great Depression. Since the beginnings of agriculture in California, various groups sought solutions to the "labor problem." Large growers sought to maintain a stable but temporary army of workers to labor in the fields during peak periods of the season, while state administrators sought to reduce the numbers of unemployed farmworkers on the relief rolls. Early in the history of California, agricultural growers found the answer in the recruitment of foreign labor, first Chinese, then Japanese, Hindu, Filipino, and Mexican workers. It was not until the combination of economic depression, climatic changes, government policy, and traditional farming techniques (sharecropping, land tenancy) created a migration of American native-stock southwesterners from Oklahoma, Texas, Arkansas, and Missouri that white workers predominated in California's fields. With the arrival of the white farmworkers, who, unlike their predecessors, traveled in family groups, came scrutiny of the conditions of farm labor in the California agribusiness system.

Throughout the 1930s, academics, community groups, chambers of commerce, and others widely discussed the migrant problem in speeches, conferences, newspapers, and radio broadcasts. Some proposed to solve this problem by giving land to each of these families in order to create a class of yeoman farmers, or by supporting government subsidy of farm labor housing under the control of the growers who employed the farmworkers. What was unique about all these proposals was the desire not only to produce relief for the migrant workers but also to stabilize them as a group, whether as an agricultural proletariat or a landholding citizenry. Efforts at solving the migrant problem inevitably ended in a discussion of what kind of social order California, and by extension the rest of the nation, should have and how it should be created.

In order to develop their envisioned social order, government administrators (through three successive organizations: the State Emergency Relief Administration, the Resettlement Administration, and the Farm Security Administration) sought both to supply the migrants with minimum standards of housing and sanitation and to create self-governing democratic citizens out of what they saw as backward and uneducated rural bumpkins. Their goals and aspirations for the migrants were often at odds with the migrants' own goals and aspirations. The cross-purposes of migrant and government underlie the pervasive and one-sided image of the Okie migrant that is at the center of this study.

The development of agriculture in California is not the typical story of rural life in the United States. Farming in California did not start out as a series of individual homesteads joined by a village or town as it did in much of the country. The Jeffersonian vision of the yeoman farmer/citizen—ruggedly independent yet an inextricable part of the whole—predominated in the West, ideally more than in reality. "California," however, according to Cletus E. Daniel, "with nearly a century of development under successive Spanish and Mexican colonial administrations behind it, entered the Union in 1848 to be Americanized rather than civilized."[3] Americanization in the mid–nineteenth century consisted of changes in national allegiance and economic transformations resulting from industrialization. The agrarian ideal of small landholders and homesteaders did not materialize in California.

From the earliest days as a state, most of California's land was privately held. Before statehood, the Mexican government granted large tracts of California land to its citizens, and these remained intact, for the most part, once California became a possession of the United States. The gold rush of 1849, California's admission as a state in 1850, and the completion of the transcontinental railroad in 1869 encouraged population growth and agricultural production for local markets and those accessible by rail. As small family farmers moved to California looking for homesteads in the Golden State, many found there simply was not any available land on which to settle. Some settled on privately owned land for which they were charged rent, which increased considerably once they had improved the land. Much of the land was not parceled out and sold but rather maintained in large tracts. Carey McWilliams points out that "these vast feudal holdings, which should have been purchased by the Government and held as part of the public domain, were never disrupted." This pattern of large holdings, according to McWilliams, "has had important social consequences in California."[4] In addition to the pattern of ownership established by the Mexican land grants, the government granted large tracts of the public domain to railroad companies as alternate sections of government land along the rights-of-way of railroad lines. By 1870 railroad companies held approximately twenty million acres in California.[5] Vague and easily corruptible land laws furthered the ambitions of the large landholders, who speculated in land to the detriment of settlers. All these factors led Henry George to comment in 1871 that "California is not a country of farms, but a country of plantations and estates. Agriculture is a speculation."[6]

Because agriculture was a speculative business, it naturally fell to entrepreneurs, rather than family farmers, to develop California's agricultural economy. Large amounts of capital were needed to work a California farm, due to necessary improvements such as irrigation, roads, and distribution transportation. These factors led to a boom mentality among California growers. Wheat was the first bonanza cash crop to be exploited in California, with wheat production skyrocketing from six million bushels in 1860 to over sixteen million bushels by 1870.[7] The production of agricultural commodities on a large scale, due to landownership patterns and the use of machinery, was perhaps the greatest legacy of the wheat bonanza era. Experimentation with exotic crops, such as grapes, started during the 1850s and led to the diversity of crops found in California during the early twentieth century. Besides a variety of grapes, deciduous fruits such as apples, peaches, pears, plums, and cherries appeared on the California landscape, along with walnuts, almonds, and olives.

The production of citrus fruits in the warmer climate of southern California did not develop until the subdivision of large ranches made land available and irrigation provided the water necessary to cultivate the semiarid region. The population of southern California grew more slowly than that of the north; likewise, transportation lines appeared in the north before the south. By 1870, however, approximately forty-five thousand orange and lemon trees bore fruit in southern California.[8] From 1870 to the start of the Great Depression, land cultivated in tree crops or vines increased from around one hundred thousand acres to over two million acres.[9] In the 1880s and 1890s the introduction of sugar beets helped a sagging fruit market, and in the post–World War I era, cotton stimulated declining prices in California agriculture. By the time of the Wall Street crash and the great dust storms on the central plains in the 1930s, California agriculture consisted of a wide array of products, with a long growing season that lasted from early spring to late fall.

Along with the intensive production of a diverse agricultural economy, California agribusiness developed the need for a corps of agricultural laborers to provide the intensive and seasonal work necessary to harvest the state's crops. In the early stages of California agriculture, native Californian Indians worked the missions and pueblos of the Spanish and later the Mexican churches and governments. This practice continued until the completion of the transcontinental railroad in 1869 released a number of Chinese workers who had been imported to build the railroad. These Chinese laborers worked the large farms during the harvest season and then congregated in urban centers, mainly San Francisco, during the off-season. Animosity toward the Chinese led to the adoption of the Chinese Exclusion Act of 1882 and the anti-Chinese riots in 1893, both of which curtailed this source of labor.

It was not until the introduction of sugar beet farming that growers imported Japanese labor to California on an organized basis. In the 1890s the development of the sugar beet industry along the lines of Hawaii's sugar industry led growers to import Japanese labor to fulfill the specific requirements of beet growing, mainly the intensive handwork of thinning and harvesting the beets. By 1903, Japanese laborers held the predominant place in California's agricultural workforce:

> As laborers, they [the Japanese] occupied a dominant position in most of the intensive, specialized agriculture, which at the time produced about half of the entire amount of agricultural products marketed. Their position thus was substantially the same as that of the Chinese except that the sector of agriculture which they occupied had grown to be very much more important than it had been at the time of the Chinese.[10]

Yet, once again, anti-Asian sentiment prevailed in California, and in 1913 the State of California enacted the Alien Land Act, which forbade aliens not eligible for citizenship, mainly Asians, from owning property. This act, along with federal restrictions on Japanese immigration in 1924, further curtailed the use of Asian labor in the fields.

Growers exploited other groups as farm labor—Hindus, Armenians, and other eastern Europeans—but the next important influx of foreign labor came from Mexico, starting around World War I. By 1920 farm journals noted that over 50 percent of the farmworkers in the state were Mexican.[11] Like earlier farm labor groups, the Mexicans followed the harvests and either "hibernated" during the winter, mostly in the urban barrios of Los Angeles and San Diego, or returned to Mexico until the following season.[12] For this reason, growers found Mexican workers a cheap source of labor, until threatened restrictions on

Mexican immigration forced growers to look to the Philippine Islands for farm laborers. Together Mexican and Filipino workers constituted the majority of the field labor force in the 1920s, and they used their dominant position to strike for higher wages and union recognition. Growers upset over labor troubles searched for other groups of workers to break their dependence on Mexican and Filipino labor. With increasing unemployment in the cities and other parts of the United States, growers found themselves with an oversupply of labor, while the state and federal governments found themselves with increasing relief roles. Both groups saw the solution to their respective problems in the repatriation of Mexican and Filipino workers.[13] With this expulsion of foreign labor, the era of the dust bowl migrant began.

The migration of white American southwesterners to California did not begin during the Great Depression, but the characteristics of the migrant population during the depression were markedly different from those of previous migrations. Before 1930, migration rested on the "pull" of California's mild weather and economic opportunities. Migrants to California consisted of those who were looking to make a new start and had the resources to do it.[14] Southwesterners constituted a substantial part of this predepression migration. During the Great Depression, however, migration to California rested on the "push" of agricultural modernization, failing crops, foreclosures, and economic depression that hit farmers in the southwestern and southern states.[15] Or, as one migrant put it, they were "blown out."[16]

Although this depression-era migration is most commonly refered to as the "dust bowl migration," the phrase is actually a misnomer. The majority of the dust bowl migrants were not actually from the areas of the country affected by the great dust storms of the early and mid-1930s. According to Gregory, "Confusing drought with dust, and assuming that the dramatic dust storms must have had something to do with the large number of cars from Oklahoma and Texas seen crossing the California border in the mid-1930s, the press created the dramatic but misleading association between the Dust Bowl and the Southwestern migration."[17]

Statistics on the dust bowl migration show that it consisted mainly of people from cities and towns, with only 43 percent of the migrant population identified as farmers. These percentages roughly mirror the characteristics of the nonmigrating population of the Southwest. Differences between those who left and those who stayed can be seen in the occupations of those from urban areas. Blue-collar workers left in large numbers, while white-collar workers, for the most part, stayed behind. In agriculture, tenants migrated in greater percentages than did farm owners. Ninety-five percent of the migrants were white (most blacks leaving the South and Southwest preferring to move north), and for the most part they were young, under the age of thirty-five. The educational level of the migrants was, on the whole, higher than that of those who stayed in the Southwest. Just over half (53 percent) were male, a low figure for migrant or immigrant populations; the majority came in families, not as individuals. The average migrant family consisted of 4.4 members, while the average Californian family had only 3.9 members.[18]

James Gregory has noted that the pattern of migration to California rested in family and community ties. Most newly arrived migrants settled near or joined other family or community members already in California, and in this sense the migration was similar to other migratory patterns in the United States. Gregory writes, "All this suggests that the Dust Bowl migration was not an atomistic dispersion of solitary families but a guided chain migration of the sort very typical for both trans-Atlantic immigrants and rural-to-urban migrants."[19] In this pattern of migration there is also a direct correlation between point of origin and place of destination: most of those migrating from southwestern cities relocated to the urban centers of California, especially the southern cities of Los Angeles and San Diego, and most of the people from rural areas ended up in the farming communities of the San Joaquin and Imperial Valleys.[20]

These statistics bring out an important point. The group commonly referred to as dust bowl refugees or migrant farmworkers made up only a portion of the total migrant population from the Southwest, and therefore an even smaller portion of the total population of migrants during the depression. These Okies, as they were derogatorily named, became the center of concern for many Californians during the depression, even though migration from the dust bowl was smaller during the depression than in either of the decades before and after the 1930s.[21] This group differed from earlier migration populations in what they found in California. They discovered, as Walter J. Stein has stated, that "they intruded upon an agricultural system that contravened every myth in the Jeffersonian pantheon."[22] The agricultural economy of California was not similar to the rural economy of the Southwest, and the disparity between the two economies was best illustrated in the existence of the white, native-born American migrant farmworkers.

The rural southwestern migrants found themselves not only in an agricultural economy with which they were unfamiliar but also in a social setting where industrial and political interests battled over the agricultural economy and therefore characterized the migrants as either victims of the system or the cause of the system's current problems. Within this battle, reformers used the migrant to illustrate the uneven and unjust distribution of wealth in California agriculture, while farm owners and growers blamed the influx of these migrants for high tax rates and large relief roles, which hampered efforts to pull California out of the depression.

The leading publicists of the reform movement were Paul S. Taylor and Carey McWilliams, both writers and government advisers. Taylor, a professor of economics at the University of California, served as the regional labor adviser for the Resettlement Administration. He made extensive studies of the reasons and conditions of migration to California. Together with his wife, FSA photographer Dorothea Lange, he published *An American Exodus: A Record of Human Erosion* (1939), which chronicled the transformation of agriculture in the United States and the migration resulting from this transformation. Taylor published many articles on the conditions of farm labor in California and spoke widely on the topic throughout the state.[23] In a paper presented to the Commonwealth Club of California in September 1935, Taylor described typical migrants:

> They travel in old automobiles and light trucks, some of them homemade, and frequently with trailers behind. All their worldly possessions are piled on the car and covered with old canvas or ragged bedding, with perhaps bedsprings atop, a small iron cook stove on the running board, a battered trunk, lantern, and galvanized iron washtub tied on behind. Children, aunts, grandmothers, and a dog are jammed into the car, stretching its capacity incredibly. A neighbor boy sprawls on top of the loaded trailer.[24]

He went on to say that the migrants illustrated the fundamental problem of California agriculture, the need for a migratory workforce to fill the demands of intensive farming in the diverse crops of the state. The migrants had not caused the poor wages and unsanitary conditions of farm work; rather, they illustrated the existence of these conditions.

This image of the dust bowl migrant, reinforced by photographs by Lange and others, led to the characterization of the migrants as refugees. As refugees, migrants were viewed by experts as victims of disaster, unable to cope with the changing world around them. Lange's famous photograph *Migrant Mother* exemplifies this image of victimization. The photograph of a mother with her children, her face etched with concern, looking out into the unknown, very quickly became more than a document of migrant farmworker conditions in California.

This generalization influenced efforts to help migrants by placing their problems in the larger context of economic and social structures, an approach that seemed to dictate reform of existing methods of agricultural employment rather than proposals for local and specific relief and assistance. Paul Taylor believed that better treatment of the migrants as laborers, efforts on behalf of the migrants as a "rural proletariat," would alleviate the destitute condition of the migrants. He did not suggest changes in what he saw as the deviant aspects of California agriculture—intensive, large-scale farms as opposed to homesteads—but suggested ways in which the demands for labor created by this system could be met in a humane and just manner.

Carey McWilliams was a young writer and attorney when he headed the state's Division of Immigration and Housing, a Progressive-era creation used to monitor conditions in labor camps. His book *Factories in the Field,* published in 1939, focused attention on the historical context surrounding the dust bowl migrants and their place in California agriculture. Like Taylor, McWilliams saw the solution to the problems of the migrants in the creation of an agricultural working class strong enough to fight for and win decent wages and working conditions, and eventual control of the farms. Unlike Taylor, he suggested changes in patterns of landownership as a solution to the "migrant problem." These changes, however, would come about not from government intervention but through organized action by the migrants themselves.

While this solution considered the economic and social ramifications of integrating the migrant population into the native population of California, it did not consider the effects of the migrants' regional culture on the culture of California. The migrants brought with them an ideal of landownership and independence. As a sociologist studying a community of southwestern migrant workers concluded:

> They came to California in the hope that they might re-establish themselves somewhere in agriculture. They are anxious to settle here, to find employment, and to build homes. "This is the way I figured. . . . I'd get a few month's work and then lay by enough for a down payment. Once we had our own place, we'd be all right."[25]

Even though it is difficult to determine clearly what many of the migrants hoped for when they moved to California, it is possible to determine what they thought about the agricultural situation in the state, and therefore to come up with a partial indication of the type of agricultural system they were used to and wanted to reproduce. One migrant, Wiley Cuddard Sr., argued that large growers should not call themselves farmers: "What you call the big farmers are not farmers, they are just holders of the farm and the other man does the labor."[26] John Bailey stated:

> I went to see one [a native Californian rancher] the other day about thinnin' apricots and he gave me to understand he wasn't havin' them thinned. That's all there was to it. When we go up to ask fer a job and after statin' our business we may try to start a conversation but never git nowhere. They are just a little distant and make you feel like they don't want to talk. Sort of cut you off short. . . . Last year I worked fer a man who come out here from Texas and made good as a rancher. It was just sort of like bein' among home folks. He knew just exactly how to handle us fellers.[27]

Bailey's animosity was not directed toward ranchers as a group but against ranchers who were typically Californian, as he saw them, and therefore coldly businesslike. The impersonal and unfriendly attitude of Californians was a constant theme in migrants' assessments of their situation, together with a nostalgic longing for the feeling of community back home, real or imagined.

A study undertaken by James Bright Wilson, a graduate student of sociology at the University of Southern California in the early 1940s, sheds light on migrants' aspirations. As part of his research, Wilson asked several migrant workers what should be done in order to solve the problems of migratory labor in California. One worker, Homer Towney, suggested that the government give each person a farm of his own: "There ought to be forty to sixty acres to the man accordin' to the size of his family. . . . Let the people farm with teams rather than with machinery. That would mean more work fer more people and so do away with a lot of relief."[28] Once again, the proposed solution recalled a type of farming practiced "back home" in the past. Likewise, the poetry of the migrants, featured in the newsletters produced in the government camps, indicated a longing for "the old homestead" and a way of life now past. Roy Turner, of the Tulare Farm Workers' Community, expressed his idea of the good life in a poem entitled "With the Poets":

> I sat on the creek with my feet in the sand.
> With my hook, pole, and line and my little bait can.
> The rocky old road and the clear little stream,
> But when I woke up it was only a dream.
> If I had the money and I could get through
> I believe I would go back and I'll bet you would to.[29]

The Thornton Farm Workers' Community's newsletter, *New Hope News*, featured a drawing titled "A Camper's Dream." It consisted of a farmhouse and barn on a small hill surrounded by trees with the sun rising in the background.

This desire to return to a former way of life is echoed in "America Today" by Mrs. L. Thrasher of the Woodville Farm Workers' Community:

> There was a time when we were content,
> Living at home even tho we must rent.
> We had no intentions or craving to roam
> Tho' ever so humble, we cherish our home.
>
> What of the future of the poor fruit tramp,
> Who is forced to move from camp to camp;
> Dragging his family from place to place.
> The way he lives is a eternal disgrace. . . .
>
> The brain may be trying but all their red tape,
> This land of the free is in a h ___ of a shape;
> I'm not blaming the people, they're forced to do it,
> But darn a condition that forces them to it![30]

The migrants' desire to remake their southwestern communities in California led sociologist Lillian Criesler to conclude that "these people wanted fiercely to resettle on property of their own; many had owned homes and farms in the past and it was inevitable that they should have attempted to buy land and establish homes in their new locale."[31] Migrant worker Charles Robinson found the answer in relocation and landownership: "About the only way I see to ever help this is to take the money that is bein' paid on relief and set a man up back East on a little piece of land and say to him, 'Now work or starve.' "[32] Robinson, like many of his peers, expressed a belief in a strongly individualistic work ethic based on a "sink-or-swim" attitude. Many migrants expressed a negative attitude toward relief that was not conditional on work for wages. One migrant, simply calling him- or herself "A Camper," wrote: "All we people want is a place to live in, decent surroundings, a job to provide us the necessary things in life so that we may live like all American People should live. We don't want just what we have to have given to us, but we want to work for it."[33] Despite their resistance to relief, conditions forced many migrants to seek assistance from the government. The government relief agencies, relying on the studies of academics and journalists like Taylor and McWilliams, focused their efforts toward shaping the migrant into a class-conscious agricultural laborer. The migrants, on the other hand, were trying to avoid permanent employment as wage laborers.

Migrant labor reformers repeatedly suggested land colonization as a solution to the problem of a wandering mass of laborers roaming the California countryside. One of the first attempts at land colonization was undertaken by Claus Spreckles, the Hawaiian sugar magnate, and the Salvation Army. Conceived in the spring of 1897, the Salvation Army–Spreckles project proposed to create a "peasant class" to assist the production of sugar in the Salinas valley, where Spreckles had set up his processing plant. The next year, the Salvation Army purchased a tract of land near Soledad and set up the community of Fort Romie. Divided into lots of ten to twenty acres each, the community was settled by indigent families, mainly from San Francisco, who purchased the lots under a long-term loan program. These families were to raise their own food and work in the Spreckles plant for additional earnings. Spreckles would thus have at his fingertips a settled labor force that he could employ when necessary. Though successful in its aims, the Fort Romie experiment eventually died due to the introduction of less expensive "coolie labor" imported from Japan. The idea of placing "landless man on manless land," however, survived and persisted.[34]

In 1917 Dr. Elwood Mead launched the State Land Settlement Project at Durham in Butte County. Conceived as a way to stabilize farm labor in California, Durham and a similar project at Delhi in Merced County founded a year later were experiments in both land colonization and social planning. Carey McWilliams described the administrators of the projects as "social idealists and not practical economists."[35] Efforts to force communal behavior, along with post–World War I deflation in real estate prices, led to the dissolution of both projects by 1930. The state concluded that land colonization was impractical in California and that "few human beings are fashioned from sufficiently rugged fiber to withstand the weakening influence of paternalism."[36] Yet, when circumstances again called for a solution to the labor problem of California agriculture, the idea of planned settlement emerged once more.

In 1934, in the midst of proposals to remedy the conditions of the migrant farm laborers publicized in newspapers and magazines, Harry Drobish, state director of rural rehabilitation in the California Emergency Relief Administration, wrote to Robert Clarckson, director of rural rehabilitation in Helena, Montana, about his plan to resettle the migrant laborer:

We also have in mind establishing colonies of subsistence homesteaders. These will be located in areas where seasonal labor is needed either in agriculture or industrial fields. The soil must be of a good type, suitable for truck gardening, and there must be sufficient irrigation water, etc. We plan to have this tract subdivided into from one to five acre blocks. On this tract a family may build a house and establish a home. They will raise vegetables for their family needs, also possibly rabbits, chickens, etc. The subsistence farm will afford a place for the head of the family to work in idle times producing food for their own use.[37]

Drobish was aware of the problems inherent in this proposal, in view of the historical precedents of land colonization: "The experience in California can be summed up by saying that colonizing land by the State is considered to be a failure financially and otherwise." Therefore, he suggested, this project should rely on colonizers' purchasing the land from private owners with the help of the State Emergency Relief Administration (SERA).[38]

Though a subsistence homestead program was the goal of Drobish and the SERA, more immediate concerns presented themselves as the "problem" of migratory labor increased. Rural counties depended on the labor supplied by the migrants, yet many were not financially equipped or willing to provide for the workers during times of unemployment. County supervisors found the best solution was to chase away the migrants after the harvest by imposing vagrancy laws. One county voted to fill the gas tanks of the workers, thus enabling them to leave the county. The neighboring county, outraged at having the migrant problem dumped on it, threatened to meet the workers with shotguns at the county line if such a measure was repeated.[39] Responding to this situation, Drobish proposed labor camps to temporarily house workers as they followed the crops around the state.

In a memo entitled "Camp Program for Migrants," Drobish outlined his rationale for such a program. He reasoned that the unique characteristics of California agriculture, along with the substandard conditions of existing privately run labor camps, made necessary camps run by the state, which would provide sanitary facilities and housing. The goal of the program would be more than just cleaning up and housing the migrants. The camps would foster the "elevation of all rural living standards by education and example." This program, Drobish noted, would not undermine the "principle of 'grower responsibility' for housing," which had informed the work of the State Immigration and Housing Division, but would supplement those areas where growers could not supply proper housing conditions. Though the memo focused on improving the conditions of the migrant worker, justification for the project centered on the advantages to growers in the stabilization of farm labor. Drobish saw the camps as a first step in the creation of a permanently settled farm labor supply residing not in temporary camps but in subsistence homesteads and "part-time farms" created through the programs of the Division of Rural Rehabilitation.[40]

In the application for funds to Frank Y. McLaughlin, administrator of the SERA, Drobish explained that these camps provided for "the 'forgotten men, women and children' of rural California."[41] In quoting one of Roosevelt's campaign speeches, Drobish placed his proposed camp program within the larger goals of FDR's New Deal, in particular the specific goals of Rexford Tugwell and the Resettlement Administration/Farm Security Administration.

In his study of the FSA, Sidney Baldwin observed, "The genesis of the Farm Security Administration, like that of the New Deal itself, was rooted in an idealism in which escape from materialistic defeat was a central motivating force."[42] This motivating force complemented the belief that the problems of agriculture in the United States could be solved through collective state intervention. Underlying this assumption were two strains of thought concerning agriculture in the United States. One viewed agriculture as a business, a simple working of product and profit, while the other saw agriculture as a way of life, "with faith resting on the trinity of agrarian tradition, folk sociology, and Christian love."[43] In the end, the business perspective won out in shaping government policy, yet throughout debates over legislation and policy, policy makers paid lip service to the agrarian view. Even though the language of reform often spoke of tradition and the family farmer, it worked to the benefit of industrialized agribusiness.

The development of government farm policy shows the compromise that took place between these competing ideological assumptions. Efforts to alleviate the plight of sharecroppers and tenant farmers in the South started from a concern with the landless, chronic rural poverty so dramatically documented by such FSA photographers as Walker Evans, Ben Shahn, Russell Lee, and Arthur Rothstein. Proposed solutions ranged from the rehabilitation of marginal lands through improved farming techniques and equipment to the resettlement of displaced families on farms. Low-interest or long-term loans to farmers caught in a cycle of debt and dependence on creditors, brokers, and merchants also emerged as a way to stabilize the family farmer against the overwhelming competition of technologically more advanced industrial agriculturalists. The first act of legislation specifically aimed at the woes of farmers, however, the Agricultural Adjustment Act of 1933, targeted the price of farm products as the chief factor in agricultural recovery. Seeking to bring "parity" to agriculture, the Agricultural Adjustment Administration (AAA), created by the act of 1933, exercised control over farm production, prices, and markets. Designed to assist the recovery of agriculture as a whole, the AAA did virtually nothing to help the small farmer and, in fact, added to problems brought about by drought and depression.

Small farmers received aid not through the agency created for agriculture but through the Federal Emergency Relief Administration (FERA), created to relieve the plight of the unemployed. The FERA, which in turn oversaw the programs of the State Emergency Relief Administrations (SERAs), developed three main programs for the relief of small farmers, tenants, sharecroppers, and farm laborers through its Division of Rural Rehabilitation and Stranded Populations under the head of Colonel Lawrence Westbrook. Loans would assist farmers on productive land, with the stipulation that the farm operate on an approved farm and home budget and the prescribed methods of the division. Community programs for stranded populations would settle part-time industrial and agricultural labor on subsistence farms and homesteads. Land reform would encourage "the purchase of submarginal land and its retirement from production as a means of improving land use, conserving fertility and resources, raising the social and economic standards of chronically depressed rural areas, and helping to reduce crop surpluses."[44] The FERA included the migrant labor camp program in the proposed community programs for laborers.

Harry Drobish developed the migrant camp program under the auspices of the SERA. To convince the SERA of the need for the camps, Drobish collected information and photographs, with the help of Paul Taylor and Dorothea Lange, and presented his proposal. The SERA approved two hundred thousand dollars to be used to establish twenty camps throughout California. Next, FERA approval was needed to allocate funds to the SERA, and Drobish submitted an application in March 1935. In his application he highlighted the benefits of the camp program, citing an improved standard of living for the migrants, a decreased possibility of contagious disease, a stable supply of workers for growers, and a decrease in strike activity. He also noted the support for the program by California officials, county governments, and many other interested parties who gathered at several conferences on migratory labor. In conclusion, Drobish stated: "Living conditions are unsanitary, and low in the extreme; they are utterly unfit surroundings in which to raise American citizens." He continued:

THIS PROJECT MEETS A NEED CLEARLY AND PUBLICLY RECOGNIZED BY FEDERAL AND STATE AUTHORITIES, AND BY CIVIC BODIES IN CALIFORNIA. IT IS AN IMPORTANT STEP TOWARD REHABILITATION OF A SUBMERGED GROUP, TOWARD BETTER INDUSTRIAL RELATIONS IN A STRIFE-TORN FIELD, AND TOWARD TRAINING OF TENS OF THOUSANDS OF MEN, WOMEN, AND CHILDREN IN BETTER STANDARDS OF AMERICAN CITIZENSHIP.[45]

Drobish's application was denied by FERA director Westbrook, who believed that migrant labor camps were not the solution to the problem of migratory labor. In his opinion these people should be placed on farms after completing a course on a teaching farm to be set up by the Rural Rehabilitation Division of the FERA. Dr. Lowry Nelson, regional director of the FERA in charge of the western states, agreed with Drobish that the camps were a necessary part of agricultural recovery in California. But "the officials in charge in Washington," according to Drobish, "having never been in California and unfamiliar with our local problems, could not become interested in meeting the problem by building camps for migrant workers."[46] Eventually, under constant prodding by Drobish, with reports from Taylor and photographs by Lange, Westbrook agreed to fund one camp as a demonstration of the program; he allocated twenty thousand dollars for the camp to be erected at Marysville in Yuba County.

Drobish started construction of the camp in the late spring of 1935 and selected Tom Collins as the first camp manager. Building almost came to a halt during the summer of 1935 as the Roosevelt administration transferred the programs of the Division of Rural Resettlement in the SERA to the newly established Resettlement Administration (RA) under the direction of Rexford Tugwell. Walter Packard and Jonathan Garst, representatives of the RA, came west from Washington to oversee the office's western projects. Both men opposed the camp project and believed that the RA was involving itself in a potentially explosive situation. The position of Packard and the administration changed after a meeting in Salt Lake City in which Drobish and Paul Taylor presented arguments, illustrated by photographs by Lange, in favor of the camp program. In attendance was the assistant administrator of the RA, Dr. William Alexander, and other RA officials, including Packard. Alexander gave the project his encouragement and the support of the administration. Irving Wood took charge of the migrant labor camp program and was responsible for the management of the camps.

The migrant labor camp program, as proposed, was more than an effort at relief, an effort to alleviate a temporary condition. It was a program designed to create a stable class of agricultural laborers, thereby benefiting the growers and large farmers, under the presumption of protecting the rights of neglected citizens. This is not to say that Drobish and the government agencies involved intended to deceive anyone by implementing this program; indeed, they saw their efforts as addressing the plight of the migrants and not the needs of the growers. The greatest opposition to their efforts actually came from the growers, who would conceivably profit most from such an arrangement.

After construction had started on the Marysville Camp, several conferences on the housing of migratory farm labor were held in various parts of the state. Growers and local officials voiced their opposition to the camp program, arguing that the camps would become a breeding ground for radical and communist activities. Lee A. Stone, county health officer for Madera County, presented his argument against the camps in a paper written for the California Conference on the Housing of Migratory Agricultural Laborers at Santa Cruz in November 1935. Stone argued that the migrant laborer was not in need of relief since he provided a "type of labor decidedly expert in character" upon which the growers of California depended. Stone proposed the erection of camps by the growers themselves, who would have control over the labor they hired. These camps would be funded through long-term loans from the government but placed on the private property of the growers. In this way growers could assure the migrants of a living space free of the possibility of radical, and even communistic, influence. Thousands of "squatters" lining the roads of rural California were the real problem, and not the housing of highly skilled agricultural workers. With workers housed by employers, those remaining in squatter camps could be effectively removed by local officials under the public nuisance laws.[47]

Against this opposition, the RA completed the construction of the camp and, on October 12, 1935, officially opened it for business. By December 1935 a second camp opened at Arvin in Kern County. The everyday management of the camps rested with the camp manager, who followed a set of instructions provided by the director of the camp program, Irving Wood. "Your camp is established primarily for the purpose of providing sanitary camp facilities for migratory farm workers," Wood said. "Camps for migratory agricultural workers should be so conducted as to be regarded by the worker as communities in which they can establish and maintain homes with the same freedom, rights, duties and privileges enjoyed by American workers dwelling in town and city homes."[48] Camps should be "organized on a self-governing, democratically controlled basis." A camp committee should be "selected, by the Manager, or preferably, elected by the camp inhabitants, whose responsibility it will be to confer with the Manager and to enforce camp rules and regulations." In this way the camp manager would be "freed from petty policing activities" and could function as a "community leader." "In his capacity as leader the Camp Manager should strive to become the campers' guide, counselor and friend,' placed there by the Administration 'to help the workers help themselves.' "[49]

In a paper presented to the Santa Cruz Conference on Housing of Agricultural Laborers, Wood elaborated on the role of the camp manager:

> A camp manager must be at all times in charge of the camp to maintain conditions of sanitation and order. He can aid the employment services to make available to growers an adequate supply of workers. The Resettlement Administration desires to avoid paternalism and regimentation, but at the same time it is expected that camp managers will protect the camp population from abuses by contractors, peddlers and others.[50]

In both of these descriptions of the role of the camp manager, it is evident that the attitude of Wood and the RA toward the migrant worker was one of paternal protection, despite the explicit disavowal of paternalism. Wood assumed that the migrants were unaccustomed to modern life, having spent their lives on backward farms and towns in the Southwest. The migrants carried the stigma of "poor white trash" engendered by the growing publicity about the condition of white southern tenant farmers and by characterizations such as Jeeter Lester in Erskine Caldwell's *Tobacco Road* (1932). They faced ridicule from local citizens and misguided concern from reformers and government agencies dedicated to the elevation of their standard of living.

A vivid example of this paternal and nurturing attitude can be found in the fill-in-the-blanks constitutions created for the camps in which the campers were to "write" their own constitution when they organized themselves into a community. The preamble to the constitution states:

> We the people of the _____ Migratory Labor Camp, in order to form a more perfect community, promote the general welfare, and insure domestic tranquility, do hereby establish this constitution for the _____ Migratory Labor Camp.[51]

Upon entering the camps, the migrants were told to respect the self-created government that had been created for them. Managers forced the migrants into being democratic, but since a strong veto power lay in the hands of the camp manager—who was in no way dependent on the approval of the occupants of the camp—the result was a democracy in name alone.

Not only the structure of the camps but their operation by the camp managers illustrated the government's view of migrants as children, uneducated in the more civilized aspects of cleanliness, cooperation, and self-government. Tom Collins, founding manager of both the Marysville Camp and the Weed Patch Camp at Arvin, recounted the trials of setting up a migrant labor camp in a paper entitled "The Human Side in the Operation of a Migrants Camp." In this address, delivered at the California Conference on Housing for Rural Workers and the Dedication Exercises of the Marysville Migrants Camp, Collins stressed the deplorable conditions of the Marysville migrants before the introduction of the camp program: "Here was a small city, a city without order, a city of neglected souls." Approaching these "neglected souls" became Collins's first concern.

> We decided to make our first step forward through the children. Within a few days we organized a playground, fully equipped with those little things which are the joy and rightful heritage of every American child.
>
> We eagerly watched results. Children came, gaped wild eyed, tempted, but went away. They returned with other children. There was more gaping, more wild eyes, but not a child responded to the temptation. On the second day some tiny tots were bold enough to venture on the ground. Their screams of delight as they frolicked with the playthings soon drew many others and by early in the afternoon of the second day approximately ninety children were on the playground.[52]

Collins went on to recall how suspicion "changed to bewilderment, bewilderment in the knowledge someone was taking an interest in them and their welfare." First the children, then the mothers and the rest of the migrant population, came to trust Collins and the migrant camp program. In essence, Collins treated the entire migrant population as if it was composed of children, induced into doing something that would be good for them, even though they did not know it.

To foster cleanliness and order, Collins approached "the four best gossipers" among the women of the camp and encouraged them to assist their neighbors in cleaning up. Suggesting to the gossipers that their untidy neighbors were messy simply because they did not have time to clean, Collins involved the campers in one another's affairs. "In other words, we developed the 'Good Neighbor' idea," and with it, "bewilderment gave way to confidence." Collins concluded that "with the proper person in charge of a Resettlement Administration Migrants Camp, one who is a real leader, one who has a keen understanding of human problems, these camps can be successfully operated by giving the migrants *some* voice in solving their own problems of community life."[53]

What looked like an effort to give the migrants a voice in their lives often turned out to be the product of successful manipulation. Mindful that the migrants' leisure time might result in actions not sanctioned by the administration ("danger points if left to themselves," as Collins put it), managers created recreational schedules designed to fill the campers' time. As a way of preserving "folk traditions," the schedule included square dances, a camp orchestra, community sings, sporting events, and women's clubs. Ironically, the migrants sought to preserve the ideological traditions of their culture rather than the recreational rituals of folk life.

When asked if the migrants appreciated what was being done for them, Collins answered:

> We believe you will agree when we say that "appreciation" is not the concern of a public agency supported by public funds. We are interested in results and we believe we have accomplished what we have set out to do. We have brought order out of chaos. As contrasted with former conditions, we have a well-planned city, each family with its own lot. . . . We have our own departments of fire, health, education, sanitation, police, playground, day nursery, our own park, our own well planned social life. We are a city of a thousand souls living in tents instead of houses but we have everything well regulated and organized communities have.[54]

The camp was not, however, the self-sustaining community he described. It lacked the ability to sustain its members through employment, and the migrants lacked the power to shape the community beyond the limits placed by the camp manager and the federal government.

The goal of creating a stable and docile working force lay beneath the rhetoric of Collins's speech. After claiming success in creating equal democratic citizens, Collins concluded his talk by stating: "[The camps] will make available for the farmers of the State of California, CONTENTED, CLEAN and WILLING workers."[55]

The aims of the migrant labor camp program developed out of pressing economic and social conditions, and the degree to which the camps mitigated these conditions is not to be discounted. The introduction of the government camps greatly improved the miserable conditions of migrants living in roadside camps, and the human concern shown to the migrants by camp managers psychologically assisted many of them. Margaret Sloan of the Brawley camp wrote to the camp paper to express her gratitude for the camp program: "Here's to the sucess of the (Migratory Camps of California) And hope they may continue to be a haven of rest to the tired (Migratory Worker) For surely they are appresiated after months spent in temory camps."[56] Yet a tension existed between the aims of the camp managers and the desires of the migrants, which can be seen in the reactions of migrants to the government camps.

Praise for the friendliness of camp workers and the living conditions of the camps is found in letters and poems written by migrants and published in the camp newsletters. Not surprisingly, praise directed at the camp program as a whole appears frequently in the weekly reports of camp managers to Irving Wood, director of the camp program. These reports, which include statistical data and a visitors' log, recount weekly events and comments. In one report, Collins wrote:

> One of the greatest compliments ever paid our camp came from a man the day he registered with us. Said he—"now I kin go any place I wants ter wuk, and if he dont pay rite I kin tell him 'nufin doin' and go sum place else. At this govmnt camp *I is a free citizn.*" This month we celebrate the natal day of Abraham Lincoln, We wonder if the blacks of those days did not use the VERY SAME LANGUAGE contained in this quotation from our own camper?[57]

The comparison of the migrant to a freed black slave and the feeble attempt to characterize the language of the migrants illustrate Collins's attitude toward the migrants and his job. In his role as an Okie emancipator, Collins saw the camps as fulfilling the migrants' democratic birthright. The man quoted in Collins's report realized his freedom as he exerted his rights as a worker, withholding his labor for a fair price. Yet what we see in this statement is not the transformation of a slave into a freedman but the transformation of an independent family farmer unfamiliar with matters of labor and management into a class-conscious worker secure in his rights. The camps were designed to assist this transformation, and in many cases they succeeded. Tensions in the camps developed, however, because many of the migrants did not want to be transformed into workers. They hoped to secure enough land to own a home and to farm with their families as they had done in their home states. The dream of landownership and economic independence was part of the cultural heritage migrants brought from the Southwest even though many were neither landowners nor economically independent. The largest portion of the white migrant farm laborers was from Oklahoma, home of the land rushes and homesteads of the 1890s and "the last expression of nineteenth-century democratic agrarianism."[58] Even during the period of greatest socialist strength in Oklahoma in the early twentieth century, many socialists, eager to include farmers in the industrial proletariat, lamented the interpretation of socialism many farmers devised: "Many farmers did seem loath to accept socialism as anything other than a scheme of relief devised to deliver land into willing hands and make its yields worthwhile."[59] One migrant in the Marysville Camp used frontier rhetoric in describing "The Whys of the Migrant": "We are looking for the answer some day for, after all, we are the pioneers of the depression."[60]

The desire to become landowners, along with the conception of landowner- ship based on working the land and not necessarily holding title to it, was height- ened by the belief that California was the land of opportunity and possibility. Many had been drawn to California out of a sense of adventure: "Probably the final analysis will show that they were people a little too romantic, adventurous and impatience, stamina and courage often failed and, as a group, had all the sins and weaknesses of the impatient, the restless, the adventurous and the re- bellious."[61] Letters from friends and family who migrated to California during better economic times further enhanced the attraction of opportunities to be found. Okie migrants came to California in the belief that after working in the fields for a season or two they would be able to afford a down payment on a piece of land where they could live in the tradition of the yeoman farmer.

Even if the transformation to laborer was inevitable, the belief on the part of the migrants that it was not so led many of them to resent the treatment offered in the government camps. Ray C. Mork, manager of the Indio Camp, seems to have been a particular target of animosity. In the February 4, 1939, issue of *The Covered Wagon*, the newsletter of the Indio Camp, Mork made this statement:

A couple of folks in camp have said that the manager is a so and so and a dictator. Well maybe I am and if so I am not sure what should be done about it. Funny thing folks who say things like that are usually some who don't seem to be able to obey our rules or who are just naturally trouble makers. Folks who have an idea that maybe they could run this camp themselves better than anyone else. There are over one hundred and sixty families in camp and I dont expect to please all of them.[62]

The animosity displayed toward Mork can be attributed to his treatment of the camp population. In a letter to the children of the camp, Mork asked them not to cause him trouble: "Course if that is what you want to do, lets be above board about it and I will see that your family looks for another place to live."[63] While this threatening attitude may explain some of the tension at the Indio Camp, incidents at other camps suggest that the migrants and managers looked upon the camp experience differently.

Reginald A. F. Loftus, camp manager of the Calipatria Mobile Unit, found it necessary to urge the migrants to "face facts":

> One of these facts is that here in this camp we are a community. The word "community" does not mean a collection of individuals working independently[,] living independently for themselves alone, it means the opposite; it means that we are a group who because we live together, play together, share together, hope together, pull together, and only by pulling together can we get done those good things we all want.[64]

In fact, of course, economic necessity, not mutual understanding, brought the people in the camp together. That Loftus needed to tell the campers that what they had was a community indicates a lack of community feeling, which was evident in the low participation rates in council elections and meetings and in the often overheard exclamations of "to hell with the council."[65] Conrad C. Reibold, community manager of the Firebaugh Camp, wrote in his monthly narrative report that attendance at council meetings was so low that council vacancies could not be filled.[66] John Spencer, manager of the Shafter Camp, questioned the readiness of the migrants for democratic participation since they had so little concern for camp governance.[67]

At the Tulare Farm Workers' Community, Camp Manager Michael P. Bruick prohibited publication of a flyer issued by the Tulare County local of the United Cannery, Agricultural, Packing and Allied Workers of America (UCAPAWA) in the camp newsletter, *The Hub*. He justified his action on the grounds that he was upholding an ordinance of the community council, which prohibited the distribution of handbills in the residential sections of the camp. Bruick determined that publication of the handbill would constitute a violation of this ordinance. The handbill in question called for a meeting to discuss the closing down of the State Relief Administration. In retaliation, the UCAPAWA issued another circular with the boldfaced heading "HITLERISM IN THE GOV'T CAMP MUST GO!" According to the handbill,

> Michael P. Bruick, camp manager, has embarked on a campaign of destroying the democratic rights and civil liberties of a large section of the people living in the camp.

Although by law the residents are guaranteed the rights of free speech and free assemblage, Bruick has denied the people these rights. Although the camp council is the law-making body of the camp, Bruick has intimidated and dominated the members of the council. He has used methods of removing members who oppose his domineering tactics which are illegal according to the camp constitution.[68]

Even though the inflammatory language of the handbill overdramatized the manager's actions, the juxtaposition of the migrants' democratic rights and the manager's authoritarian control signaled an underlying tension in the democratic aims of both sides. Bruick's democracy relied on strict adherence to established laws and rules. Order, even if it was lightly imposed, was necessary to a smoothly running democratic community. The migrants, on the other hand, saw democracy as a set of individual rights, with freedom from control as its essential element. James Gregory saw this individualism in action when efforts to unionize the migrant workers fell short of success. He saw this affirmation of individual rights as part of the "plain-folk Americanism" apparent in Okie culture. In *American Exodus* Gregory describes the attitudes—political, social, and economic—that the Okie migrants held and maintained in California and labels it "plain-folk Americanism." These attitudes include a political populism based on "the dignity of hard work and plain living and promised deliverance from the forces of power, privilege, and moral pollution, near and far"; a "cult of toughness" fostering courage, determination and "grit"; a dedication to agrarian ideals of landownership and independence; and a fierce strain of nativism and racism.[69] The disparity between the "plain-folk Americanism" of the migrants and the dominant Californian outlooks of "business conservatism" and "urban liberalism" further alienated the migrants and became an identifying aspect of the group as a whole.

Both the conservative growers and the liberal government reformers sought to transform the migrants into farm laborers dependent on the farm owner and aligned with their fellow workers. The "plain-folk Americanism" of the migrants, however, sought to transplant an agrarian/populist system of farming from nineteenth-century Oklahoma to twentieth-century California. These cross-purposes were the result of differing conceptions of democracy and the migrants' place in it.

Returning to the quotations with which this chapter began, it is evident that Bruick's attempt to equate the migrants with the Founding Fathers, much like Collins's attempt to equate them with freed black slaves, was more an effort to lend historical significance to the migrant camp program than to describe the actual circumstances of the camps. The creation of a farmworkers' community was not a spontaneous gathering of concerned citizens who decided to write a constitution for the governance of their community; it was a carefully planned endeavor in which the government preprinted a constitution for the migrants and placed numerous restrictions on the migrants' control over the camps. Bruick's parallel of the camp's formation with the democratic creation of the nation revealed his idea of democracy as an adaptable and recurring concept in the collective consciousness of Americans. But he and the other directors of the camp program believed that migrants were not quite capable of democratic governance without the assistance of educated and concerned social workers.

On the other hand, S. K. Blackmon saw democracy as a thing of the past, a set of ideals quickly fading from the American scene. Hence he spoke of the "twilight of democracy." He believed that the common bond of God, family, and liberty no longer held people together. The ideals of God, family, and liberty were the essence of "plain-folk Americanism," the elements most incongruous with the efforts of the migrant camp program. While the migrants tried to hold on to the moral teachings of their predominantly Southern Baptist upbringing, the stability of their family ties, and their dedication to individual autonomy, the camp managers and government administrators tried to foster a reverence for secular rights, class consciousness, and collective cooperation. The democracy of workers envisioned by the FSA left no place for the democracy of individuals hoped for by the migrants. Each sought a goal contrary to the other.

The importance of these cross-purposes extends beyond the success or failure of the migrant camp program and raises questions about the image of the migrants constructed by reformers such as Paul Taylor, Harry Drobish, and Tom Collins. It was this constructed image, given evocative form by Dorothea Lange, that provided the basis for the public image of the migrants.

2

For better or for worse, the destiny of the photographer is bound up with the destinies of a machine. In this alliance is presented a very special problem. Ours is a time of the machine, and ours is a need to know that the machine can be put to creative human effort. If it is not, the machine can destroy us. It is within the power of the photographer to help prohibit this destruction, and help make the machine an agent more of good than of evil. Though not a poet, nor a painter, nor a composer, he is yet an artist, and as an artist undertakes not only risks but responsibility. And it is with responsibility that both the photographer and his machine are brought to their ultimate tests. His machine must prove that it can be endowed with the passion and the humanity of the photographer; the photographer must prove that he has the passion and the humanity with which to endow the machine.

—Dorothea Lange (with Daniel Dixon), "Photographing the Familiar," 1952

THE PASSION AND

THE HUMANITY

Dorothea Lange

and *Migrant Mother*

With her famous photograph *Migrant Mother* (1936), Dorothea Lange produced one of the clearest examples of the photographer endowing her camera with "the passion and the humanity" necessary not only to stir emotions in the viewer but to stimulate action and change. And while the single photograph of the *Migrant Mother* has become the classic icon of the Great Depression, Lange's approach to documentary photography relied on viewing her pictures in context with other photographs accompanied by explanatory text of a sociological or historical nature. She developed this approach to documentary photography at first from a simple desire to touch the lives of those around her, which in depression-era San Francisco meant the unemployed. Her association with Paul Taylor supported this new endeavor. Giving up her career as a studio portrait photographer, Lange was able to support herself and her family working for the California State Emergency Relief Administration (SERA) and later the Historical Section of the Resettlement Administration's (later the Farm Security Administration's) Information Division under the leadership of Roy Stryker. Lange and Taylor also developed a new documentary form beginning with their joint reports to the government on the conditions of migrant labor in California, and later in their book *An American Exodus: A Record in Human Erosion* (1939), in which photographs and text work together to form a complete statement about the migration.

In *An American Exodus*, Lange and Taylor describe the dust bowl migration as the result of the battle between man and machine. In this battle it is not the machine that is bad but the uses to which man puts the machine. In this battle the power of the large landholders and giant corporations is represented by the tractor, while the hard-working tenant farmers and sharecroppers become refugees in their own country. The book builds a powerful argument for what is wrong and why, and concludes that mechanization is inevitable and therefore must be dealt with in as humane a way as possible. In the book, Lange and Taylor suggest industrial expansion as the answer to the migrant problem, and celebrate such development projects as the damming of the Columbia River and other reclamation projects. Yet Lange and Taylor realized the long-term nature of these vast projects and suggested furthering the government's support of relief programs already under way, such as the camps for migratory farmworkers. By reinforcing the need to assist the migrants' adjustment to an industrial economy, Lange and Taylor supplied additional clout to the idea that the migrants were unable to deal with their circumstances and needed the helping hand of government reformers. With *An American Exodus*, Lange and Taylor brought the agenda of the government experts to a larger audience and further supported the positions of experts like Harry Drobish, Irving Wood, and Tom Collins.

However, the audience for *An American Exodus* pales in comparison with the exposure received by the photograph *Migrant Mother*. Lange's photograph of stranded pea picker Florence Thompson and her children quickly transcended the specific context of a flooded pea crop and stranded workers and became an image representing the distress of dislocation for all of the depression's victims. The message Lange wished to relate concerning the conditions of farm laborers and her desire to support and promote programs to help these people fell victim to the more general uses of the photograph as an all-encompassing record of what the depression had done to Americans.

However, *Migrant Mother* did perform the function Lange had intended (it brought attention to the conditions of workers during the depression and channeled support for the government's programs to assist the poor), even though it did not function in the way Lange would have liked. While she saw her photographs as social documentation, part of an academic foundation for social change and therefore an instance of using the photographic machine with passion and humanity, it was precisely the passion and humanity expressed by the single photograph, *Migrant Mother,* that created an emotional imperative for social change. Lange based this emotional imperative on the idea that the migrant was a victim of nature, technological progress, and an advanced industrial society. As such, *Migrant Mother,* and Lange's other photographs neglected the migrant's own desires and ambitions. Lange created most of her photographs to gain the support of administrators, legislators, and the general public for government-sponsored relief programs. In this sense Lange's work reinforced the expert representations of the migration while purporting to speak on behalf of the migrants. While she gave voice to the migrants through her photographs and publications, she focused on those voices that reinforced her ideas about relief and the rights of the migrants in an advanced industrial society.

Ironically, just as the tractor displaced the migrants in the agricultural economy by making their way of farming obsolete, Lange, her camera, and the images she created removed the migrants from their traditional culture and utilized them as evidence of the devastating effects of mechanization and the need for worker solidarity. For better or worse, the passion and the humanity with which Lange endowed her work were not those of the migrants but her own.

Even before she took her first photograph, Dorothea Lange knew she wanted to be a photographer. In 1914, at the age of nineteen, she told her mother of her intention to become a photographer: "But I had announced that I wanted to be a photographer, and I had no camera and I'd never made a picture."[1] Growing up in Hoboken, New Jersey, and New York City helped to develop Lange's observational abilities. She remembers having to walk home from school in the city, through the Bowery and across the river to Hoboken, and how she developed the ability "to keep an expression of face that would draw no attention, so that no one would look at me."[2] She later used this technique to capture her subjects unposed and unaware of the camera. Also, at the age of seven, Lange contracted polio, and the lack of a proper vaccination and treatment program left her crippled in her right leg and caused a pronounced limp in her walk. This too became an asset in her chosen career. She found that "where I walk into situations where I am very much an outsider, to be a crippled person, or a disabled person, gives an immense advantage. People are kinder to you."[3]

Having declared her intention to be a photographer, Lange proceeded to learn the trade. She took several successive jobs working for commercial portrait photographers in Manhattan, learning how to solicit business and how to mount and frame pictures. One of her earliest mentors was famed portrait photographer Arnold Genthe, who photographed presidents and celebrities. Lange felt Genthe succeeded in his portraits of women because "he loved women, understood them, could make the plainest woman an illuminated woman. When he photographed her, he understood her." And she learned that "you can photograph what you are really involved with."[4] Yet while working with Genthe and at succeeding jobs at other studios, Lange did not take any photographs. However, she did learn how to run a portrait studio and business. While Lange was working at a portrait studio on Fifth Avenue, one of the staff photographers quit, giving Lange the opportunity to make her first portrait. Though inexperienced, Lange succeeded and soon became a regular camera operator for the studio. Also during these years (1914–18), Lange created her own darkroom in an abandoned chicken coop with the help of an intinerant photographer who happened upon the Lange household. In addition, she took a class on photography from Clarence H. White at Columbia University. White was a member of the influencial Photo-Secession Group led by Alfred Stieglitz. Advocating "straight photography," the Photo-Secession claimed that the photographer "does not have the painter's opportunity to consider, transpose, eliminate, augment. He must, in an instant, create enduring beauty out of transient actuality."[5] White showed Lange the beauty in ordinary objects and subjects and helped to develop her critical eye. She still did not think of herself as an artist in any sense; to her photography was a trade.[6]

In January 1918 Lange and a friend, Florence Ahlstrom, left New York to see the world. They traveled by boat to New Orleans, west by train to Los Angeles, then north to San Francisco, where upon their arrival they were robbed, leaving them with less than five dollars between them. They were not down on their luck for long, though. The next day Ahlstrom, a Western Union clerk, got a job at the San Francisco office, and Lange got a job at a store that also did photo-finishing. At this photo counter Lange met Roi Partridge and Imogen Cunning-ham, he an etcher and she a photographer, who introduced her to the San Fran-cisco art community. Lange also joined the San Francisco Camera Club so she could have access to a darkroom. By 1919 Lange had opened her own portrait studio on Sutter Street and quickly became the favorite photographer of the city's leading citizens. Her studio also became the center of a Bohemian crowd of artists and friends who congregated at Lange's studio in the evenings. One of the artists at Lange's studio was painter Maynard Dixon, who became Lange's husband in March 1920. Though she was surrounded by artists, Lange's work during this time was strictly business and a trade. "I wasn't trying to be a great photographer," she recalled, "I never have. I was a photographer, and I did every-thing that I could to make it as good as I could. And good meant to me being useful, filling a need, really pleasing the people for whom I was working."[7] She would follow this philosophy for the rest of her career.

In 1928 Lange moved her studio to Montgomery Street, just a few doors down from Dixon's studio. After the crash of the stock market in 1929 and upon their return to California after a working trip to Taos, New Mexico, Lange and Dixon each moved into their respective studios to save money on rent. With a diminishing clientele due to the depression, Lange spent much of her time gazing out of her window to the streets below. "I was surrounded by evidence of the depression," she said.

> I was on the corner where the sun came in and I remember well standing at that one window and just watching the flow of life. Up from the waterfront it came to that particular corner, that junction of many different things. There was the financial district to the left, Chinatown straight ahead, and the Bar-bary Coast and the Italian town. The unemployed would drift up there, would stop, and I could see they did not know where next.[8]

Lange remembers looking down at this situation until "one day I said to myself, 'I'd better make this happen,' and that started me." What that started in Lange was the desire to document what was happening. "I was compelled to photo-graph as a direct response to what was around me."[9]

Aware of what was around her, Lange took her camera outside of the studio and began photographing people on the streets. Unlike her portraits, in which she posed her subjects, Lange found it necessary to find and select situations to photograph, mainly people in a context and not removed from their surroundings. One of her first attempts at documenting the depression resulted in a photograph of a small overcoated man, his hands folded around a tin can, leaning against a wooden rail, his eyes obscured by his dirty hat. Around him are the backs of other overcoated men waiting in a breadline. The photograph, *White Angel Bread Line, San Francisco, 1932,* has become an enduring image of the Great Depression by communicating both the widespread nature of the depression (the crowd of men waiting in line) and the solitary feelings of helplessness it provoked (the singular figure in the center of the photograph).

For months the photograph hung on the wall of Lange's studio and prompted her customers to ask her, "What do you want to do this for?"[10] Lange knew she wanted to help these people she saw on the streets, but she had no way of knowing how to go about it. Lange knew she wanted to do more in her photographs than portray a person. Concerning her photograph *Man Beside Wheelbarrow, San Francisco, 1934* she said:

This photograph of the man with his head on his arms for instance—five years earlier, I would have thought it enough to take a picture of a man, no more. But now, I wanted to take a picture of a man as he stood in the world—in this case, a man with his head down, with his back against the wall, with his livelihood, like the wheelbarrow, overturned.[11]

In this description Lange illustrated her early attempts to confer meaning on a subject through the objects of his or her surroundings.

For Lange, the value of photographic context preceded lessons on the value of written context in the form of captions and accompanying text. She continued to photograph the world around her—demonstrations and rallies—and upon seeing these photographs a friend introduced Lange to the magazine *Survey Graphic*. The magazine, described by Lange as "more a social welfare magazine, more connected with settlement houses and social welfare problems, not political commentary," bought a photograph of Lange's in which a street speaker is talking into a microphone and printed it with the caption, "Workers of the world, unite!" "Which was no favor to me," Lange recalled. "But that's what they did. Made me a Communist right away, quick."[12] "It wasn't my caption and it, of course, gave the picture a turn which a good documentary photographer is very punctilious about."[13] This was Lange's first lesson in the importance of captions in documentary photography. Later in life she stated: "All photographs can be fortified by words. . . . I like the kind of material that gives more background, that fortifies it without directing the person's mind."[14]

The article accompanying the photograph in *Survey Graphic* was written by University of California economist Paul Taylor, who contacted Lange about working with him on an investigation into California agriculture. Taylor had received a grant from the SERA, and he hired Lange as a stenographer since there was no official designation for a photographer. Together they documented the labor problems of California farms and Lange received her first experience with social scientific fieldwork. She noticed how in the field Taylor "got the broad answers to questions without people really realizing how much they were telling him."[15] It was also during these field trips that Lange became aware of the problems of California agriculture and noticed the growing stream of migrants entering the state. She realized that her task lay in bringing the plight of these people to the attention of those who could help them. "During those years farm mechanization was just starting," Lange recalled, "and it was not a matter of general public knowledge that it was starting. The extension of big farming was happening in those years. It doesn't seem possible, but very few people knew it." When asked about the people affected by these changes, Lange replied: "They were voiceless, you see, and we were the people who met them."[16] Together, Lange and Taylor sought to give voice to these migrants and to advocate and support government programs aimed at the migrant problem. Lange firmly believed that photography was one way of bringing problems to the attention of the government since "it is in the nature of the camera to deal with what *is*." With her son Daniel Dixon (also a photographer) she criticized photographers for trying to photograph "what *might be*. We suggest that, as photographers, we turn our attention to the familiarities of which we are a part. So turning, we in our work can speak more than of our subjects—we can speak with them; we can more than speak about our subjects—we can speak for them."[17]

In 1935 Lange divorced Maynard Dixon and married Paul Taylor. She had left the business of portrait photography behind and devoted her career to government photography work. For ten years (1935–45) Lange did little else than work for one government agency or another. Her early government work was for the SERA, photographing the living conditions of migrant agricultural workers. Her photographs, accompanying Taylor's reports, provided the crucial push to establish camps for migrant workers in California. Lange shaped the reports through her photo layouts and captions, and implemented her beliefs in the necessity of context for documentary photography.[18] Lange spent many hours writing captions and arranging photographs to achieve the greatest impact. "It's not the individual captions that take the time but its the arrangement and grouping. If this is not done I believe that half the value of field work is lost."[19]

Crucial to the context surrounding the photographs was Lange's method of note taking in the field. After observing Taylor and many of his collegues and students interviewing subjects in the field, Lange saw the importance of recording the migrants in their own words, their own voices. Upon arriving at a migrant camp or workplace, Lange would talk to her subjects and listen carefully to them before she even attempted a shot. After speaking with the migrants, Lange would jot down in her notebook bits of what the migrants had said. In these field notes Lange's methods and objectives become clear not so much from what she wrote but from what she left out. Lange's notes, like her photographs, strive for objectivity (save for the subjective function of selectivity). Lange, as a person, an individual, never appears in the field notes. There are a few of her own descriptions of the conditions she witnessed, but she does not moralize or suggest psychological explanations. Zoe Brown noticed this lack of self-reflection in her study of Lange's field writings: "Her focus is outward, to facts and figures, life histories; the entries are terse and unemotional. Her personal reactions are rarely recorded, and pejorative terms and other value judgements are avoided."[20] However, Lange left out more than just her personal feelings. She often did not record the names of those she photographed, choosing instead to place them into certain categories of home state, length of time in California, former property status (owners, tenants, sharecroppers, or wage laborers), reasons for migrating, and so on. She also asked questions concerning the number in each family, their ages, the number of them working, in school, at home. Many times she and Taylor would ask these subjects what they thought the government could do to help them.[21]

Several themes appear in these field notes. The most apparent is the search for evidence to justify government relief programs such as the migrant camp program. Lange quoted one woman as saying: "I really feel that this is something the gov't will have to go into from now on—these camps." Below this quote in the field notes Lange remarked, "camps at no expense to growers," and she wrote a suggestion to herself to "do comparison in the cost to gov't & what it would cost to keep them on relief."[22] As with the government "experts," Lange found the justification for government intervention into the lives of the migrants in the processes of dislocation, migration, and migratory work. "Constant movement does not favor the development of normal relationships between citizens and community, and between employer and employee, nor the proper function of democracy."[23] Just as the camp managers and program administrators sought to create democratic citizens out of the migrants, Lange felt it was the government's responsibility to create a situation where the migrants could fulfill their democratic birthright, and she felt it was partly her responsibility to point out to the government that the conditions of California agriculture denied the migrant's birthright. Lange realized that her work was intended mainly for a selected audience of influential government reformers. In discussing a filmstrip on migratory labor produced from the photographic files of the RA/FSA, Lange told Roy Stryker, head of the photographic division, "The Governor ought to see it, the relief administrator ought to see it, the new state research director ought to see it, and it would certainly do a lot of good."[24] Like the government reformers, Lange related the deplorable conditions of migrant life to a lack of democratic participation on the part of the migrants rather than to a different interpretation of democracy held by the migrants. Lange reinforced the idea that the camps not only would provide sanitary housing conditions but would aid in the democratic development of the migrants as well. "The camp as it stands today represents a democratic experiment of unusual social interest and national significance."[25]

The second theme in the field notes is the devastating effects of agricultural mechanization. To clarify the intent behind her many photographs of desolate highways Lange wrote, "Highways are a part of the process of mechanization."[26] This is evident in photographs of migrants on the road juxtaposed with billboards advertising modern transportation technology such as trains. She also collected quotes from people who felt mechanization was the cause of their problems. "It's machinery, you see," one migrant told her. "It's just these fellers that have tractors as has got too much land rented. You couldn't rent a place out here. I come from Oklahoma, I bought me a little car. If I paid the car out I couldn't eat so I lost my car."[27] For this migrant, not only has mechanization forced him off his land but his dependence on a machine, his car, is second only to food.

On a shooting trip around Shafter, California, Lange noted the use of new technology in potato farming. "Large scale, mechanized farming," she wrote. "Potato planter, 3 men. makes rows, fertilizes and plants—note truck on edge of field. Contains seed and fertilizer. Followed by tractor." And underneath this description she jotted: "No Promised Land."[28] On one trip through the Texas Panhandle Lange came to the realization that the migrants in California were more than drought refugees; "a lot of them were also tractor refugees."[29] For

Lange, as for the rest of the government reformers, these conditions and their effects led to a proletarianization of the migrants. In order to effectively support the government's efforts to create democratic citizens out of the migrants, Lange needed to show not only that their democratic potential was not fulfilled but also that their natural inclinations were toward democratic principles. She noted one migrant who she felt "speaks for his class": "Fellers, such as me. Farmers, such as me, right down on our knees. Got no more chance than a one legged man at a foot race. They're aimin' at keepin fellers *sich* [sic] *as me* right down on our knees, aimin at makin slaves of us."[30] Lange also highlighted the democratic principles behind the migrant camp program and the creation of camp councils as "an expression of democracy."[31]

Lange's alliance with the goals and agenda of the government reformers strengthened when she joined the Historical Section of the Information Division of the Resettlement Administration (later Farm Security Administration), headed by Roy Stryker. Though not a photographer himself, Stryker had made a name for himself in eastern academic circles for his integration of photographs and text in academic works. Hired by Rexford Tugwell to create a photographic record for use by government agencies and other media sources, Stryker assembled a team of photographers and created a file of monumental scope and proportion. The FSA was the same agency that took over the running of the migrant camp program from the Federal Emergency Relief Administration (FERA). Therefore, Lange's previous work for the California SERA and the FERA fell into the hands of Stryker as he assembled his team of photographers.

The job at the FSA gave Lange financial support for what she wanted to do and the institutional support of an active government, which gave her a tremendous sense of responsibility. She had found not only acceptable ways of expressing her concerns but effective and supportive ones as well.

> When you went into that office . . . , you were so welcome, they were glad to see you, did you have a good trip, was everything all right? What you were doing was important. You were important. Not in the way in an organizational chart, not that way at all. Which made you feel that you had a responsibility. Not to those people in the office, but in general. As a person expands when he has an important thing to do. You felt it.[32]

As a portrait photographer, Lange sought to satisfy her customers to the best of her ability; this business approach to photography translated into a sense of duty and obligation to support the programs of the FSA.

The FSA programs most important to Lange were those that centered on the migrant farmworkers. When asked about her most memorable experience at the FSA, Lange responded with a description of her first encounter with dust bowl migrants:

> I stopped at a gas station to get some gas, and there was this car full of people, a family there at that gas station. I waited while they were getting their gas, and they looked very woebegone to me. They were American whites. I looked at the license plate on the car, and it was Oklahoma. I got out of the car, and I approached them and asked something about which way they were going, were they looking for work, I've forgotten what the question was at the time. And they said, "We've been blown out." I questioned what they meant, and then they told me about the dust storm. They were the first arrivals that I saw. These were the people who got up that day quick and left. They saw they had no crop back there. They had to get out. All of that day, driving for the next maybe two hundred miles—no, three or four hundred miles, I saw these people. And I couldn't wait. I photographed it.[33]

What was significant about this event was the change it signaled in Lange herself. "I went home that day a discoverer, a real social observer. Luckily my eyes were open to it. I could have been like all the other people on that highway and not seen it. As we don't see what's right before us. We don't see it till someone tells us. But this I discovered myself. This thing they call social erosion."[34] It was "this thing" that led Lange, in collaboration with Paul Taylor, to produce her best documentary work, *An American Exodus: A Record of Human Erosion.*

Published in 1939, *An American Exodus* was Lange and Taylor's attempt to describe fully the impact of agricultural mechanization, economic consolidation, and drought. Lange's photographs illustrate Taylor's narrative about a people on the move: "Now our people are leaving the soil again. They are being expelled by powerful forces of man and of Nature. They crowd into cities and towns near the plantations. Once more great numbers of landseekers trek west. This contemporary exodus is our theme."[35] In *An American Exodus* Lange and Taylor describe the transformation of American agriculture by examining the cotton culture of the South, southern farms in the postplantation period, homesteading on the plains, and agribusiness in California. This geographical narrative envisions a development of small yeoman farmers becoming tenant farmers, sharecroppers, failed homesteaders, wage workers, migrants, and eventually a unionized labor force. The overriding theme is one of agricultural mechanization and consolidation transforming independent farmers into a rural proletariat.

However, unlike the earlier exodus of easterners moving to free land in the

West, Lange and Taylor did not view this new exodus as an expansion of American values or a growth experience for the American character. Instead, they labeled their study of this contemporary exodus "a record of human erosion," drawing a parallel between the soil erosion on the plains and the dislocating effect of drought, wind, and tractors:

> Dried by years of drought and pulverized by machine-drawn gang disk plows, the soil was literally thrown to the winds which whipped it in clouds across the country. The winds churned the soil, leaving vast stretches of farms blown and hummocked like deserts or the margins of beaches. They loosened the hold of settlers on the land, and like particles of dust drove them rolling down ribbons of highway.[36]

The effect of this poetic parallel is an unmistakable emotional sympathy for the dispossessed, but like most "expert" renderings of the migrants it places migrants in the position of victims, unable to affect the course of their own lives. The characterization of the migrants as refugees enhances the idea of victimization, as do Lange and Taylor's suggested solutions of industrial expansion and large government land reclamation projects. In both cases, external forces guide the lives of the migrants without concern for the migrants themselves.

The narrative progression of the book reinforces this idea of migrant as victim as the collapse of the plantation system, the introduction of labor-reducing machinery such as the tractor, the introduction of managed farms hiring wage laborers, drought, dust storms, and California agribusiness push the small farmer into the ranks of migratory wage laborers. Even the section on the beginnings of migrant organization and the Salinas lettuce strike describes the class consciousness of the migrants as a natural, inevitable, and therefore external, phenomenon.

For Lange and Taylor, the process they recorded in photographs and words was a natural one, implemented by men but not necessarily controlled by them. In their work Lange and Taylor sought to assist the migrants in their adjustment to industrialized agriculture by promoting government programs aimed at relief and resettlement, and by educating the general public about the plight of the migrants. They felt that through their work they gave to the migrants "an opportunity to tell what they are up against to their government and to their countrymen at large."[37] Lange and Taylor did provide an outlet for the migrants' expressions of their situation; however, they failed to promote the solutions proposed by the migrants, instead favoring the "expert" solutions of government intervention and labor organization. Both Lange and Taylor felt that the migrants lacked the capacity to solve their own problems. Not only were the migrant workers unable to afford property in California, but they would be unable to deal with the peculiarities of California agriculture. "The mysteries and hazards of fluctuating markets for highly commercialized crops confound the uninitiated."[38]

Both Lange and Taylor utilized the migrants to illustrate weaknesses in the agricultural political economy and, in so doing, obscured the unique culture of the migrants. Completely discounting the possibility of self-sufficient family farmers, they discounted the migrants' own concerns of independence. Lange and Taylor placed a priority on economic status and political participation over cultural perseverance.

Lange and Taylor attempted to do more than describe this contemporary exodus; they sought to reach the American people through a whole new form of presentation. Their work, as they conceived it, was neither a monograph accompanied by photographs nor a photo book with captions. "Its particular form is the result of our use of techniques in proportions and relations designed to convey understanding easily, clearly, and vividly."[39] The photographs are presented in a large format, "bleeding" off the sides of the pages, while captions are mainly quotes from the field, quotes from experts, or short descriptive lines. Each of the six sections (Old South, Plantation Under the Machine, Midcontinent, Plains, Dust Bowl, Last West) consists of a photographic narrative (with occasional added documents such as newspaper headlines and help wanted advertisments) followed by a short essay further illuminating the theme of human erosion with statistics and occasional quotes from migrants and experts.

The aim of *An American Exodus* is objectivity. Personal observations and reactions are not included in the narrative, but the subjective selection and placement of carefully chosen photographs and words belie any surface objectivity. In recording the world around them, Lange and Taylor failed to realize the process of selection involved in all aspects of their endeavor. For Lange, taking photographs was itself an act of editing as she moved about her subjects and took multiple exposures from various angles, changing the composition of the photographs. Once taken, the photographs selected for inclusion in the book had to meet certain criteria, such as picture quality, descriptive or emotional appeal, continuity with other photographs, and relationship to the work as a whole.

Informing each of these selective processes was Lange's knowledge of the migrants' situation, which was, for the most part, derived from Taylor or at least influenced by his agenda. What Lange added to Taylor's analysis was an identifiable human element. By visually presenting the destruction of family farms, the displacement of farmers and their families, and recurring images of desolate highways, Lange gave a face to the disembodied statistics and trends described by Taylor. In seeking to humanely assist the migrants' entrance into an industrialized economy, Lange not only attempted to imbue the technology of her camera with passion (by capturing emotionally charged scenes and situations on film); she also sought to give a human face to the methods of social science (by utilizing photography as a tool of research and preservation). Photography, for Lange, was a way to introduce the general public to the methods and uses of social scientific inquiry while also being an effective tool in shaping government policy.

The methods Lange and Taylor developed in *An American Exodus* did succeed in gaining support for government relief efforts, but the audience for the book, published late in 1939 in the midst of international concern about war, never materialized. And while many critics proclaimed *An American Exodus* to be the best example of the documentary photographic books, "it didn't have its chance at the market for which it was intended."[40] This fact, however, did not diminish Dorothea Lange's impact on the nation's consciousness of the depression. In her most famous and most frequently reproduced photograph, *Migrant Mother*, Lange discarded most of her ideas about documentary photography and created an icon of the depression and a lasting symbol of victimization.

Even though Lange did not like to be considered a "one-picture photographer," she is best known for a single photograph, *Migrant Mother*.[41] The image of Florence Thompson, a migrant worker in the pea fields of Nipomo, California, and her children was the last of six exposures taken by Lange on a rainy March day in 1936. On her way home at the end of a month-long field assignment, Lange passed a sign indicating a pea-pickers camp just off the highway. Already having a box full of exposed film documenting the conditions of California agriculture, Lange passed the sign. Twenty miles later, Lange turned her car around and returned to the pea-pickers camp. "I was following instinct, not reason; I drove into that wet and soggy camp and parked my car like a homing pigeon. I saw and approached the hungry and desperate mother, as if drawn by a magnet."[42] Lange began to photograph the mother and children, without asking her usual questions about local conditions or the family's history. The woman did provide Lange with some information: her husband was a native Californian, she was thirty-two years old, they had been living off the frozen vegetables they found in the fields and the birds caught by the children. The family had just sold the tires from their car to buy food. Lange did not find out the woman's name, or the names of her children. Most of the encounter took place in silence.[43] As Lange remembered, "There she sat in that lean-to tent with her children huddled around her, and seemed to know that my pictures might help her, and so she helped me. There was a sort of equality about it."[44]

In the course of this encounter Lange took six exposures, starting with a long shot of the lean-to with the mother and four children inside. In this first shot, one child is smiling at the camera while the other people in the frame do not seem to be aware of the camera. The second shot is a longer view of the tent, now with the figures arranged and looking at the camera. Next Lange focused in on the mother and her baby in a medium shot that excluded the other children. The fourth shot moved in a bit closer to the woman and reintroduced one of the younger children, her head resting upon her mother's shoulder. Next Lange rotated her camera to take a vertical shot of the mother, baby, and small child, pulling back to reveal a worn trunk with a tin plate resting on the top. For the final shot Lange called back another of the children and had the children lean upon their mother with their backs to the camera. The woman raised her hand to her chin and struck the now famous pose of the *Migrant Mother*, which Lange photographed in a close-up shot. After taking these six exposures, Lange did not approach the tents of the other migrants. "It was not necessary," she said. "I knew I had recorded the essence of my assignment."[45]

The essence Lange captured that day was not the specific documentation of a unique situation, that of a failed pea crop and the effects it had on the Thompson family; rather, she captured a powerful image of victimization, an image of the challenges imposed on motherhood in depressed times, dramatically illustrated by the look of worry in Thompson's eyes. The theme of New Deal reform, the necessity of government assistance for the "forgotten" men, women, and children of the depression, is clearly supported by the photograph. By excluding the context in which Thompson found herself (the lean-to tent, muddy ground, abandoned crops), Lange removed Thompson from her specific wants and needs (food, shelter, and employment) and presented her as a symbol for the nation's wants and needs (assistance in troubled times). Without a specific context (provided through captions, accompanying text, or other photographs), the photograph could represent just about any injury caused by the depression. This photograph represented unemployment, dislocation, the effects of agricultural mechanization and industrialization, the deterioration of the family, poverty, and a host of other social ills.

In many ways, *Migrant Mother* is different from Lange's other documentary photographs. She failed to collect any background information on the

Thompsons, such as where they came from and why they came to California. She did not include other shots of the rest of the pea-picker's camp or the surrounding fields but focused her attention exclusively on Florence Thompson and her children. When Roy Stryker selected the final shot of the sequence for circulation to newspapers and journals, the context of the photograph was lost, especially when photo editors created new captions that failed to even mention the state in which the photo was taken.

The first photographs in the *Migrant Mother* series to appear publicly were two exposures (not the famous last shot) in the *San Francisco News* on March 10, just days after Lange took the photographs. Lange took the photographs to the *News* office and the editor notified the United Press, which in turn contacted relief authorities, who then rushed food to the pea-pickers' camp. The *News* story that included Lange's photographs described the "chance visit of a Government photographer" and how this led to the rescue of twenty-five hundred men, women, and children. The caption explaining the two photographs (one of Thompson, her baby, and one small child, the other of the tent with Thompson, baby, and small children inside and an older child in front in a chair) leads the reader to believe that the photographs are of two different families, part of the "scores of weary, discouraged and hungry families."[46] Both of these photographs illustrated the living conditions of the Thompsons better than did the famous close-up shot, and their use best served the function of specific government relief, but once the government remedied the particular conditions of the starving pea pickers, *Migrant Mother* took on the more general concerns of national relief.

Later in March, *Survey Graphic* printed the last exposure of the *Migrant Mother* series with the title *Draggin' Around People*, and the caption "A blighted pea crop in California in 1935 left the pickers without work. This family sold their tent to get food."[47] While the state of the Thompson's condition was inaccurate (they had sold their tires, not their tent), the caption did provide a locality and a cause for the look of worry on Thompson's face. Furthermore, an article by Paul Taylor following the photograph explains the conditions of California agriculture and the plight of migrant workers.[48] The goal of the photograph and article was public support for government-sponsored programs to relieve the distress of migratory farm labor, and not necessarily the dissolution of the particular distress felt by Thompson and her fellow pea pickers in March of 1936. The differences between the photographs in the *News* and *Survey Graphic* can be found in both content and context. The content of the *News* photos centers on the living conditions, while the *Migrant Mother* photograph centers on the emotions of an individual. However, this individual does not have an individual identity since no name or any other identifiers are given in its presentation. We do know she is in California, and an agricultural worker, but little else.

The difference in context between the articles in the *News* and in *Survey Graphic* can be seen in the form of presentation. As a newspaper, the *News* is characterized by immediacy in its reporting and locality in its concern, while *Survey Graphic,* as a magazine, is more concerned with describing trends over time and situations that affect a national audience. The choice of photographs in each instance reinforced the specific requirements of each form.

In October 1936, *Migrant Mother* appeared in the magazine *Midweek Pictorial* accompanied by the headline "LOOK IN HER EYES." The accompanying story on farm tenancy began: "This woman is watching something happen to America and to herself and her children who are part of America."[49] Taken completely out of context, the photograph became a larger symbol of the perseverance of American motherhood in the face of great adversity. Within the popular form of a weekly illustrated magazine, *Migrant Mother* became a national symbol of the depression. No longer an individual, Thompson's image had become an American version of the Madonna and child, signifying the strains imposed on the sacred duty of motherhood.

The pervasive theme of Lange's work—the effects of mechanization and industrialization—is missing from *Migrant Mother.* In this instance the machine (the camera) was a tool in assisting humanity and not a tool of destruction. Technology had made it possible for Lange to capture this image of Thompson and for this image to be transmitted all over the world. Lange saw her use of this photograph as an act of passion, a way for her to help Florence Thompson and her children, if not directly, then indirectly by helping those in similar situations. Even though technology created the situation whereby Thompson and her children ended up in a pea-pickers camp in California, this does not enter into the photograph, or into any of the photographs in the series. Lange did not include this photograph in *An American Exodus* since it did not suit the theme of mechanization and change, but the image of concerned motherhood that she produced provided more empathy for the migrants and their plight than any government report or news article. It succeeded in gaining the support of a middle-class audience for the poverty-stricken by appealing to the universal emotion of a mother's concern for her children. Any contextually created explanation for this situation took a back seat to the overwhelming emotional impact of the photograph. Viewers empathized with a character type, a worried mother. By creating this symbolic figure, Lange discounted the specific concerns of Thompson and her family, and, in turn, ignored any analysis or solution that Thompson may have proposed.

As a symbol, *Migrant Mother* succeeded in supporting the government's relief and reform efforts but failed to give the migrants a voice "to their government and countrymen at large." As a character type, and not an individual character, Thompson's specific concerns—as well as the particular concerns of the migrants as a group—were overshadowed by the generalizing effect of symbolism. Lange left it to others to give names and individual characteristics to this type. The most successful of these attempts was John Steinbeck's *Grapes of Wrath.*

3

The ancient commission of the writer has not changed. He is charged with exposing our many grievous faults and failures, with dredging up to the light our dark and dangerous dreams for the purpose of improvement. Furthermore, the writer is delegated to declare and to celebrate man's proven capacity for greatness of heart and spirit—for gallantry in defeat, for courage, compassion and love. In the endless war against weakness and despair, these are the bright rally flags of hope and of emulation. I hold that a writer who does not passionately believe in the perfectibility of man has no dedication nor any membership in literature.—John Steinbeck, "The Nobel Prize Acceptance Speech," 1962

THE PERFECTIBILITY OF MAN

John Steinbeck and

The Grapes of Wrath

With these words John Steinbeck accepted the Nobel Prize for literature and forcefully stated his philosophy and his motives for writing. A faith in the perfectibility of man informed and shaped his work. Seldom taken seriously, Steinbeck's vision of the revolutionary and educative potential of literature underlay all his work, especially *The Grapes of Wrath* (1939).[1]

Early in his career, Steinbeck developed his ideas about the role of literature in society and the role of the writer in producing literature. He based his ideas on an organic (or, as he put it, "organismal") conception of the world and man's place in it. For Steinbeck, man was simply one of many "cells" that make up a universal organism. Man would survive by working in harmony and understanding with nature and would perish by exploiting or otherwise working against nature. This was simply the way of things. The role of the writer, according to Steinbeck, was to educate and bring this organic understanding to the mass of people, who, in thinking that man was at the center of the universe, misunderstood man's place in the grand scheme of things. Man must learn to adapt to life instead of controlling it. Steinbeck believed he could help teach people this important lesson through his work, not by explaining theories and presenting arguments but by writing imaginative literature.

In practice, Steinbeck's organic determinism did not come through, in part because of his staunch desire to "hide" theory under his stories and characters. Steinbeck's more immediate concern lay in changing society by understanding the way in which groups of people became more than the sum of their parts. Steinbeck's organic philosophy found its fullest expression in his strike novel *In Dubious Battle* (1936), in which the mob (the phalanx, in Steinbeck's terminology) becomes an organism in its own right apart from the individuals who compose it. The power of the mob, especially an economically motivated proletariat, would be able to effect tremendous change toward a more rational, and therefore perfect, system of survival for the organism (society, the universe), which, for Steinbeck, was the tendency of all things. Steinbeck saw his role in this process as an educator, one who understands and conveys the potential of group action while remaining scientifically detached from the action.

The Grapes of Wrath sits uneasily between conservative representations of the California migrant farmworker problem as the result of the degenerate living habits of backward Okies and the radical critique of the capitalist system of agribusiness for creating such a distressed and oppressed group. The novel is less political than philosophical. Steinbeck did not teach the migrant workers how to reap the benefits of their labor. Rather, he taught them how to see life and their place in the universe. More precisely (since his chosen form, the novel, largely excluded the subjects of the book from its audience), he taught an educated and reform-minded audience how the migrants should see the world.

Steinbeck's rather paternalistic view of the migrants rested on a genuine concern for their situation, a reliance on "experts" such as Tom Collins for information on the migrants, and a belief in the federal government's ability to reshape the migrants into class-conscious democratic citizens. Steinbeck's paternalism can be seen in the form and content of the novel, especially through the interchapters and the characterizations of the migrants. This dynamic of migrant as subject, elite audience as students, and Steinbeck as teacher distinguishes *The Grapes of Wrath* from other dust bowl migration documents, and this difference is rooted in the conviction that the migrants' culture was not sufficiently developed for direct education in the role of a democratic government in an organic universe. Steinbeck believed the migrants did not have the capacity to understand their own situation; they needed assistance in learning to cope with modern industrial society. The migrants had to be taught their role in Steinbeck's democratic America.

John Steinbeck's childhood exemplified the life of a native son of postfrontier, post–gold rush California.[2] Born in 1902 and raised in the small agricultural town of Salinas, surrounded by the fertile lettuce and sugar beet fields just off the coast from the Monterey Bay, Steinbeck felt the tension between a frontier homestead environment of bindle stiffs and wranglers and an emergent "respectable culture" of universities and middle-class businessmen. His father was one such businessman who held the respectable post of Monterey county treasurer, and his mother was a schoolteacher before marrying. Both parents instilled in John a love of reading. At the age of nine he received a version of Thomas Malory's *Morte D'Arthur.* Years later, Steinbeck recalled the gift and suggested that it kindled his ambition to be a writer: "I loved the old spelling of the words—and the words no longer used. Perhaps a passionate love for the English language opened to me from this one book. I was delighted to find our paradoxes—that "cleave" means both to stick together and to cut apart. . . . For a long time, I had a secret language."[3]

Steinbeck's schooling was unimpressive, but the influence of his mother and various other family and community members reinforced his appetite for literature and interest in writing. An avid storyteller, the young Steinbeck wrote short stories, which he submitted to magazines unsolicited and unsigned. Unsure of his family's support for a writing career, he entered Stanford University in the fall of 1919 with his ambition to become a writer unavowed.

By most criteria, Steinbeck's collegiate career was a failure. Sporadic attendance, difficulty in conforming to administrative policies, a distaste for socially respectable college life, and financial constraints produced a record of incompletes, semester- or year-long leaves of absence to earn tuition and living expenses, and a failure to receive a degree. But Steinbeck received training and support from teachers impressed with his work and from fellow members of the Stanford English Club, which consisted of a small group of students described as "the in-group of the out-crowd."[4] Some of the students Steinbeck met became longtime friends and correspondents; letters to them remain the major sources of information on Steinbeck's method of composition and the intellectual influences on him.[5]

Upon leaving Stanford for the last time in 1925, Steinbeck embarked on a writing career and a typically spartan, Bohemian lifestyle, which included manual labor and seedy dwellings in New York, San Francisco, and Los Angeles. Through it all, the privileged position of the Steinbeck family afforded John a haven to fall back on—the family's summer home in Pacific Grove, on the Monterey peninsula. Though his early days of writing saw many lean years and empty kitchen pantries, he never lived in life-threatening poverty, and for a time after his first marriage, he and his wife lived rent-free in Pacific Grove, supported by a monthly allowance from his father. Steinbeck did, on occasion, work and live among the working-class people who were so often the subject of his writings, and in certain respects he gained an appreciation for the struggles of workers and others outside the mainstream of capitalist society. But the safety net of Steinbeck's family hindered a complete understanding of and brotherhood with his working-class, or impoverished, characters.

Steinbeck also distanced himself from his characters through philosophical beliefs that led him to view his characters as cellular components of an organism to be studied and explained. Armed with an early interest in nature and biology, Steinbeck spent a summer term studying at the Hopkins Marine Station in Monterey. In a zoology course, the ideas of William Emerson Ritter prevailed. Ritter argued that "in all parts of nature and in nature itself as one gigantic whole, wholes are so related to their parts that not only does the existence of the whole depend upon the orderly cooperation and interdependence of its parts, but the whole exercises a measure of determinative control over its parts."[6] This scientific theory, according to Ritter, applied not only to instinctual as opposed to intelligent behavior but even to "the human spirit," which was "inseparably and essentially identified with it all."[7] For Ritter, science and philosophy had to be combined in order to mend the intellectual break between science and aesthetic and ethical experiences.

In pursuit of Ritter's organic conception of the universe, Steinbeck read many of the philosophers who shaped Ritter's biological ideas. He regarded Jan Smuts, Robert Briffault, and John Elof Boodin as three organic philosophers who "share John Dewey's feeling that the facts of evolution forced a modesty on philosophy by which it had acquired a sense of responsibility, a new teleology in terms of its usefulness as a method of moral and political diagnosis and prognosis."[8] In reading these philosophers, Steinbeck enlarged his ideas about the physical world into the realm of the mind and spirit, and found a rationale that connected intellectual endeavor to social action. By seeing human thought, as expressed in action, as having an effect on the whole of the universe, Steinbeck reinforced his idea that a writer, educating his audience through literature, could help change the world. Steinbeck became more than an observing scientist seeking understanding for its own sake; he became a pragmatic philosopher seeking to reorganize the human organism through literature.[9]

Steinbeck's early works reveal his interest in the educative function of literature. *To a God Unknown* (1933) tells the tale of Joseph Wayne, a Vermont farmer who moved to California in search of land on which to build his dynasty. Set in the valleys just east of California's central coast, the novel presents the battle between man and nature and the realization by Joseph Wayne that the two are interrelated—that the larger forces of nature can and should consume the human forces that presume to supplant them. Wayne seeks to override the forces of nature through the strength of his will to build and farm in a valley plagued by recurring droughts. His defiance of nature costs him his individuality and his life. As Joseph Wayne lies dying, his severed wrists watering the ground with blood, he realizes his connection to the land:

He lay on his side with his wrist outstretched and looked down the long black mountain range of his body. Then his body grew huge and light. It arose into the sky, and out of it came the streaking rain. "I should have known," he whispered. "I am the rain." And yet he looked dully down the mountains of his body where the hills fell to an abyss. He felt the driving rain, and heard it whipping down, pattering on the ground. He saw his hills grow dark with moisture. Then a lancing pain shot through the heart of the world. "I am the land," he said, "and I am the rain. The grass will grow out of me in a little while."[10]

Combining myth and religion with a pragmatic concern for resources, Steinbeck uses the story of Joseph Wayne as a parable of man's place in nature. The environmental necessity of rain for farming and ranching is equated with man's need to know his place in the universe. Only through a knowledge of both these necessities can man live at peace with himself.

Steinbeck repeats this combination of myth and pragmatism in his next novel, *Tortilla Flat* (1935), in which the exploits of the inhabitants of a Monterey neighborhood are narrated with all the splendor of the Arthurian knights of the Round Table. The "Paisanos" (mixed-blooded, ne'er-do-wells of Tortilla Flat) spend their days devising plans for the acquisition of wine or helping a friend in need. The *paisanos* live by a distinctive code of ethics from which they never stray. Their actions (petty theft, drunkenness, unemployment) are often viewed as deviant in the eyes of the society outside of Tortilla Flat, yet Steinbeck reveals each action to be the result of living by the code. These are, in Steinbeck's eyes, noble people who do not fit into modern society. Their inability to change society results in their destruction. In the end the *paisanos* walk off in different directions, dispersed and forgotten among the masses of modern society. But Steinbeck's rendering of the *paisanos* is more than a sympathetic view of misunderstood people. What is important in this novel is not the sympathy Steinbeck displays for the common man but his use of the struggles of the common man as an example of the futility of resisting change. Steinbeck's belief in progress, or more precisely the progression of events, is not celebratory but cautionary. In recounting the struggles of common people, Steinbeck is in no way suggesting an adoption of their ideals for all of society, but neither is he happy about the loss of their ideals. He presents this episode as an illustration of a social fact: societies change. This social fact is equivalent to the physical fact of nature in *To a God Unknown,* and in both cases man must adapt to these facts or cease to be.

In *Tortilla Flat* Steinbeck makes no suggestions for dealing with these facts; he just states them. In his next book, *In Dubious Battle* (1936), he does suggest ways in which people can learn from the experiences of others in the struggle for social change. It is important to note that Steinbeck is not trying to educate the oppressed and depressed subjects of his writings but rather is using them as examples of his worldview, a case study for a lesson to be learned by an educated, literate, and socially concerned audience.

In Dubious Battle recounts the struggles of a group of migrant farmworkers striking against the low wages offered by apple ranchers. In this work Steinbeck utilizes the phalanx theory of group action: a group of people become a new being, a creature larger than the sum of its parts, and the way to understand this organism is to study the whole and not the parts. In relating the story of the strikers, Steinbeck gives a running commentary, mainly through the characters of Mac and Doc Burton, concerning the actions of the mob and various tactics employed to utilize the power of the mob. The protagonist of the novel, Jim Nolan, is a new Communist Party member learning the ins and outs of organizing from Mac, the veteran organizer. Mac's pragmatic approach—"we've got to use whatever material comes to us" in order to gain the confidence of the strikers—is counterpoised by Doc Burton's scientific detachment and interest in "group-man."[11]

> I want to watch these group-men, for they seem to me to be a new individual, not at all like single men. A man in a group isn't himself at all, he's a cell in an organism that isn't like him any more than the cells in your body are like you. I want to watch the group, and see what it's like. People have said, "mobs are crazy, you can't tell what they'll do." Why don't people look at mobs not as men, but as mobs? A mob nearly always seems to act reasonably, for a mob. (148)

Doc continues by positing the idea that group-man may act not for a specific cause but for the sake of action itself:

> It might be like this, Mac: When group-man wants to move, he makes a standard. "God wills that we re-capture the Holy Land"; or he says, "We fight to make the world safe for Democracy"; or he says, "We will wipe out social injustice with communism." But the group doesn't care about the Holy Land, or Democracy, or Communism. Maybe the group simply wants to move, to fight, and uses these words simply to reassure the brains of individual men. I say it might be like that, Mac. (148)

Mac counters by asking, "What's all this kind of talk got to do with hungry men, with lay-offs and unemployment?" When Doc defends the need for scientific knowledge, Mac replies, "If you see too darn much, you don't get anything done" (149).

These two positions illustrate Steinbeck's own ambivalence between theory and practice. Steinbeck, like Mac, sees a need and a way to fill it, while intellectually he feels incapable of effecting necessary change. His ambivalence is evident when the central figure, Jim, opts for the pragmatic approach of Mac and is killed with the strike left unresolved, though defeat is imminent. Jim opts for action over understanding and meets the wrong end of a rifle. Doc mysteriously disappears and is never heard from again. The antistrike forces have set up imposing obstacles, and the novel ends with Mac using Jim's dead body as a rallying point for the strike. Jim's physical sacrifice, Mac's pragmatic approach, and Doc's philosophical ponderings have all failed to make an immediate difference. The long-term effects of each of these positions are left open to the reader. The need for social change is never questioned, however; the way to go about change is the issue. Steinbeck never resolved this dilemma in *In Dubious Battle* because he viewed the strike apart from the larger context of political, economic, environmental, and cultural change. In the months following the publication of *In Dubious Battle,* Steinbeck embarked on a series of projects that taught him much about this context and resulted in his novel *The Grapes of Wrath.*

In August 1936, eight months after the publication of *In Dubious Battle,* George West of the *San Francisco News* asked Steinbeck to write a series of articles on the migrant farm laborer situation in California.[12] West and the editorial pages of the *News* were among the few vocal supporters of the FSA's migrant camp program. Steinbeck's research for the series resulted in a personal tour of the camp program in the San Joaquin valley conducted by the regional director, Eric H. Thomsen, who introduced him to Tom Collins. Collins, then managing the Weedpatch Camp at Arvin, informed Steinbeck about the operations of the camp and showed him a few of the squatters' camps in the area. Collins also gave Steinbeck a stack of papers, mostly reports written by Collins, as research materials. Many of the "human nature" stories recorded by Collins are found in descriptions of Okie behavior in *The Grapes of Wrath.*

Steinbeck presented the preliminary findings from his research in an article for the *Nation* published on September 12, 1936, under the title "Dubious Battle in California."[13] The same month, a strike of lettuce workers broke out in Salinas, Steinbeck's hometown. The suppression of the strike by vigilantes angered Steinbeck, who years earlier had planned to write a satirical novel about the "respectable" people of Salinas. He vented his anger in a story called "The Great Pig Sticking," which, upon completion, he threw into the fire.[14]

From October 5 through 12, the series for the *News* appeared under the title "The Harvest Gypsies." In seven articles Steinbeck described the living conditions of the migrants in roadside squatters' camps and placed the blame for their situation on a system of agribusiness dependent on a peon class of workers who were deprived of the rights guaranteed to all American citizens.[15] Yet even though Steinbeck blamed patterns of landownership and the corporate structure of California agriculture for the plight of the migrants, his suggested solutions did not confront these aspects of the problem. Steinbeck's solutions, consistent with the programs of the federal government, looked toward alleviating the miserable living conditions of the migrant worker and finding ways of stabilizing a workforce for the large farms and ranches of California. One of Steinbeck's solutions, the creation of subsistence farms for migratory workers, was based on economic rationalization.[16] He noted the relative inexpensiveness of creating such farms and camps compared with the cost of arming and maintaining a security force necessary to combat the inevitable revolt of the oppressed workers. Furthermore, he suggested that if California agriculture

> requires the creation and maintenance at any cost of a peon class, then it is submitted that California agriculture is economically unsound in a democracy. And if terrorism and reduction of human rights, the floggings, murder by deputies, kidnappings and refusal of trial by jury are necessary to our economic security, it is further submitted that California democracy is rapidly dwindling away. (61)

The civil rights of the migrants were uppermost in Steinbeck's mind, especially since the migrants did not have the capacity to gain these rights by themselves. Just as their ignorance of the relief codes hampered their efforts to gain relief, their lack of "social responsibility"—brought on by the destitute nature of their situation—limited their own efforts to claim their civil rights. Only when socially responsible people denounced the "fascistic methods" of growers' groups and vigilante gangs could democracy be saved: "It will require a militant and watchful organization of middle-class people, workers, teachers, craftsmen and liberals to fight this encroaching social philosophy, and to maintain this state in a democratic form of government" (61–62).

It is here that the contribution of Tom Collins became important. Collins fit Steinbeck's vision of a militant and watchful advocate of democracy. What Steinbeck received from Collins was more than "bits of migrant wisdom"; in Collins he found a kindred spirit. As Steinbeck biographer Jackson Benson observes:

> They both had a knack for getting close to ordinary people and winning their confidence. . . . They both had a deep sense of justice and injustice, while at the same time, they both had faith that our democratic institutions, through

the pressure of an enlightened citizenry, could and would correct the inequities which appeared at that time to be tearing the fabric of society apart.[17]

Collins's belief that the problems of the Okie migrants could be solved through the migrant camp program reinforced Steinbeck's conviction that education and understanding might lead to human perfection.

In a weekly report written at the Kern Migratory Labor Camp, Collins described the results of a recent camp election and the lesson it taught the men of the camp. After seeing direct results from casting their ballots in the camp election, the men decided to register as voters in California. Collins called this experience "the repatriation of American exiles," commenting that in the government camps the migrants are "humans once again."[18] This education in democratic participation was key to Steinbeck's goal of education in organic unity. For Steinbeck, the goal of the organism was survival through an increasing efficiency of functions. He saw democracy as the most efficient social structure since, theoretically, it allows for individuals to contribute according to the ability of each.

Both Steinbeck and Collins agreed that the migrants must be taught their role in a democracy by what Benson calls an "enlightened citizenry" and what Steinbeck referred to as the "socially responsible." What Steinbeck gained from Collins, aside from a few stories, was reinforcement of his ideas and agenda from the man he believed to be the preeminent expert on the subject of the migrants. "In this sense," Benson says, "the most important contribution by Collins to *The Grapes of Wrath* may well have been to the spirit at the heart of the novel, rather than to the details and color of its surface."[19] The mere fact that much of Steinbeck's information about the migrants came secondhand from Collins illustrates Steinbeck's faith in expertise as a tool in solving the migrants' problems, in the role of experts and the "socially responsible" in a democracy. Steinbeck concluded his series for the *News* by declaring:

The new migrants to California from the dust bowl are here to stay. They are of the best American stock, intelligent, resourceful; and, if given a chance, socially responsible. To attempt to force them into a peonage of starvation and intimidated despair will be unsuccessful. They can be citizens of the highest type, or they can be an army driven by suffering and hatred to take what they need. On their future treatment will depend which course they will be forced to take. (62)

Steinbeck expressed two important aspects of his thought here. First, he conceived of democracy as the equal distribution of rights and duties. Drawing on the camp managers' ideas about the democratic potential and significance of the migrants, Steinbeck urged recognition of the rights of the migrants as American citizens. Not only was it the government's responsibility to restore these rights to the migrants, it was imperative that the democratic heritage of these migrants be preserved: "They have come from the little farm districts where democracy was not only possible but inevitable, where popular government, whether practiced in the Grange, in church organization or in local government, was the responsibility of every man" (23).

Second, Steinbeck saw the migrants in the same light as the strikers of *In Dubious Battle*, as a group that reacted to outside stimuli. Just as the strikers responded to the wage cut by becoming an angry and hungry mob, the migrants reacted to the treatment they were accorded. Control of the situation rested in the hands of the socially responsible—the literate, concerned readers of a liberal newspaper such as the *News*. To say that the solutions offered in the articles were tailored to the audience for which they were written may be obvious. Nevertheless, it is important to note the similarities between Steinbeck's ideas about the educative potential of literature and such paternalistic reforms of the federal government as the migrant camp program. Both addressed an elite, educated audience and held it responsible for the continuation of a deplorable situation and encouraged it to assist in the revitalization of a people stripped of their dignity. For Steinbeck and the camp managers, dignity was more than a condition of self-respect, it was "a register of a man's responsibility to the community." The loss of a man's dignity was a threat to the community: "We regard this destruction of dignity, then, as one of the most regrettable results of the migrant's life, since it does reduce his responsibility and does make him a sullen outcast who will strike at our Government in any way that occurs to him" (39).

In this light the most important concern of reform was not the economic welfare of the migrants but their social status. By restoring their dignity (a task for the socially responsible), the reformers hoped to place the migrants in a position to demand what was rightfully theirs. Steinbeck's representation of the migrants as undeniably American further chastised his readers for their lack of concern and respect for the migrants. In educating his audience about the migrant situation and the ramifications of inaction, Steinbeck fulfilled his role of teacher and, for a moment, resolved the tension between philosophy and practical action in favor of the latter. This resolution resulted from his belief that journalism was an eminently more practical endeavor than literature. Once he returned to the novel form in *The Grapes of Wrath,* the ambiguity between theory and practice reemerged.

While Steinbeck's attitudes concerning the migrants had not changed between the publication of the *San Francisco News* series in October 1936 and the writing of *The Grapes of Wrath* (May to October 1938), his role in solving the migrant problem shifted from that of a political advocate to novelist. The *News* articles offered a pragmatic agenda for the resolution of the migrant farm labor problem: subsistence farms, union organization, and the standardization of the employment process. For the moment, Steinbeck himself was an advocate rather than merely an observer. In general, however, Steinbeck's fear that notoriety would taint the creative process of literature led him to shun publicity and to avoid becoming an active spokesman for the migrants. Constantly denying requests to speak or to lend his name to causes, he withdrew into the realm of literature to express his concerns and ideas about the migrants. He once asked his agent, Mavis McIntosh, to make an arrangement with his publisher so he would not have to supply biographical data for publicity. "Good writing comes out of an absence of ego," he wrote, "and any procedure which is designed to make a writer ego-conscious is definitely detrimental to any future work." [20]

In attempting to write a "big" book on the migrants, Steinbeck took working trips with Tom Collins into California's central valley and as far south as the California-Arizona border at Needles. [21] Two aborted attempts during this time—the unfinished and lost manuscript "The Oklahomans" and the completed but destroyed satire "L'Affaire Lettuceberg"—illustrate the difficulty Steinbeck had in finding the "right" tone, even the right medium, for what he felt would be his most important novel. [22] In May 1938 he started the first draft of *The Grapes of Wrath* and feverishly worked on the manuscript until October. A journal kept during the writing of the novel served as a warm-up for the day's writing and as a record of the writing process. In the journal Steinbeck's concern for accuracy of detail and honesty of character was evident, as was his concern that his abilities as a writer might not be equal to the task of representing the noble qualities of the migrants. For example, this entry for June 30, 1938, was written after the completion of Book 1, or what in published form became the first ten chapters:

Yesterday the work was short and I went over the whole book in my head—fixed on the last scene, huge and symbolic, toward which the whole story moves. And that was a good thing, for it was a reunderstanding of the dignity of the effort and the mightyness [sic] of the theme. I felt very small and inadequate and incapable but I grew again to love the story which is so much greater than I. To love and admire the people who are so much stronger and purer and braver than I am.[23]

Steinbeck had consciously created the migrants as stronger, purer, and braver than the average person in his attempt to express the "over-essence" of these people. "But my people must be more than people," he said. Through intricate description and abundant detail Steinbeck sought to define his characters' reality. "Slow but sure, piling detail on detail until a picture and an experience emerge. Until the whole throbbing thing emerges."[24] The "whole throbbing thing" presumably was the understanding of the situation and the realization that something can be done about it.

To express this understanding, Steinbeck tells the story of the Joads, tractored off their Oklahoma farm by a combination of natural causes, economic rationalization, and changing cultural values. Drought and wind combined to create the great dust storms vividly described in the first chapter. Subsequent chapters introduce the problems of sharecropping in the face of mechanization and economic consolidation, which resulted in changing conceptions about land use, productivity, and man's connection to the land. For the owners and banks, the land had become a commodity, a resource to be bought, used, and sold. For the Joads and their people, the land shaped their lives by giving each family a boundary and a connection to the larger whole. By settling the land, working it, and maintaining it the dust bowl migrants had developed a relationship to the land that was more than economic. The land became a part of them.

The tenant pondered. "Funny thing how it is. If a man owns a little property, that property is him, it's part of him, and it's like him. If he owns property only so he could walk on it and handle it and be sad when it isn't doing well, and feel fine when the rain falls on it, that property is him, and someway he's bigger because he owns it. Even if he isn't successful he's big with his property. That is so."[25]

The Joads, stripped of their land, are cast out on the road. An extended family consisting of Tom (the protagonist), his parents, grandparents, siblings, an uncle, and one brother-in-law, the Joads, along with ex-preacher Jim Casy, embark on a journey westward under the assumption that good jobs and high wages can be found in the California fields. Tom, just paroled from the penitentiary, becomes aware of the family's plight as they prepare to head out. Grandpa refuses to leave his home and, after being forced to comply, dies before they reach the western border of Oklahoma. Along the way, the Joads catch glimpses of what life in California is really like through the stories of people heading back to the Southwest, even though they have no home or job there. Poor living conditions, scarce resources, the death of Grandma, brother Noah's departure, and Connie's abandonment of Tom's pregnant sister, Rose-of-Sharon, all mark the Joads' crossing to California.

Once in California, a harsh reality grips the Joads and destroys their dream of a small farm. Forced to live in a Hooverville, the Joads learn about the hiring practices of large owners and growers. Realizing the futility of fighting the system by themselves, they seek refuge in the government camp at Weedpatch. There the Joads are treated with respect, offered the sanitary necessities of showers, toilets, and washtubs, and schooled in the process of democratic self-governance. Unable to find work near the government camp, they migrate north to a peach ranch, where they are hired as strikebreakers. Learning firsthand about the underhanded tactics of the growers and owners, Tom Joad defends himself from vigilantes who attack him and kill Jim Casy. With Tom forced into hiding, the family finds work in the cotton fields and a home in an abandoned boxcar. In fear of being caught and jailed, Tom leaves the family, hoping in some way to effect change in favor of the migrants. In the boxcar, Rose-of-Sharon delivers a stillborn baby, and a flood forces the family to leave their limited possessions behind in search of dry ground. In the novel's final image, Rose-of-Sharon gives her childless breast to a dying man. As their own family disintegrates, the Joads join the family of man.

The future of the Joads is unclear, but the lesson is not. The unity of the migrants is the key to regaining their dignity, their proper place in society. By understanding their place in society, the Joads will be better able to cope with the situations that confront them since they will see them as problems facing them as a group and not as individuals or separate families. Through the experiences of the Joads, it becomes evident that serious deficiencies in the political economy, brought on by the mechanization and corporate rationalization of agriculture, caused the migrants' situation. Blame is not placed solely on the political economy, however. In Steinbeck's eyes, the migrants' lack of understanding and experience with the new industrialized corporate state contributed to their inability to cope successfully with it. Natural forces such as drought and land fertility added to the combination of political-economic change and lack of Okie awareness to create a group of unemployed people without dignity.

For Steinbeck, the organic unity of nature, society, and individual requires an understanding of the complex of forces working on any given situation. He passes on this understanding to his readers. He illustrates man's attempts to exploit natural resources rather than living in accord with nature; the inadequate structure of American society, which causes great inequities in wealth and power; and the problems arising out of feeble attempts to cope with a problem with no understanding of it. In short, Steinbeck illuminates the problem and, through carefully selected facts and situations, leads the reader to conclude that the difficulties of the migrant workers can be solved through government-sponsored camp programs, subsistence farms, and union organization, all of which foster migrant unity. In each of these cases the solution requires *someone* (through the apparatus of a democratic government) to give dignity to the migrants by encouraging and teaching self-government and self-sufficiency. That someone is Steinbeck's audience: educated, socially responsible, voting citizens concerned about democratic rights in a free society. In Steinbeck's view it is only by giving the migrants the opportunity to be self-governing and self-sufficient that the migrants can ever learn these essential democratic practices. Steinbeck's audience is in a position to give the migrants these opportunities by supporting the policies of FDR's New Deal, and specifically the programs of the Resettlement Administration and the Farm Security Administration.

The Grapes of Wrath is not a proletarian novel but a novel aimed at teaching a middle-class, progressive audience its role in the shaping of American society and the future of American democracy. *The Grapes of Wrath* succeeds in creating an experience—and an understanding of it—that touches a reader's sense of justice. It seeks to provoke the reader into action. This is most evident in the scene in which the Joad family pulls into the Weedpatch government camp. As Tom Joad learns about the democratic orientation of the camp and its supply of health and sanitary necessities, he asks the simple question: "Why ain't they more places like this?" The watchman answers Tom by saying: "You'll have to find that out yourself" (393). In essence, Steinbeck is planting a suggestion in his readers' minds by presenting a solution to the Joads' plight that is limited, both in terms of the numbers served by the camps and by their ability to relieve the migrants' unemployment. Steinbeck's philosophical position restrains him from lapsing into outright advocacy of government reform. The actions of men are only a small part of the universal organism, and an understanding of the organism as a whole is the ultimate goal. Literature, in Steinbeck's view, is philosophical, whereas journalism seeks to evoke political action. Literature, through the grandeur of its themes, can enlighten its audience on many levels. As the Joads learn about their place in society—their membership in a group and the group's position in regard to other groups—readers are made aware of their own place and of the place of mankind in the universe.

> The last clear definite function of man—muscles aching to work, minds aching to create beyond the single need—this is man. To build a wall, to build a house, a dam, and in the wall and house and dam to put something of Manself, and to Manself take back something of the wall, the house, the dam; to take hard muscles from the lifting, to take the clear lines and form of conceiving. For man, unlike any other thing organic or inorganic in the universe, grows beyond his work, walks up the stairs of his concepts, emerges ahead of his accomplishments. (204)

Knowledge of this drive in man leads to an understanding of the migrant situation and an acceptance of the inevitable unity of the migrants in their biological drive to survive. Steinbeck warns the men of property and wealth that their lack of this human understanding will result in their demise:

> And in the night one family camps in a ditch and another family pulls in and the tents come out. The two men squat on their hams and the women and children listen. Here is the node, you who hate change and fear revolution. Keep these two squatting men apart; make them hate, fear, suspect each other. Here is the anlage of the thing you fear. This is the zygote. For here "I lost my land" is changed; a cell is split and from its splitting grows the thing you hate—"We lost *our* land." . . . This is the beginning—from "I" to "We." (206)

Men of property and wealth, according to Steinbeck, cannot understand this drive since "the quality of owning freezes you forever into 'I,' and cuts you off forever from the 'we' " (206). The migrants, in the course of the novel, are learning this lesson on a practical level, but understanding of the whole situation—the drives of man, the forces of nature, relative positions of owners to migrants—is reserved for the middle-class audience.

While telling the story of the Joads, Steinbeck addresses his audience directly in intermittent general chapters, or interchapters, in which he generalizes the migrant experience and gives his readers additional information beyond the experiences of the Joads. In other words, the reader is privy to knowledge unknown to the Joads and the migrants as a whole. For instance, in a chapter about used-car salesmen, Steinbeck describes the tactics used by these men to gain a large profit from the ignorance and dire conditions of the landless men. In another episode Steinbeck reveals the cynical sympathy of truck drivers and hash slingers for the migrants. He uses these chapters to place the migrant experience into the larger scheme of the natural world by describing the dust storms of the Great Plains, the coming of a rainstorm over the coastal hills of California, and the trek of a land turtle across the concrete expanse of a highway. In most of the interchapters a natural progression is described: loose topsoil is blown by the wind and the dust obscures the sun; thunderclouds form and drop their rain as water levels rise in streams and rivers; the turtle diligently makes its way across the highway in the face of all obstacles. Other interchapters describe natural progressions of a different order: the transformation of farmer into migrant as the farmer loses his land; the consolidation of California farms in the hands of a greedy few; and the inevitability of a people's revolt.

> And the great owners, who must lose their land in an upheaval, the great owners with access to history, with eyes to read history and to know the great fact: when property accumulates in too few hands it is taken away. And that companion fact: when a majority of the people are hungry and cold they will take by force what they need. And the little screaming fact that sounds through all history: repression works to strengthen and knit the repressed. The great owners ignored the three cries of history. . . . the changing economy was ignored, plans for the change ignored; and only the means to destroy revolt were considered, while the causes of revolt went on. (324–25)

In all these instances an understanding of the situation, the causes and effects, is foremost. Acceptance of change, both natural and social, must be accompanied by appropriate adaptation to that change. A lack of understanding and concern for these changes results in the owners' perpetuating an unjust system, while the ignorance of the migrants prevents them from adequately challenging the power of the owners. Complete understanding belongs to Steinbeck and, through the novel, to his audience.

The educative function of Steinbeck's novel, along with his philosophical theory of organic unity, created a portrait of the migrants as victims incapable of reversing their victimization without assistance from the government, supported by a socially responsible elite. The victimization of the migrants results not only from the greed of property owners but also from the undeveloped nature of their agrarian existence.

There in the Middle- and Southwest had lived a simple agrarian folk who had not changed with industry, who had not formed with machines or known the power and danger of machines in private hands. They had not grown up in the paradoxes of industry. Their senses were still sharp to the ridiculousness of the industrial life. (385)

Even though the migrants are aware of the "ridiculousness of the industrial life," their lack of adaptation to it proves detrimental when their agrarian way of life disappears.

Not only are the migrants ignorant of economic change, but their old way of life is wholly inadequate in modern society. Steinbeck characterizes the migrants as ignorant of basic sanitary and health concerns, superstitious, vulgar, and petty. In the government camp scenes, migrants must be taught how to use a toilet, how to take care of their children's health, and how to get along with one another. Just as little Ruthie is taught how to play nicely and according to the rules by the children's chaperon, the migrants are forced into a cooperative existence, even though the advantages of that existence are not readily evident; after all, the camp is incapable of finding all the men employment. Descriptions of the tactics used to teach the migrants various lessons render them childlike. In entering the government camp, the Joads hit a speed bump, which jolts their truck. The night watchman informs the Joads that "you tell folks to go slow and they're liable to forget. But let 'em hit that hump once and they don't forget" (390). As in teaching a child not to play with matches, getting burned is the best lesson. This holds true for other lessons the Joads must learn. Returning migrants tell the westward-bound Joads about the scramble for work, low wages, and living conditions, but the Joads do not learn the lessons of labor exploitation until they experience it firsthand in California.

The superstitions of the migrants add to the sense that they are backward and not fit for modern society. Uncle John constantly worries over the possibility that his sinful transgressions are bringing the family bad luck, and Rose-of-Sharon believes that "touch dancing" and playacting will adversely effect her pregnancy. The moral values of the migrants, characterized by Steinbeck as distinct from those of the larger American society, are displayed through crude allusions to sexual promiscuity—even in respectable preachers—and a tendency toward violence. Tom Joad's matter-of-fact description of knocking a guy's head "plumb to squash" and the migrants' general solution of finding those at fault for their plight and shooting them illustrate a frontier justice that is out of place in twentieth-century America.

In both content and form, Steinbeck addressed an audience presumably capable of understanding the migrants' situation and sympathizing with the downcast Okies. Aware of the migrants' shortcomings, as well as those of the owners and growers, Steinbeck's audience was privileged in its understanding and in its position to effect change. With *The Grapes of Wrath*, Steinbeck filled his self-imposed commission as a writer by teaching a socially conscious audience the necessity of government intervention on behalf of the migrants, as part of the struggle for a more rational form of social, economic, and political life. Exposing the inequities caused by property accumulation and industrialized agriculture while at the same time portraying human dignity, compassion, and courage, Steinbeck created what he called a "bright rally flag of hope and of emulation," from which the perfectibility of man might emerge. His evaluation of the migrants, like that of the camp managers, rested on a notion that knowledge and training in the modern democratic functions of an industrialized state would release the migrants' capacity for action on their own behalf. Education by the socially responsible would secure a place for the migrants in a democratic America.

The crucial difference between the camp managers and Steinbeck lay in Steinbeck's philosophical detachment from the world he created. This detachment allowed him to advocate change on behalf of the migrants without considering the realities of the migrants' everyday existence. By seeing the migrants' position in a context beyond the migrants' own conception, Steinbeck placed himself—and his audience—in a position to know what was best for the migrants; their lives must fit into the unity of the larger organism. The camp managers, however, were government employees, hired to fulfill the purposes of the government, theoretically controlled by the American people. In seeking to help the migrants, these New Dealers had to gain the cooperation of the migrants as well as the support of the general public. They had to fulfill at least some of the needs of the migrants in order to be successful. It is in this context of practical political necessity that Dorothea Lange worked so successfully. Lange and the government reformers worked in a context of political reality and economic power in which performance, not philosophy, was crucial. Steinbeck sought to illuminate the human condition by telling the migrants' story. By these measures the migrant camp program failed to reach its goals, while *The Grapes of Wrath* succeeded. Steinbeck became, for his educated audience, the voice of the migrants.

Steinbeck's concerns, however, went beyond those of the migrants and ultimately to the universal human condition. His concern for an organic understanding of the universe obscured the migrants' specific concerns behind the unity of man, society, and nature. The film version of *The Grapes of Wrath*, directed by John Ford, also obscured the particularities of the migrant experience in favor of generalizations about the human condition. Yet Ford's rendering of this condition is quite different from Steinbeck's, and it is to Ford's story that we turn in the next chapter.

Was it [the FSA photographic project] education? Very much so, and in more ways than one. For me, it was the equivalent to two Ph.D.'s and a couple of other degrees thrown in. I know it was an education to every photographer we had, too. And I'm sure it's made a contribution to public education. If I had to sum it up, I'd say, yes, it was more education than anything else. We succeeded in doing exactly what Rex Tugwell said we should do: *We introduced Americans to America.*—Roy Emerson Stryker, *In This Proud Land,* 1973

INTRODUCING AMERICANS

TO AMERICA

The Image of the Migrants

As chief of the Historical Section of the Resettlement Administration, and later the Farm Security Administration, Roy Stryker led the most impressive collection of photographers ever to work for the government.[1] The section included sociologists, economists, and other social scientists, as well as such photographers as Walker Evans, Ben Shahn, Arthur Rothstein, Carl Mydans, Marion Post-Wolcott, Russell Lee, and Dorothea Lange. The mission of the camera team was to document rural America, its people, its problems, and the success of the government's solutions to those problems. In their desire to "introduce Americans to America," the photographers, directed by Stryker, turned their cameras on a particular vision of America.

These photographs, as part of the larger documentary movement of the 1930s, illustrate the pervasiveness of the paternalistic rendering of the rural poor as victims of the environment and the economy. Dorothea Lange, in her work for the photographic unit, focused on the problems of poverty in the rural West, particularly in California, and on the creation of the migrant camp program. The visual techniques Lange used to illustrate the migrants' plight were reinforced by Steinbeck's words, Ford's cinematography, and Guthrie's songs. Together, these artists presented an image of the migrants that focused on the representational nature of the migrant experience to the exclusion of the specific concerns of the migrants themselves.

The most prominent descriptions of the dust bowl migrants focused on several key facts in presenting the migrant population to the public. Most descriptions included the fact that the migrant population consisted of families rather than single men, and that environmental factors were instrumental in the causes for the migration. These two factors contributed to the dramatic rendering of the migrants since both themes reinforced the idea of victimization. Whole families cast adrift by the forces of nature represented the precariousness of life in depression America. Dorothea Lange presented these two themes, along with the feeling of alienation produced by the process of migration, in this photograph of a homeless family walking on the long, desolate road.

Dorothea Lange, "Homeless Family, Oklahoma, 1938." (Copyright the Dorothea Lange Collection, the Oakland Museum, the City of Oakland. Gift of Paul S. Taylor.)

This photograph of children playing in an automobile reinforces several key themes evident in representations of the dust bowl migrants. The theme of families migrating, as opposed to single working men, is presented in the use of children as the subject of this photograph. Mechanization is represented by the automobile, which is here used not as transportation but as a home and playground. Despite their situation, the children play like all American children, reinforcing the idea that this situation is not due to the migrants themselves, as racially inferior, but to forces beyond their control. These are not just migrant children, they could be our own children.

Dorothea Lange, "Migrant Children
from Oklahoma on a California Highway.
March, 1937." (Library of Congress.)

The process of mechanization has not only left these displaced farmers without a home and livelihood; as this photograph illustrates, it also has left them out of touch with the modern conveniences of rail travel. In this photograph Lange places the farmer in a modern context, one filled with fast and efficient transportation and a tourist mentality, which has displaced the farmer. For this photograph, context is central to an understanding of Lange's intentions. Not only are the families placed within the context of a modern society (symbolized by the billboard), but the photograph itself is placed in the context of a narrative, *An American Exodus,* which describes historical change and questions the ideology of technology and progress. Once again, children are the focus of attention, reiterating the main themes of dust bowl representations.

Dorothea Lange, "3 Families, 14 Children, U.S. 99,
San Joaquin Valley, November, 1938."
(Library of Congress.)

Again, the irony of white Americans living in deplorable conditions is illustrated using the migrants and their experiences. In this 1936 Lange photograph, the conventional snapshot format of proud homeowners in front of their home is mocked by the desolate terrain, the skeletal attempt at a fence and the relative size of the house compared with the automobiles. The inhabitants stand on their doorstep, seemingly unaware of their failure to achieve the American Dream. The fault, this photo states, lies not with the people living in these conditions but with forces beyond their control and understanding.

Dorothea Lange, "Kern County, California, February 1936.
Shack in 'Little Oklahoma'." (Library of Congress.)

According to many reformers, the reason
the migrants themselves were not to blame
for their situation was because of their lack
of understanding and experience with the
modern world of technology and
California agribusiness. In representations
of the migrant experience this lack of
understanding was presented by Lange and
others in terms of traditional practices and
dress. This photograph of a migrant from
Texas emphasizes the fact that the
sunbonnet was not worn by this woman
alone; rather, it represented all women who
had migrated from Texas. Making note of
the woman's hat draws attention to both
the typicality of the hat for women from
Texas and the fact that it is unique for
California. This picture represents the
cultural clash between traditional
southwesterners and progressive
Californians that was created by the
migration.

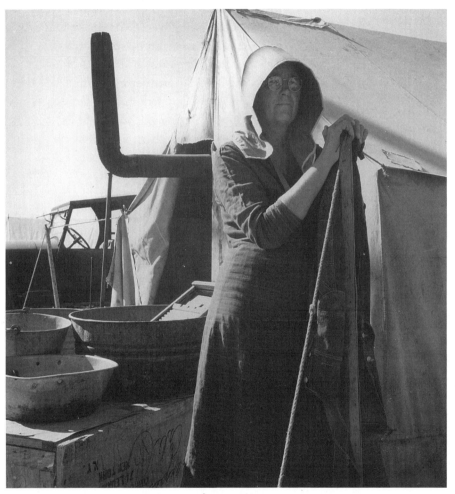

Dorothea Lange, "Imperial Valley, California, February 1939. Texas woman in a carrot pullers' camp. This sun-bonnet is typical of women who come from Texas." (Library of Congress.)

In order to resolve at least some of the disparities between rural southwesterners and Californians, the migrant camp program was designed to provide a clean and orderly place to live for agricultural workers, and also to serve as a training ground for modern cooperative society. In the camps, migrants would learn the basics of democratic self-government and orderly conduct. This order can be seen in the layout of the camp, in which blocks of "camping spaces" form separate sanitary units (groups of campers sharing laundry and rest room facilities). Sanitary units were more than just physical divisions in the camp; they also designated political representation in the camp council.

Dorothea Lange, "Schafter, California, June 1938.
FSA camp for migratory agricultural workers."
(Library of Congress.)

The order seen in the layout of the camps was maintained and enforced by the camp manager, who oversaw the workings of the camp council and all other organizations in the camp. The manager was responsible for keeping a record of all camp inhabitants and events. Tom Collins, pictured here, was the first manager of a FSA migrant labor camp and helped to define the role a manger should play. Collins often described his dealings with the migrants as an exchange between a teacher and children in which the manager assisted the migrants' education in everything from the use of a flush toilet to democratic governance.

Dorothea Lange, "Kern County, California, November 1936. The Arvin migratory farm workers' camp of the Farm Security Administration. Tom Collins, manager of the camp, with a drought refugee family." (Library of Congress.)

The main element in the migrants' education at the FSA camps was participation in the camp government, as seen here in this photograph of the Farmersville Camp Council meeting. The actions of the camp council usually filled the pages of each camp newsletter as well as the weekly reports of the camp manager. Both Steinbeck and Ford emphasized the self-help nature of the camps as signs of the migrants' democratic potential. The camp manager took responsibility for cultivating this potential, inherent in these white, native-born Americans, as the migrants adapted to life as laborers instead of farmers.

Dorothea Lange, "Farmersville, Tulare County, California, May 1939. Farm Security Administration camp for migratory workers. Meeting of the camp council." (Library of Congress.)

The transition from farmer to laborer also included, in the minds of most reformers, a radicalization of the migrants and their values. The creation of a rural working class was utmost in the mind of Carey McWilliams, John Steinbeck, and Woody Guthrie, while other reformers like Paul Taylor, Dorothea Lange, and John Ford sought a less radical class consciousness among the migrants. In both cases, all the artists and reformers neglected the migrants' own traditional, conservative political and economic views. In those cases of radical migrant activity, such as the United Cannery, Agricultural, Packing and Allied Workers of America (UCAPAWA), government reformers tried to downplay the participation of the migrants in favor of more acceptable reform groups such as the John Steinbeck Committee to Aid Agricultural Organization and the Simon J. Lubin Society. Both the Steinbeck Committee and the Lubin Society sought government reforms as the answer to the "migrant problem."

Dorothea Lange, "Bakersfield, California, November 1938. Speaker, a migratory worker and leader in the cotton strike, at the Steinbeck conference committee to aid agricultural organization, saying; 'Brother, 'hits pick 75 cent cotton or starve. Brother, 'hits pick 75 cents cotton or else.' " (Library of Congress.)

Before reformers could suggest proper reforms they needed first to collect information on the situation, in the best Progressive tradition. Documentary photography in the 1930s was based on this idea of bringing the problems of the depression to the public's attention. Dorothea Lange's first forays into documentary photography, however, focused on the relationship of individuals to their environment as opposed to her training in portrait photography where the individual is taken out of context and photographed in a studio. *White Angel Bread Line* illustrates Lange's use of context to make a statement about the life of the individual at the center of the photograph. Alone in a crowd, head down and hands folded as if in prayer, the figure evokes feelings of isolation and desperation, yet we see no indication of the causes of his plight. The photograph does not illustrate a specific deplorable situation but evokes the feeling of the "forgotten man." Emotion is more important than information.

Dorothea Lange, "White Angel Bread Line,
San Francisco, 1932." (Copyright the
Dorothea Lange Collection, the Oakland
Museum, the City of Oakland. Gift of
Paul S. Taylor.)

In *Man Beside Wheelbarrow* Lange turned the individual's context into symbols of his economic and emotional state. "I wanted to take a picture of a man as he stood in the world—in this case, a man with his head down, with his back against a wall, with his livelihood, like the wheelbarrow, overturned."[2] This use of symbolism illustrates Lange's concern for ideas and feelings over specific information. The elements in the picture are important not because they exist but for what they represent.

Dorothea Lange, "Man Beside Wheelbarrow, San Francisco, 1934." (Copyright the Dorothea Lange Collection, the Oakland Museum, the City of Oakland. Gift of Paul S. Taylor.)

Once Lange learned of the problems of migrant farmworkers from the Southwest, she began to focus specifically on the context from which these workers came, using her camera to document the effects of agricultural consolidation on the environment. *Tractored Out* was only one of many photographs illustrating the effects of mechanization on agriculture. The long rows of cultivated soil reach all the way to the abandoned house. These photographs are significant not only in content but in quantity as well, because they express Lange's concerns about the situation that caused farmers to migrate to California. She took many photographs similar in content (cultivated rows and abandoned houses) though different in setting to illustrate the widespread nature of the phenomenon. These photographs have their greatest impact when viewed in a series, within the context of each other. Lange's concern for context led to a search for causes. The causes she found included technology and its improper use.

Dorothea Lange, "Tractored Out, Childress County, Texas, 1938." (Copyright the Dorothea Lange Collection, the Oakland Museum, the City of Oakland. Gift of Paul S. Taylor.)

The use of technology is highlighted in this photograph in which the lack of modern technology is the major characteristic of the migrants. The disparity between the walking migrants and the reclining train passenger reinforced notions of migrants unaware of technology and its uses. The billboard's slogan, "Next Time Try the Train," suggests not only the migrants' lack of ability to ride the train (money) but also a lack of understanding about the various transportation options available.

Dorothea Lange, "Toward Los Angeles, California. March 1937." (Library of Congress.)

Trained as a portrait photographer, Dorothea Lange possessed an ability to capture people on film during moments of introspection. This unnamed migrant woman, looking down at the child below her, expresses a certain melancholy due to the positioning of her body and head. The downcast eyes, the body turned in upon itself, express sadness and isolation. The photograph says very little about the conditions of migrant life or the specific circumstances of this woman, but it does present a feeling of displacement and depression, presumably as a result of economic dislocation. By using this woman to express these ideas, Lange presents the feeling of economic loss as a direct expression of this woman, rather than as her interpretation of this migrant's condition.

Dorothea Lange, "Calipatria, Imperial
County, California, February 1939. The
Farm Security Administration emergency
camp for migratory workers in the pea
harvest. Daughter of a migrant who was
formerly a tenant farmer in Oklahoma."
(Library of Congress.)

Many of Lange's most provocative photographs combined her abilities as a portrait photographer with her approach to documentary photography, creating a portrait defined by a subject's context. In this photograph of another unnamed migrant, Lange showed the living conditions of this woman and used them to reinforce the woman's feeling of disruption and uncertainty. The tattered tent flap and unmade bed present a picture of a life in transition, on the move. The woman's questioning look adds to the disconcerting feeling of the photograph. Though the context is narrowly defined, the tent and its contents, the main subject and its context reinforce each other, and when placed in the context of other photographs of migrant laborers, the feeling of isolation increases.

Dorothea Lange, "Sacramento, California (vicinity). November 1936. Daughter of a migrant Tennessee coal miner living in the American river camp." (Library of Congress.)

In the first two photographs taken in a pea-picker's camp in Nipomo, California, Lange documented the living conditions of a migrant family by showing the tent and possessions, as few as they are, of the migrants. In these photographs the context of the family is the essential element. Lange enlarged the context of the second shot from the first to include the surrounding terrain. She also caught the attention of the family and had them look directly at the camera. Again, despite the posed look of the photograph, the main element is the depiction of the migrants' living conditions.

In the third shot of the *Migrant Mother* series, Lange focused on the mother and her smallest child but still retained elements of the migrants' context, such as the wood crate used for a chair, the makeshift tent pole, the lantern, and the dirty plate. The idea of motherhood is reinforced by the act of nursing taking place in the photograph. The viewer's sympathy lies not just with an individual living in such squalor but with a mother facing such circumstances.

In the fourth and fifth shots of the series, Lange reintroduces another child and places her in a dependent position just behind the mother. Elements of the migrants' context are still included, though not as evident or essential as previously. The theme of motherhood becomes emphasized more by the introduction of the second child.

Dorothea Lange, "Migrant Mother #3, Nipomo, California, 1936." (Library of Congress.)

In the final shot of the series, Lange eliminates all elements of the migrants' context and centers on the idea of motherhood by adding yet another child and turning the children (both leaning dependently on their mother) away from the camera. The position of the children enhances the feeling of dependency since their identity is determined only by their relationship to the mother. The mother, and her thoughtful expression, dominate the photograph, which is more a symbolic representation of motherly concern than a documentation of migrant living conditions. The editorial choices Lange made during this series of shots show how her desire to use the camera in a humane and passionate manner overwhelmed her desire to mechanically document the context of the migrant experience. *Migrant Mother #6* is more artistic (symbolic) than scientific (documentary), more passionate than mechanical. As such, it reveals more about its creator than its subject.

Dorothea Lange, "Migrant Mother #6, Nipomo, California, 1936."
(Library of Congress.)

This Dorothea Lange photograph, which is similar in content to the famous *Migrant Mother* photograph, served as the cover for the first reprint of John Steinbeck's *San Francisco News* articles on the dust bowl migration, "Their Blood Is Strong" (1938), published by the Simon J. Lubin Society. In this photograph Lange illustrates the migrants' context as well as focusing on the relationship of the mother and her child. (Another photograph of this scene includes the father lying next to the mother with his face prominently in the foreground.) The use of Steinbeck's words with Lange's photographs reinforced the authority of each artist and their representations of the dust bowl migrants.

Dorothea Lange, "Drought Refugees
from Oklahoma, Blythe, California,
1936." (Library of Congress.)

Lange took this photograph of camp manager Tom Collins, who provided materials on the migrants for John Steinbeck and also served as a technical director on the film version of *The Grapes of Wrath*. Jim Rawley, in the novel, and the nameless camp manager in the film were both modeled after Collins. In this photograph we see Collins outside the tent, standing protectively between the viewer and the young woman and child in the tent. The tent serves as a division between Collins and the migrants, while Collins himself serves as a mediator between the viewer and the migrants. This mediated relationship between viewer and subject underlies all the representations of the migrants. In this case the relationship between audience and migrant is mediated by Collins the reformer, Lange the photographer, and the photographic medium itself.

Dorothea Lange, "Kern County, California, November 1936. The Arvin migratory farm workers' camp of the Farm Security Administration. Tom Collins, manager of the camp, with migrant mother and child." (Library of Congress.)

In addition to the artists' and reformers' function as mediators between the public and the migrants, the authority of the artists and reformers reinforced each other through the use of common themes and ideas. In this photograph of striking cotton pickers, Lange has captured visually a migrant characteristic that Steinbeck emphasizes in *The Grapes of Wrath.* In an early interchapter, Steinbeck describes the process by which the tenant farmers were displaced by tractors and businessmen: "The tenant men squatted down on their hams again to mark the dust with a stick, to figure, to wonder." This questioning led to anger, an anger which the farmers' wives saw as a danger: "And the women went quickly, quietly back into the houses and herded the children ahead of them. They knew that a man so hurt and so perplexed may turn in anger, even on people he loves. They left the men alone to figure and to wonder in the dust."[3] In this narrative Steinbeck created the impression that the act of migrants squatting on the ground in groups was the first step in the direction of more violent action. The photograph, therefore, reinforces the idea by showing striking workers at a similar stage of confusion and building anger. These mutually reinforcing ideas are just a part of the larger overall impression presented in numerous photographs, written descriptions, and accounts. While direct influence is hard to detect, the overall impact is unmistakable.

Dorothea Lange, "Kern County, California, November 1938. Striking cotton pickers talking it over. The strike is failing. 'I don't care: let them throw me in jail. There's somebody will take my place.' " (Library of Congress.)

Another mutually reinforcing idea presented in *The Grapes of Wrath* and seen in this Lange photograph is the idea that other working people, both laborers and small business owners, were sympathetic to the plight of the migrants. This gas station sign, indicating an anticorporate message from the owner of the station to passing migrants, recalls the episode in *The Grapes of Wrath* in which a migrant family stopping at a roadside café ask to buy some bread. The openly hostile attitude of the waitress, Mae, changes over the course of the exchange to a sympathetic and benevolent gesture of not only selling the bread at a reduced rate but offering the migrant children nickel-a-piece candy at two for a penny. The truck drivers who witnessed the scene overtip Mae as a compensation for her good deed. The working class has shown its solidarity.

Dorothea Lange, "Kern County,
California, January 1939.
Gasoline station." (Library of
Congress.)

In the most direct instance of mutually reinforcing representations, John Ford's *Grapes of Wrath* brought to life Steinbeck's characters in a setting reminiscent of Lange's photographs. In this advertisement for the film, the name of John Steinbeck is larger than those of Darryl Zanuck (the producer), Ford (the director), and Henry Fonda (the star), lending the authority of the novel to the film. Also, the dominant visual element in the advertisement is a drawing by Thomas Hart Benton taken from the illustrations included in the book. The advertisement makes the connection between the novel's characters (as represented by the drawing) and the film's characters (as represented in the collection of faces in the lower left-hand section of the advertisement).

20th Century–Fox, advertising art from
The Grapes of Wrath, 1940. (Courtesy of
the Academy of Motion Picture Arts and
Sciences.)

This cast photograph from *The Grapes of Wrath* gave the public its first glimpse of the film and served as a link between reality and the film. This publicity photograph circulated in the press and could be presented along with, or mistaken for, photographs by Lange and others of actual migrants. The look of the characters recalls the look captured by most of the FSA photographers: melancholy, questioning, and uncertain.

20th Century–Fox, publicity photograph
from *The Grapes of Wrath,* 1940.
(Courtesy of the Academy of Motion
Picture Arts and Sciences.)

John Ford reinforced many of his own ideas about the migrant situation and American history by using many of the same actors in a number of different roles. Henry Fonda, pictured here as the lead in *Young Mr. Lincoln* (1939), also starred as Gilbert Martin, a small farmer and member of the militia during the American Revolution in *Drums Along the Mohawk* (1939) after appearing as the young lawyer and politician, Abe Lincoln. In both roles Fonda exemplified the simple and honorable American, acting upon firmly set moral principles and triumphant in the end. The actor, Fonda, became the embodiment of these American values.

20th Century–Fox, still from *Young Mr. Lincoln,*
1939. (Courtesy of the Academy of Motion
Picture Arts and Sciences.)

Fonda followed up his roles in *Drums Along the Mohawk* and *Young Mr. Lincoln* by portraying Tom Joad in *The Grapes of Wrath*. Fonda was readily accepted as a virtuous character because of his previous performances, despite the fact that Tom Joad is an ex-con and murderer. Audiences saw Fonda, and by extension Tom Joad, as embodying the same values as Gil Martin or Abe Lincoln. The unjust treatment accorded to Tom Joad in the novel becomes more unjust when it is imposed on Henry Fonda. The film also places Tom Joad in the tradition of American revolutionaries and the Great Emancipator by having each portrayed by the same actor. The studio elaborated on this idea in a press release for *The Grapes of Wrath* that proclaimed: "Abe Lincoln becomes an Okie."

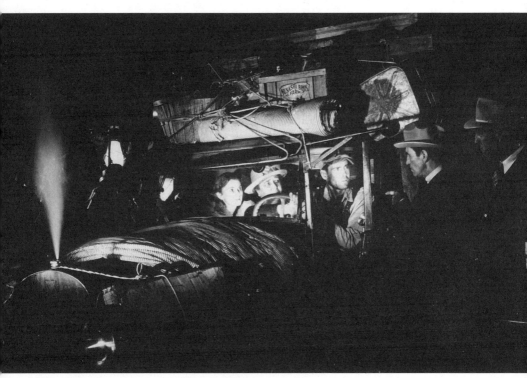

20th Century–Fox, still from *The Grapes of Wrath,* 1940.
(Courtesy of the Academy of Motion Picture Arts and
Sciences.)

John Ford, like Dorothea Lange, used context to reinforce ideas about certain characters. In *Young Mr. Lincoln* Ford often placed Fonda within a frame of vertical and horizontal lines, creating a formal structure that commands respect. In this still from the film, Fonda, as Lincoln, strikes a pose reminiscent of the statue in the Lincoln Memorial in Washington, D.C. The railing and bookcase behind Fonda frame him, as the sleek classical lines of the memorial frame the statue of Lincoln. By posing Fonda in this manner, Ford used the memorial to reinforce accepted ideas about Lincoln, as a great president and martyr, and lent authority to Fonda's portrayal of Lincoln.

20th Century–Fox, still from *Young Mr. Lincoln,* 1939.
(Courtesy of the Academy of Motion Picture Arts and
Sciences.)

In *The Grapes of Wrath* Ford used context in a very different manner from his portrayal of the young Lincoln. Instead of monumental framing, Fonda as Tom Joad is often enclosed by his surroundings, be it men, machines, or darkness. This technique reinforces the feeling of Joad as a character trapped in his circumstances and straining to escape. The visual tension in the film strengthens the emotional tension of the character. In this shot Fonda is surrounded by his family and all their possessions: they, in turn, are surrounded by the vigilante mob.

20th Century–Fox, still from *The Grapes of Wrath,* 1940.
(Courtesy of the Academy of Motion Picture Arts and
Sciences.)

The role of Ma Joad is also defined through character placement and context. In this scene Ma Joad feeds her family supper, leaving some remaining food for the hungry children of a roadside Hooverville. This action on the part of Ma Joad signals her developing understanding that the problems of her family are rooted in the problems of the people and, therefore, that any solution to their problems must come through cooperation and concern, not just for the family but for all the people. Visually, Ma stands between the family, safe and protected in the tent, and the outside world. While standing guard over her family, she nonetheless shows her concern for others; she provides the link between the Joads and the rest of the people.

20th Century–Fox, still from *The Grapes of Wrath*, 1940.
(Courtesy of the Academy of Motion Picture Arts and
Sciences.)

Unlike many dust bowl migrants, Woody Guthrie quickly found employment in California with his cousin Jack "Oklahoma" Guthrie, a cowboy singer in the Jimmie Rodgers style. While Jack cultivated a cowboy persona, Woody created a hillbilly character as Jack's comic sidekick for "The Oklahoma and Woody Show." Woody quickly realized that there was an audience ready and willing to identify with a "down-home" character. Many listeners were recent migrants themselves and saw Guthrie as a nostalgic reminder of home, but since they did not all come from Oklahoma like Guthrie, he had to create a character versatile enough for a heterogeneous audience, and that character was the hillbilly.

Upon Jack's departure, Woody took center stage and continued the show with a new partner, Lefty Lou (also known as Maxine Crissman, pictured here). They described themselves as "easy goin' country folk, plain ole Woody and Lefty Lou."

Photographer unknown, Woody Guthrie
and Lefty Lou, California, ca. 1935.
(Courtesy of the Woody Guthrie Archives.)

This 1941 concert by Guthrie in Los Angeles is interesting in the way the description of Guthrie attempts to connect him to the "common people." Making it clear that he will be singing his own songs, the sign further describes these as "songs of the common people," which Guthrie is dedicating to skid row and dust bowl refugees. The announcement performs the curious act of dedicating to the people something that already belongs to them. It is in this curious act of dedication that Guthrie's position outside of the migrant culture becomes clear.

Seema Weatherwax, Skid Row Sign Board,
Los Angeles, California, 1941. (Courtesy of
the Woody Guthrie Archives.)

By 1940, Guthrie had attracted a following of radical intellectuals and New York sophisticates. Further cultivating his image as a rural bumpkin, Guthrie played the role of organic intellectual, but his audience remained outside the dust bowl migrant population. This CBS radio publicity photo presents Guthrie the hillbilly with a fellow performer, Margaret Johnson, but Guthrie's appearance is more stylized and therefore more appealing to a sophisticated audience.

Photographer unknown, Woody Guthrie
and Margaret Johnson, New York, 1940.
(Courtesy of the Woody Guthrie Archives.)

Guthrie's position outside of the migrants' culture becomes even clearer in this flyer for the CBS radio program *Pipe Smoking Time*. In this lineup, Guthrie is the corncob pipe–smoking hillbilly in a group of sophisticated urbanites. Guthrie's function is not to voice the ideas of a rural audience but to attract a rural, pipe-smoking audience while not offending an urban audience.

Photographer unknown, Flyer for *Pipe Smoking Time,* ca. 1940. (Courtesy of the Woody Guthrie Archives.)

This photograph was taken by Seema Weatherwax, wife of sometime Guthrie singing partner Jack Weatherwax. On this occasion the CIO in Los Angeles had arranged for a fund-raiser for the migrant camps, and Guthrie and the Weatherwaxes headed to Schafter to round up some migrants to join in the event. Guthrie entertained the migrants at the camp while Weatherwax arranged transportation for "several carloads of people who came to the party, which turned out to be a big success."[4] In this instance Guthrie received the institutional support of the CIO and not the grassroots support of the migrants. In fact, the CIO used Guthrie to attract the migrants to their cause. This illustrates Guthrie's ability to speak in the language of the migrants, but it also shows his failure to see their basic distrust of labor organizations.

Seema Weatherwax, Woody Guthrie at Schafter
Farm Workers Community, Schafter, California, 1941.
(Courtesy of the Woody Guthrie Archives.)

Inspired by the plight of the dust bowl migrants, folklorists Charles Todd (with headphones) and Robert Sonkin (seated on table) traveled to the migrant camps of California in search of authentic folk songs. Todd and Sonkin collected what they saw as a dying tradition. In their attempts to preserve traditional folk culture, the folklorists ignored elements of a changing migrant culture, such as the introduction and prevalence of mass-marketed country music. The recordings made by Todd and Sonkin favored older musicians playing regional variations of English ballads, like fiddler Will Neal pictured here, over younger migrants imitating the latest country and western singers like Gene Autry.

Robert Hemmig, Fiddler Will Neal, recorded by
Charles Todd and Robert Sonkin, Arvin Farm Workers
Community, Arvin, California, 1940. (Photo by
Robert Hemmig. Courtesy of the Archive of
Folk Culture.)

Charles Todd (in headphones) believed that Mrs. Pipkin was the prototype for the character of Ma Joad in Steinbeck's *Grapes of Wrath*. Although there is no evidence that Steinbeck ever met the Pipkins, Todd's belief strengthened his claim to authenticity by associating himself with Steinbeck. Todd's use of Steinbeck to reinforce his authority included the title of an article about the migrants Todd wrote for *Common Sense* entitled "Trampling Out the Vintage," and his claim that he wrote the article at one of the migrant camps while Steinbeck collected research materials for *The Grapes of Wrath* in the camp library. The folklorists authenticated their collection of migrant songs for a liberal audience by associating it with the creative writing of John Steinbeck. In the end, fiction validates reality.

Robert Hemmig, Mr. and Mrs. Frank Pipkin, recorded by
Charles Todd, Schafter Farm Workers' Community,
Schafter, California, 1941. (Photo by Robert Hemmig.
Courtesy of the Archive of Folk Culture.)

The photographs of Dorothea Lange, both in her own work and in conjunction with Steinbeck's writing, combined with the image of the migrant created by Ford and Guthrie to present a composite migrant that represented the victimization of the poor and the sufferings of the depression. The symbolic nature of Lange's photos, especially *Migrant Mother*, reinforced the symbolic rendering of the migrants as the Joads in both versions of *The Grapes of Wrath*. Woody Guthrie added to this image through the character he portrayed in concerts and on the radio. The federal government endowed these images with its authority through New Deal reformers and folklorists whose vision of the migrants informed the artistic representations presented by Lange, Steinbeck, Ford, and Guthrie. From this series of mutually reinforcing images the migrants emerged as representative Americans in search of an ideal America.

4

Written in the universal language of visual imagery, the pictures have made appeal to the creative artistic impulses of almost all peoples and to almost every class of society. No man has been too high-brow to scorn the medium of motion pictures for his ideas, no man too humble to be denied the chance of success in this most modern medium of a world-old desire to tell a story.—John Ford, "Veteran Producer Muses," 1928

THE WORLD-OLD DESIRE

TO TELL A STORY

John Ford and

The Grapes of Wrath

For John Ford, film was a democratic art that spoke to all people and was open to all people.[1] The form was modern but the motive for making movies was the age-old need to tell a story. His own films combined modern technology and old-fashioned storytelling. His technique bordered on the innovative, yet his stories centered on such traditional values as American individualism, frontier democracy, and the fight of good people against corrupting institutions. Where Steinbeck strove to educate his audience and to convey an organic social theory, Ford sought simply to tell a story, one with a clear and definite moral, to be sure—an education of the heart rather than of the mind. While Steinbeck targeted a specific audience by selecting literature as his medium, Ford tried to include everyone in his audience by telling stories in the popular and easily understood medium of film.

These differences in approach resulted in very different renderings of the dust bowl migrants. Steinbeck and Ford each emphasized different aspects of the migrants' story. The same people who praised the accuracy with which Steinbeck illustrated the plight of the migrant workers blamed Ford for placing his portrayal of the Joads into a prefabricated Hollywood narrative complete with a happy ending.[2] Steinbeck championed progressive ideas about reform and relief, while Ford reinforced more traditional beliefs in moral values and the family. Elite reformers embraced Steinbeck's novel, while most of the public, migrants included, flocked to Ford's *Grapes of Wrath* (1940). Utilizing a medium capable of reaching the entire nation, Ford told his story in universal terms that touched all segments of society, but in doing so he too diluted the specific concerns of the migrants (fair wages, housing, representation) and fostered little more than an understanding of human perseverance and courage. Like Lange's *Migrant Mother,* Ford's Joad family became symbolic of a troubled America in which the strength of the American character endured despite the depression. It was this understanding, this visual description of their goals and aspirations, with which the migrants identified. Steinbeck's attempt to express a philosophy through the story of the Joads did become a part of the national consciousness about the 1930s. But Ford's use of images and myth in the Joads' saga created perhaps the most widely recognized document of the Great Depression.

John Ford's ability to tell a story in images using elements of American mythology can be traced to the manner in which his career paralleled the rise of Hollywood and the studio system. Ford's directorial career (1917–65) witnessed the most significant changes in the Hollywood film industry: the transition to sound, the rise and decline of the studio system under the control of powerful executives, the introduction of color film, and enhanced technical capabilities in cinematography, sound, and projection. Ford's ability to adapt to these changes, while maintaining a consistency of theme and style, marked him as an artist, a creator, rather than just a technician or a filmmaker. The themes foremost in Ford's films celebrate Jeffersonian democracy and the frontier spirit embodied in such common men as the cowboy, the farmer, and the dust bowl migrant.

John Ford's personal life remains obscure. Because of confusion, much of it fostered by Ford himself, various biographers have reported conflicting accounts of his birth and early years.[3] Reminiscences of friends and family offer conflicting views of Ford's personality. He was, in the words of biographer Tag Gallagher,

> a complex, perhaps multiple, individuality. Direct and devious, charismatic and sardonic, amusing and caustic, he generally dominated those around him, or at least retained his independence. He read voraciously, history especially, surrounding himself with books. . . . But he posed as illiterate, hiding his erudition, as he did his wealth under baggy clothes and his sensitivity under a tough crust. He was a man of many masks, a joiner who stayed an outsider, a man of action self-consciously reflective, a big man, Irish and Catholic.[4]

John Ford arrived in Hollywood in the summer of 1914 and worked as an assistant for his older brother Francis, who had made a name for himself as a director, actor, and writer with his own production company working out of Universal Studios. John quickly learned all aspects of filmmaking by performing stunts, acting, and eventually directing two-reel Westerns. The pioneer nature of Hollywood encouraged the careers of hardworking and persistent newcomers. The Hollywood in which Ford found himself had just witnessed its first acknowledged classic, D. W. Griffith's *Birth of a Nation* (1915). Filmed entirely in southern California under the auspices of a Hollywood studio, the film was more than a landmark of film artistry; it marked the ascendancy of Hollywood in the film industry.[5] Ford himself remembered the impression Griffith's film had on him: "I went to the premiere of *The Birth of a Nation* and at the end I actually strained my voice yelling. Before it, everything had been static."[6] Griffith's attention to detail in the midst of epic action would figure largely in Ford's own work. The growing myth of Hollywood in the wake of Griffith's masterpiece provided the perfect setting for the growing myth of John Ford.

Ford's first feature, *Straight Shooting* (1917), starred veteran Western film hero

Harry Carey. Even though the film industry was still very young, the Western genre already had firmly established conventions, established and reinforced by the hundreds of Westerns produced before Ford directed *Straight Shooting*. Agrarian settings and situations focusing on the family proved successful devices for the action-dominated Western genre. Ford thrived in the genre and while at Universal made few pictures outside of it. Whether by chance or conscious decision, John Ford enhanced and adopted many of the genre's basic themes—the independent nature of the hero, the primacy of the family, and the importance of a connection to the land.

In 1921 Ford moved from Universal to the more dynamic Fox studio, where he built his reputation and filled his wallet. Ford expanded his vision of the West across the American landscape to include various genres, yet he retained a reputation as a director of Westerns. By 1924 Ford's status as a director led Fox to lavish the grand sum of $280,000 on the transcontinental railroad epic *The Iron Horse* (1924). Grossing over $2 million, *The Iron Horse* solidified the standing of both Ford and Fox. Meanwhile, Ford built a reputation as lord and master over his productions by strictly disciplining his film crews and actors. Cultivating a tough image, Ford hid his compassion and charity. Through the depression, Ford anonymously sent weekly checks to twenty-two families via his friend, actor Frank Baker. The sensitive man under a gruff exterior had become part of the John Ford legend.[7]

While Ford was taking control of his film productions, William Fox and his successors successfully transformed the Fox Theaters Corporation and Fox Film Corporation from a twenty-theater outfit targeting blue-collar audiences into the third most successful corporation of the studio era.[8] William Fox was a pioneer of the film industry, opening his first movie theater in 1904. Building a string of theaters around New York City, he fought the all-powerful Motion Pictures Patent Trust and, with the decline of the trust, entered the production and distribution ends of the business. By the mid-1920s Fox had become a studio poised on the verge of industry leadership. Lacking the financial resources of the powerhouse studios of Paramount and Loew's Metro-Goldwyn-Mayer, Fox successfully gambled on the emerging technology of sound film production, developing the newsreel division of Fox's Movietone. In addition, the acquisition of key theater chains across the country and the takeover of Loew's, after the death of Marcus Loew in 1927, made Fox the largest film production-distribution-exhibition enterprise in the world.

Eight months after the creation of Fox-Loew in March 1929, the Hoover administration brought suit against the corporation for violating the Clayton Anti-

Trust Act. Seven months later, the stock market crash of October fell especially hard on a financially strained William Fox. A series of ineffective executives left Fox facing the harshest years of the depression in the worst financial condition of the "Big Five" studios. Taking over the presidency of Fox in 1932, Sidney Kent, former head of Paramount, brought the studio out of its financial woes through effective reorganization and a more dedicated approach to film production. In 1935 Kent maneuvered the merger of the recently formed Twentieth-Century Pictures with Fox and installed Twentieth-Century's two top men, Joseph Schenck and Darryl Zanuck, as chairman of the board and head of production, respectively. In addition to effective management, Fox was fortunate to have the two most popular film stars of the 1930s, Will Rogers and Shirley Temple, in its employment.

It was fortunate for Fox that John Ford successfully made the transition to sound, which proved tragic for other silent film directors, and that he continued to work within the studio system rather than to challenge it. Ford's films from the late twenties and early thirties show an increasing complexity and the desire to "amplify irreconcilability while still suggesting a higher harmony," that is, to illustrate tension within the confines of a larger unified theme.[9] The narrative tool of confining a group of people in dramatic circumstances allowed Ford to "make individuals aware of each other by bringing them face to face with something bigger than themselves." He said, "The situation, the tragic moment, forces men to reveal themselves, and to become aware of what they truly are. This device allows me to find the exceptional in the commonplace."[10] The growth of Ford's personal style took place within assigned film projects that were not always of his own choosing. Although there were some projects he simply refused to make, Ford's repertoire expanded to include war films, literary adaptations, gangster films, and historical dramas.[11] While the Will Rogers trio of Americana films (*Dr. Bull,* 1933; *Judge Priest,* 1934; and *Steamboat Round the Bend,* 1935) seem like typical Ford fare in placing traditional values in the face of encroaching "civilization," a film such as the dark and expressionistic *The Informer* (1935) seems uncharacteristic, as does the Shirley Temple vehicle *Wee Willie Winkie* (1937). Yet all these films share the distinctly Fordian elements of a protagonist caught between worlds and acting (either consciously or subconsciously) in ways that affect both worlds, strengthening one at the cost of the other. Each film demonstrates Ford's ability to work within the Hollywood studio system while maintaining a personal style and consistency of theme.

Taken as a prime example of Ford's major theme and use of characters, *Judge Priest* (1934) recounts a 1890s episode in the life of Circuit Court Judge William

(Billy) Priest of Kentucky. Will Rogers plays the wisecracking southern judge who favors the spirit of the law over the letter of the law, just as he favors a mint julep (which is mostly mint) over ice cream–eating, hypocritical politicians seeking votes. Billy Priest is caught between a past he cannot give up and a future in which he has no place. This film captures the tensions of a nation in the midst of industrialization. Kentucky of the 1890s, while retaining a veneer of the antebellum South, is succumbing to the "civilizing" effects of jurisprudence and politics and the "moral order" of the Daughters of the Confederacy. Priest is not a politician, and he mocks his sister-in-law's smug pride as a leading citizen; he is a veteran of the "War for the Confederacy" and has a frontier sense of right and wrong. He recreates an ideal Old South within the confines of his home as his black maid (in apron and bandanna) joyfully sings at the clothesline: "I've got to take down the Judge's clothes, oh Lord, that's what I'm a-gonna do." Black character actor Stepin Fetchit plays Billy's slow-talking, slow-walking, "Dixie"-playing sidekick. Rogers plays Priest as the benevolent master who sings "My Old Kentucky Home" with his servants and does the morally right thing even if it means using a bit of deception. Yet, as we see Billy reflected in the photograph of his wife and children who have long since died, we realize that the past is a memory and Priest is woefully alone in the present. In the end of this courtroom drama, which pits Priest against the despicable prosecutor Senator Horace K. Maydew, Judge Priest (reduced to lawyer by the letter of the law) is victorious in his defense of a man accused of assault; yet for him and his kind, it has been a last stand.

While Judge Priest wins his minor battle against the tide of time, for another Ford character time has run out. In *The Informer,* former Irish Republican Army member Gypo Nolan (Victor McLaglen) is caught between the IRA and the Black and Tans of the Sinn Fein rebellion in Dublin in the 1920s. Dropped from the IRA for not following an order to murder a prisoner, Gypo informs on his friend Frankie McPhillip in order to get ship fare to America. After fingering someone else as the informer, Gypo squanders his money on drink for himself and some fair-weather friends, is convicted by the IRA as the informer, and is sentenced to die. He escapes, only to be gunned down in the street. He dies in a church where Frankie McPhillip's mother forgives him for not realizing what he has done. Gypo belongs neither to the IRA nor to the Black and Tans and therefore has no place in Dublin. He seeks the safety of an American Eden, but his transgressions prevent him even from leaving Ireland. Dark and expressionistic, this film is stylistically very different than the bright and happy *Judge Priest.* Ford's mistrust of institutions and authority creates a world in which morally good characters (however confused) cannot exist. They may temporarily resolve the tensions of their world, but eventually one side will triumph over the other—whether or not this eventuality is contained within the confines of the film's narrative.

A case in point is Ford's version of Rudyard Kipling's *Wee Willie Winkie,* in which Shirley Temple plays Private Winkie, an American child who comes with her widowed mother to live with her grandfather, a British colonel, in 1890s India. Innocent of the circumstances surrounding British control of India, Winkie seeks to stop a war between her grandfather and the rebel forces of Khoda Khan. Shaming the natives by calling them "mean and angry men," Winkie secures peace while finding a husband for her mother, uniting her grandfather with his daughter-in-law (as well as herself), and gaining new friends of all nationalities. It is Winkie's innocence that brings about this peace, yet youthful innocence is a fleeting thing. We know Winkie will grow up and lose her precious youth, and with the loss of youth will come the loss of peace.

In expressing his doubts about the benefits of progress, Ford glossed over the inequities of the past (a common and justified criticism of his work). In *Judge Priest* Ford overlooked slavery in favor of the old Kentucky home; in *The Informer* he gave no explanation for the circumstances surrounding the rebellion; and in *Wee Willie Winkie* he used a childlike view of colonial India to obscure the historical context of imperialism. Ford universalized his stories by presenting his main characters as types, not as individual people. The already legendary persona of Will Rogers provided ample fuel for the mythologizing fire. Instead of creating a distinctive character in *Judge Priest,* Ford relied on the audience's identification of Rogers as a familiar type, the friendly and wisecracking uncle or neighbor. Rogers's characterization of Priest was barely distinguishable from the Will Rogers millions listened to on the radio or in his shows. Ford reinforced the familiar by referring to the main character as "Billy" or simply as the "Judge." Victor McLaglen played Gypo not as a character but a character type, the misguided but good-hearted man representing those caught between sides in political and economic wars. Shirley Temple, as the embodiment of youthful innocence and love, barely acted at all. She relied on the audience's identification of her as the ideal child. Ford's ability to enhance his narratives with star personalities reinforced his vision rather than diluted it.

These three films illustrate Ford's ability to work within the restrictions of the Hollywood system while maintaining a sense of personal style. His use of prevailing genre conventions (comedy for *Judge Priest,* expressionism for *The Informer,* and musical comedy for *Wee Willie Winkie*)[12] and the popular image of star performers plays an important role in understanding a Ford film and supports, rather than subverts, the basic Ford theme of a protagonist caught between forces in a changing world. Throughout the thirties, Ford developed his skill for working within conventions to achieve a desired result. In fact, Ford's particularly nostalgic vision fit perfectly into a Hollywood that favored illusion over truth and fantasy over fact. Utilizing mythic conventions, in addition to genre conventions and actor identification, Ford's vision of American history illustrated in *Stagecoach, Young Mr. Lincoln,* and *Drums Along the Mohawk* (all 1939) relied more on the lost ideal of Jeffersonian democracy than on historical fact, and favored the illusion of myth over documentary realism.

      John Ford, perhaps more than any other director, has been associated with American mythology, especially the myth of the American frontier.[13] His use of history as a narrative tool in the myth-making process has led critics to lambast the historical inaccuracy of many of his films. However, a more complex reading of Ford's use of history illustrates the function of his films. As Peter Stowell says, "Ford used film to mediate between recorded history and mythical history, so that while the tension and play between them remain, history has become myth and myth history through film."[14] For Ford, film was not art in the sense that artists revealed themselves through their work; rather, it was the medium through which filmmakers (as opposed to artists) showed the world to itself. Ford usually chose to show the world its good side through its bad. Ford's beliefs in a natural order of things (embodied in nature, the family, and Jeffersonian democracy) led him to tell stories that highlighted familial and democratic values. By utilizing the narrative structure evident in his earlier films (tension within a larger unity), Ford created stories in which conflicts tested Jeffersonian values. His films looked to what America should be through what America had been, or, more specifically, what America should have been. By placing the ideal in the past, Ford assured his audiences that the ideal was not wrong, just lost, and that the ideal was larger than the specific tensions of the narrative. By dogmatically defending the ideals of Jeffersonian democracy, Ford's films may seem naive or simple, but the way in which he presented his vision of the American past is far from simple.

Ford's first film of 1939, *Stagecoach,* illustrated the way in which he used form and content to reinforce Jeffersonian values. The film recounts the journey of nine passengers from Tonto to Lordsburg across the Southwest of the early frontier. The tensions in this film are twofold: first, the survival of the passengers against the warring Indians; and second, the struggles of the uncivilized against the civilized. The first tension is between man and nature, much like a natural disaster; indeed, the ominous name of Geronimo looms over the passengers like a flood or tornado warning. The Indians are merely another natural force to overcome. The second tension is between people—between those who live by the rules of the wilderness (natural morality) and those who live by the rules of civilization (social civility). Ford used the contained environment of a stagecoach traveling through the wilderness to represent civilization's tenuous position on the frontier. Within the coach is a cross section of society representing all classes from the social elite to the disreputable masses.

This microcosm of society reacts to its environment, and we discover that those thought disreputable are most suited to the struggles of the frontier. The intolerant social elite must either change (Mrs. Mallory accepts Dallas the prostitute after Dallas watches over her), be punished (embezzling banker Gatewood is discovered and arrested), or die (Hatfield, the southern gentleman turned shady gambler, is killed during the Apache attack). The disreputable, on the other hand, become stalwarts of the community. Town drunk Doc Boone delivers Mrs. Mallory's baby, Dallas mothers both Mrs. Mallory and her child, and the outlaw, the Ringo Kid, helps hold off the Indian attack until the cavalry arrives. The democratic nature of the community (they vote at successive stops whether or not to continue) allows each member to be valued for what he or she can do for the community. Ironically, it is the member most removed from civility—the Ringo Kid—who does the most. For Ford, society was a corruption of community, and the task of retrieving community from society lay in the hands of someone who was not of the society but instead a mediator between civilization and the wilderness.

Ford introduces Ringo (John Wayne) in the film by first showing him as a threat. Standing tall with arms and rifle outstretched, Ringo seems wild. Ford then focuses in on Ringo's face to reveal an innocence—not threatening but vulnerable. Ringo is at home in the wilderness but is not of the wilderness like the Indians. He is the only passenger to board the coach outside of town, and his role as the hero/mediator becomes clear when he takes his place in the coach on the floor between the two rows of passengers. Ringo innocently mediates between the elite and the disreputable in the same way that naive Wee Willie Winkie mediates between warring factions in India.

Ringo is the ideal frontiersman in his staunch defense of moral obligation (revenge), his independence, his impartial respect for all people, and his dream of settling down on his own farm. Antithetical to Ringo are Hatfield, whose moral fervor was misplaced with the Confederacy; Gatewood, who demands the protection of the military as one of his rights; Mrs. Mallory, with her disrespect for Dallas; and the Indians, who block the way for yeoman farmers on the frontier. Visually, the towns—never seen from a distance—are claustrophobic while the wilderness is expansive. Within the dialectical structure of the film, the winners and losers are evident, as is the heroic role of the mediator/protector. Ford creates a character of mythic proportions imbued with democratic ideals in a uniquely American setting. *Stagecoach* is not history but mythic America, and Ford's next two films brings these two elements even closer together.

In *Young Mr. Lincoln* Ford created an ideal Jeffersonian democrat by fictionalizing the early life of the country's most beloved mediator/protector, President Abraham Lincoln. Now form, content, and context all assist the myth-making process. Ford's image of Lincoln (Henry Fonda) alternates between that of a relaxed country lawyer (leaning back in a chair with his legs propped up on a rail or ledge) and the melancholy figure of greatness (low-angle shots, backlighting, framed by a doorway or some other solid and monumental structure). In this way Ford tells the simple story of a backwoods lawyer while reminding the audience of the character's future greatness. Within this story of young Abe's defense of two country boys accused of murder, Ford presents Lincoln as the ideal Jeffersonian democrat, moral ("I may not know so much of law, but I know what's right and what's wrong!"), self-sufficient (young Abe wins a Fourth of July log-splitting contest), tolerant (Lincoln accepts the town drunk as a juror since he is honest), and appreciative of a hand-built farmhouse. Surrounding this story is the audience's knowledge that this young lawyer will lead the country through civil war and become the Great Emancipator. From the opening credits underscored by the singing of "The Battle Cry of Freedom," Ford reminds his audience of the future of this man; and in the last scene, Lincoln walks off toward an approaching storm (with thunder that sounds more like cannon fire) as "The Battle Hymn of the Republic" fills the theater. In *Young Mr. Lincoln* Ford utilizes camera angles, lighting, and music to highlight the mythic potential of young Abe. This potential, combined with the audience's historical knowledge of Lincoln the president, creates a heroic narrative rather than a historical narrative. Context becomes another tool in the myth-making process.

Ford's next film, *Drums Along the Mohawk*, reinforces the myth of the heroic democrat by placing the hero in the struggle for American democracy. More than the savior of the Union, yeoman farmer Gil Martin is one of its creators. Gil (Henry Fonda again) is everything an ideal Jeffersonian democrat should be. Like the young Abe Lincoln, he is a farmer, a man of the land, not particularly adept in the ways of polite society but perfectly suited to community building on the frontier of upstate New York's Mohawk valley. The film begins with Gil's marriage to Lana (Claudette Colbert) and their departure from her home in Albany to his log cabin in the Mohawk. Lana becomes proficient in frontier life as they build their home and community around the fort at German Flats. When their home is burned in an attack by Tory-led Indians, Gil and Lana become the hired help for an old widow, temporarily involving them more closely in the affairs of the community. The approach of the British sends Gil and the other men of the community off to a battle that claims over half their numbers. An attack on the fort leaves the community isolated. One man tries to escape for help but is caught and tied to a hay wagon (arms outstretched) and then burned within sight of the fort. This martyrdom/crucifixion forces Gil to accept the responsibility of protecting the community by trying to get help. As he outruns the Indians, the Tories attack the fort. Lana, no longer the frail city girl, takes up arms to protect the community. Gil and reinforcements arrive in time to defeat the invaders, and as Gil and Lana leave to rebuild their home, the American flag is raised above the fort for the first time. Gil Martin remarks as he gazes up at the Stars and Stripes: "I reckon we better get back to work. There's gonna be a heap to do from now on." Democracy and freedom need constant attention.

With this film Ford presents the birth of his ideal community. By illustrating this ideal in three different and important periods in American history (the Revolutionary War, antebellum, and frontier eras), Ford creates a historical continuum in which the ideals of Jeffersonian democracy are seen as natural, desirable, and even necessary. Within the separate struggles of each period, the unifying thread of democracy provides continuity. This continuity of content is further reinforced by the continuity of actors in these films. John Carradine played the mysterious southerner, Hatfield, in *Stagecoach,* and the equally mysterious Tory, Cauldwell, in *Drums.* In both cases he is killed fighting for his beliefs, even though he ends up on the losing side. Carradine reappeared in *The Grapes of Wrath* as the mystical, if not mysterious, Jim Casy, again killed for his beliefs (this time on the right side). Eddie Quillan played one of the young men Lincoln saves from being wrongly convicted of murder in *Young Mr. Lincoln.* Quillian's bride-to-be was played by Doris Bowdon. Bowdon returns in *Drums* as a young neighbor of the Martins, and her wedding is one of the community-solidifying events of the film. Bowdon and Quillan appeared in *Grapes* as the recently married, parents-to-be Rose-of-Sharon and Connie. Henry Fonda appeared as the young Abe, Gil Martin, and the hero/mediator of *The Grapes of Wrath,* Tom Joad. Fonda's mild-mannered country boy Lincoln contained within its humor a sense of destiny and importance. At crucial moments in the film, Fonda's expression sinks into a thoughtful melancholy and Ford's camera frames him in an appropriately magisterial angle. These images remind one of standing in front of the monumental statue of Lincoln in the memorial at Washington, D.C., and reinforce a popular image of Lincoln. Fonda's ability to balance simple character traits with traces of mythic greatness continues in *Drums* as he transforms Gil Martin from simple farm boy and shy newlywed to the hero and savior of the community and, by extension, the creator of a nation. Through these two films, Fonda established his lanky frame and slow, deliberate speech as physical manifestations of self-sufficiency, morality, and tolerance. Not only could audiences accept Fonda in the role of Tom Joad, they held certain expectations for his character in *The Grapes of Wrath*.

By utilizing formal composition, content, and historical context, Ford created in his three films of 1939 a cohesive and coherent interpretation of American history based on the mythic ideal of American democracy. Ford's ideal of a Jeffersonian democracy, and its attainability, connects each of these films, as well as other Ford films. Ford's coherent vision was not hampered by the studio system (*Stagecoach* was made for Republic Pictures, while both *Lincoln* and *Drums* were Twentieth Century-Fox productions under the guidance of Darryl Zanuck), and his reputation as a director was clearly made. Yet Ford's vision of America was isolated in the past. His next film brought the promise of democracy to the twentieth century.

Less than a month after the publication of John Steinbeck's *Grapes of Wrath*, Twentieth Century-Fox's Darryl Zanuck bought the film rights for seventy-five thousand dollars. He quickly assigned screenwriter Nunnally Johnson to the task of transforming Steinbeck's long novel into a workable screenplay. Zanuck's control of production since arriving at Fox in 1935 focused on utilizing the notoriety of Fox's top performers: Shirley Temple, Sonja Henie, Don Ameche, and Tyrone Power. Zanuck himself was best known as a caterer to popular tastes for his role in initiating the gangster cycle of films in the thirties with *Little Caesar* (1930) and lavish musical productions like *42nd Street* (1933). Zanuck's purchase of Steinbeck's best-selling and very controversial book sparked rumors of Zanuck's intention, or the intention of the studio and its financial backers through Zanuck, to quash any film version of *The Grapes of Wrath*. Early in the screenwriting process, Johnson met with Steinbeck to discuss the adaptation, and Steinbeck's queries concerning these rumors led Johnson to publicly declare the dedication of the studio to the project.[15] Zanuck was committed to the project, though his devotion was probably economically motivated. By rushing production, Zanuck was able to release the film while the book still topped the best-seller list (the film opened in January 1940 at the Rivoli Theater in New York). Zanuck's manipulations in coercing Ford to use Fox contract player Jane Darwell as Ma Joad instead of Ford's choice of Beulah Bondi forced Ford into an adamant defense of Henry Fonda for the role of Tom Joad instead of Zanuck's choice of either Fox star Ameche or Power. Due to Ford's insistence, the freelance Fonda signed an eight-picture contract with Zanuck and the Fox studio.[16] Consequently, Ford gained in Fonda an important element in his vision of *The Grapes of Wrath*, while Zanuck gained the lucrative exclusive services of a popular actor.

Nunnally Johnson spent two months writing the screenplay for the film and claimed little interference in his work by anyone. Both Zanuck and Steinbeck approved of his screenplay. According to Johnson,

> Nine-tenths of the dramatic action of the book is in the screen play, and, to the best of my purpose and ability, the same sociological emphasis. Ninety-five per cent of the dialogue is from the book and the remainder, obligatory in instances of transition of sequences, is as shy and unpretentious as it should be. The ending, which is from the book but not as that, is one that Steinbeck himself suggested in New York, before any word of the script had been set down on paper.[17]

Devotion to Steinbeck's novel was important to Johnson, who felt the role of a screenwriter should be that of technician, someone who adapts the work of an artist for the film medium.[18] Filming proceeded in the fall of 1939 under the working title *Highway 66,* to avoid any controversy the production may have provoked. At Steinbeck's suggestion, Tom Collins was hired as technical director on the film, although there is no evidence of any significant contribution on his part.[19]

Ford's own enthusiasm for the project seems to fit his earlier concerns for simple people (Billy Priest, Gypo Nolan, Winkie, the Ringo Kid, young Abe, and Gil Martin). When asked what attracted him to *The Grapes of Wrath* Ford replied:

> I just liked it, that's all. I'd read the book—it was a good story—and Darryl Zanuck had a good script on it. The whole thing appealed to me—being about simple people—and the story was similar to the famine in Ireland, when they

threw the people off the land and left them wandering on the roads to starve. That may have had something to do with it—part of my Irish tradition—but I liked the idea of this family going out and trying to find their way in the world.[20]

Ford's interest in the universal—drawing a parallel between the dust bowl migrants and Irish potato famine victims—is clear. His focus on the family making its way in the world diffuses issues of class and politics, and his Irish parallel reinforces notions that the migrants' problems were the result of a natural catastrophe, not of economics or politics. Ford consistently denied any political intention behind the film: "I was only interested in the Joad family as *characters*. I was sympathetic to people like the Joads, and contributed a lot of money to them, but I was not interested in *Grapes* as a social study." Prodded about the social significance of the film, Ford said: "I am of the proletariat. My people were peasants. They came here, were educated. They served this country well. I love America. I am a-political."[21] Ford's storytelling ambitions for film seemed to him to be antithetical to making a political point. For Ford, storytelling was about myth and morals, and not politics.

The film begins with Tom Joad, just out of the penitentiary, returning home to find his family tractored off their Oklahoma farm and ready to head off for California and the promise of good work for high wages. The family—consisting of Ma, Pa, Grandma, Grandpa, Uncle John, Tom, his brother Noah, sister Rose-of-Sharon, her husband Connie, and children Ruthie and Winfield, along with ex-preacher Casy—embark on a journey in which they learn much about the world outside of Oklahoma and their place in it. Along the way Grandpa dies clutching a handful of the worthless Oklahoma soil that was important to him because it was his. Grandma dies as the family attempts to cross the California desert. Noah disappears, Rose-of-Sharon's husband, Connie, runs away, and Casy is taken away by the police when he takes the blame for Tom's assault on a deputy.

The family encounters other migrants in a roadside camp, a transients' Hooverville, a peach ranch, and a government camp. In each, their situation gradually improves and in each we can see a developing populist consciousness. In the roadside camp one man heading back to Oklahoma expresses his hatred of the situation in California. He tries to teach the other migrants the lesson it took him a year and a dead family to learn: the business of California agriculture is stacked against the migrant laborer, and the dream of a small piece of growing land near water is not to be realized. For his efforts, he gets chased away and the suggestion is made that he is a communist agitator. At the Hooverville, another man questions the hiring practices of a land contractor and is about to be hauled off to jail when he hits a cop and escapes. When Tom Joad knocks out the cop, Casy covers for Tom and is taken by the police. This is the first instance in the film when non–family members assist one another in an act against the system and are effective. In a similar manner, it is at the Hooverville camp that Ma first realizes her responsibility to those outside the family as she feeds the leftovers of the family's stew to a group of hungry children.

It is not until the Joads reach the peach camp that they see a concerted effort of "our own folks" taking action against the methods of California agribusiness. The Joads see angry men striking against the Keene Ranch for paying a piece rate that is not even life sustaining. As Tom searches for the meaning of the strike he finds Casy, who tries to convince Tom to join him in the struggle for workers' rights. Several "tin shield" deputies brought in to stop the strike attack Tom, Casy, and some other strikers. Casy dies in the attack; Tom kills a vigilante and thus becomes an outlaw and a threat to his family's security. Ma convinces Tom to stay with the family since she needs his help to hold the family together. In Ma's eyes the family has lost the traditional anchor of their existence when they lost their land. She explains the necessity of a strong male presence in the lives of the younger children and the abandoned mother-to-be, Rose-of-Sharon.

The family leaves the peach ranch together and finds itself at the Farmworkers' Wheat Patch Camp run by the Department of Agriculture. Here the government treats the Joads decently and gives them the sanitary necessities for a healthy existence. It is in the government camp that the greatest act of migrant worker solidarity takes place. The men of the camp devise a scheme whereby a plan by local growers to disrupt the square dance, create a riot, and shut down the camp is thwarted. Again Tom plays an important role. His presence, however, endangers the family when authorities track him to the government camp. He leaves the family after trying to convey to Ma the lessons he has learned. He himself will try to find some answers and see if there is something he can do for "the people." "Maybe a guy doesn't have a soul of his own but is just a part of one great big soul," he says, and therefore the sacrifice of one person is strengthening to the whole. As the family leaves the government camp, Ma summarizes the lessons she has learned. She realizes that persevering through the events of life "makes us tough" and is the characteristic that will enable "the people" to outlast the wealthy. "Cain't nobody lick us," she says. "We're the people who live. We'll go on forever, 'cuz we're the people." The Joads drive off, one truck in a parade of workers.

The story of this film is the moral education of the Joads, mainly through the characters of Tom (Henry Fonda) and Ma (Jane Darwell), from a worldview centered on the family to one centered on "the people." Tom, an outsider, literally cut off from society in the penitentiary, becomes a hero/protector of the people. When he is first seen, he is a lone figure traveling along a deserted road. Even though he leaves the film in the same fashion, it is clear he is no longer alone. He tells Ma as he leaves that, although he may not be with the family, "I'll be everywhere":

> wherever you look. Wherever there's a fight so hungry people can eat, I'll be there. Wherever there's a cop beating up a guy, I'll be there. I'll be in the way guys yell when they're mad—and I'll be in the way kids laugh when they're hungry an' they know supper's ready. An' when our people eat the stuff they raise, an' live in the houses they build, why I'll be there too.

He is no longer a social outcast but a man of the people. Tom has come to the realization that he must act in order to effect change. Fonda's exit over the hill in the rising sun implies hope through its association with his earlier exits in *Lincoln* and *Drums,* both of which lead to future success. Young Abe became president and emancipator, and revolutionary Gil Martin, and others like him, settled and forged the American nation. Implied in Fonda's exit from *Grapes* is his ultimate success; even his final soliloquy moves from hunger to action to results.

Ford asserted that although Tom's departure would have been the logical end of the film, "we wanted to see what the hell was happening with the mother and the father and the girl; and the mother had a little soliloquy which was alright."[22] Whether or not Ford himself filmed the final scene with Ma Joad proclaiming "We're the people" is unclear. Conflicting accounts credit either Johnson or Zanuck with writing the scene, and either Ford or Zanuck with shooting it.[23] The published version of Johnson's screenplay includes Ma's speech, followed by a shot of the Joad truck passing a Chevy on the open highway:

> The truck, steaming and rattling and churning, passes the Chevrolet and Al leans out of the window and waves a jeering hand at it. As the Joad truck pulls in front, we see Ruthie and Winfield laughing with excitement over the triumph. Even Uncle John shares the general satisfaction. Grinning, he waves. As the truck moves away along the road, all three are beaming and waving. Further along the truck passes a sign on the side of the road. It says NO HELP WANTED. The scene fades out.[24]

This final image is absent from the finished film. Johnson's version calls into question Ma's optimism and casts doubts over the Joads' future. The film's final image, a parade of trucks traveling through the orchards of California, seems consistent with Ford's imagery in other films. *Judge Priest, Wee Willie Winkie,* and *Drums Along the Mohawk* all end with parades of some sort. The image harks back to the internal theme of the road, seen in the very first shot of the film and echoed throughout. It excludes the ambiguity implied by Johnson's "NO HELP WANTED" sign but unifies Tom's initial homecoming with the Joads' homecoming to "the people." It is doubtful that Ford would have ended the film with the Joads still in the government camp, the implication being that they had arrived at their goal and went no further.

The film's ending gives no indication of what happens to Rose-of-Sharon (Doris Bowdon) and her unborn baby. Johnson's script has Ma comforting her daughter as they leave the government camp: "Try to be strong, honey. Someday it'll be different—someday you'll have another one. You're still jus' a little girl, remember."[25] This dialogue is omitted from the film. Although Rose-of-Sharon's health does not look good as she is loaded onto the truck, the implication is that she, and the rest of the family, will be fine. This impression is reinforced by the image of actress Doris Bowdon in three consecutive Ford films in which she plays first a bride-to-be (Carrie Sue in *Lincoln*), then a bride (Mary Reall in *Drums*), and then finally a mother-to-be in *Grapes*.[26]

The overall optimism of the film, Tom's eventual success and Rose-of-Sharon's health, is strengthened by Ma's declaration of perseverance. "The people" will survive because of what they are, not because of what they have become in the face of this journey. While Tom's leaving indicates the birth of a new character (the active hero/protector), Ma's final speech indicates a new understanding. Tom's call to duty is balanced by Ma's understanding that they will survive precisely because they have not changed. The values Ma holds at the end of the film are the same as earlier (keep the family together); the only difference is that at the end they encircle a much larger family. The anchor of land that held the family together is left behind in Oklahoma and replaced with the new anchor of the people. Visually, fences that abound and separate families in the early Oklahoma scenes are absent in the rest of the film; the gate around the government camp echoes the family's boundaries back home but includes a much larger family.

In keeping with Ford's ideas concerning the ideal Jeffersonian democrat, the Joads as a family and Tom as an individual are moral, self-sufficient, innocent (more so in the beginning than at the end), and looking for "a piece of growing land near water." The ideal democrat is not a member of the self-elected camp committee or the New Deal camp manager of the government camp; they lack the individual self-sufficiency of the Joads. The camp has institutionalized the democratic ideal and therefore subverted one of its main characteristics, individualism. The Joads participate in camp functions (the dance as a communal ritual), and Tom is central to the migrants' successful subverting of the growers' plan to close down the camp. But in the end the Joads' dream of landownership is not to be found within the institutional arms of the government. Democracy is natural to the Joads and the migrants. Firmly anchored in "the people," democracy will be everywhere they are, like Tom himself.

True to Nunnally Johnson's claims, the majority of the film's action and dialogue are from the book. The major difference is in the chronology. By having the Joads arrive at the peach ranch before the government camp (reversing Steinbeck's narrative), Johnson traces a progression from the squalor of the Hooverville to the oppression of the peach ranch to the benevolence of the government camp. Ford visually reinforces this progression in presenting a series of brighter scenes (there is more daytime action in the government camp than elsewhere, and night scenes there are lighted by electric lights as opposed to the fires of the roadside camp and the Hooverville). The migrants' situation in California progresses from the glazed-eyed passivity of the Hooverville occupants to the bright and happy activity of the government camp; finally the Joads head off for the promise of twenty days' work (supposedly at good wages) and a bright future.

For Ford, the migrants found what they had lost—the Jeffersonian ideal; for Steinbeck, the migrants needed to learn a new ideal, one of shared humanity, the organic universe. Just as Steinbeck and the camp managers looked forward to the social democratic potential of the migrants, Ford and his migrants looked back to the democratic ideal (Jefferson's yeoman farmer) they thought they had left behind. Steinbeck sought to change the migrants through reform programs, while Ford sought to strengthen the migrant in the face of change. Steinbeck's book provokes its readers to act, while the film does not. But the action provoked by Steinbeck was not consistent with the desires of the migrants themselves. Both Steinbeck's and Ford's versions of *The Grapes of Wrath*, as well as Dorothea Lange's photographs, characterized the migrants as victims of circumstance unable to effect change without assistance. Ford's connection to the migrants was stronger than Steinbeck's, and his film was more accessible to them in both form and content than was Steinbeck's novel. Steinbeck universalized the migrant experience in order to enlighten an elite minority, while Ford universalized the same experience in order to attract a popular audience.

Like the symbolic renderings of documentary photography, the easily interpreted images of a motion picture enabled John Ford to tell stories to a great many people. His ability to utilize accepted conventions of filmmaking and the Hollywood studio system made possible a universal rendering of the dust bowl migration. His story of the migrants, since it reinforced the widely accepted American ideal of Jeffersonian democracy so important in the "plain-folk Americanism" of the migrants, reinforced the migrants' own understanding of themselves and their place in society. But Ford did not single out the migrants as his audience; he tried to speak to as large a segment of the American population as possible, of which the migrants were but a part. Lange's photographs (through their universality), Steinbeck's novel (through its exclusiveness), and Ford's film (through its all-inclusiveness) failed to speak to the migrants on their own terms. Each, in a sense, failed to represent the migrants as the migrants represented themselves. Neither Ford, Steinbeck, nor Lange presented the Okies' unique culture. While Lange assisted government reformers, Steinbeck helped an elite understand the migrants, and Ford brought understanding to a large public; but none of them helped the migrants understand one another. The folk song, brought west with the migrants, provided a familiar medium that could be used to express the migrants' concerns and ambitions to each other and to themselves. This self-understanding was then transformed and transmitted to the larger public through the songs of Woody Guthrie.

5

You elected me to this office
Of a poet and a singer
And I think I know
What you want me to do here
Things are said in history
And they are said again
And these of today
Have got to be said
Said again
Because today is our first time
To say
What we are today—
And I will say
And sing of these things
These things
That you fight for today.*
—Woody Guthrie, undated

THE THINGS THAT

YOU FIGHT FOR

Woody Guthrie and

the *Dust Bowl Ballads*

Woody Guthrie knew he held a privileged position among his people. Self-elected as their poet and singer, Guthrie felt a great responsibility to fight on behalf of poor people's struggles. A native Oklahoman, he was perhaps the best-known "Dust Bowl refugee" next to the fictitious Tom Joad or Dorothea Lange's nameless *Migrant Mother.* Guthrie traveled across the states and wrote about what he saw. His experiences, while not typical of dust bowl migrants, became the foundation for songs that spoke to the migrant experience in a form familiar to the migrants. Guthrie utilized the traditional folk song form, sometimes simply changing the words of an old melody, in order to politicize his audience. While embodying the Okie migrant, Guthrie extended the migrant experience to include workers and the unemployed outside of Oklahoma's farms and California's fields. And while his main concern was the political education of the working class, Guthrie knew that his privileged position as an entertainer enabled him to reach a wider audience, which included the participants and patrons of the Hollywood and New York artistic and radical communities.

Just as Lange placed the migrants in a universal context, and Steinbeck placed them in a philosophical context, and Ford placed them in a mythic populist context, Guthrie included the migrants on the side of the have-nots in a highly politicized context. For Guthrie, the folk song provided a vehicle to speak directly and intimately to the working class and to those who were in a position to help them. In this sense he was a political educator; aside from singing his songs he also wrote for *People's World* and the *Daily Worker.* Though never a card-carrying member of the Communist Party, Guthrie's political sympathies lay with the party and he assisted it in fund-raising and organizing.

From Guthrie's dual role as Okie chronicler and political activist, we get a vivid picture of the dust storms, the dislocation, disruption, and despair of migration, the conditions of migrant life, and a sense of the migrants' traditions and values, along with an interpretation of the causes of the migrants' problems and suggested solutions. While Guthrie praised the same traditional values of family and morality highlighted by Ford in *The Grapes of Wrath,* he also advocated the migrant camp program and other reforms supported by Steinbeck and Lange. For Guthrie, changes in the political economy would reinvigorate the traditional, or what he called simple, values of working people. Guthrie rejected the passive resistance to corporate capitalism offered by Ford and was more radical than Lange or Steinbeck in calling for reform. Guthrie advocated a combi-

---

nation of Ford's familial values, Steinbeck's organic worker, and Lange's worthy victim. Guthrie, in essence, combined elements of each position into his role of folksinger/activist and therefore was able to speak to the migrants on their own terms while also speaking on behalf of the migrants to a larger audience. Far from the simple country boy he claimed to be, Guthrie, as an Okie activist, created an image of himself and the dust bowl migration that sought to center the migrant in the debate over American capitalism. In the end, however, Guthrie failed to understand the unity of politics, economics, and traditional values in Okie culture, and in seeking to change the migrants' status in the political economy, Guthrie distanced himself from the migrants' self-expressed concerns.

Born in Okemah, Oklahoma, on July 14, 1912, Woodrow Wilson Guthrie, named in celebration of Wilson's recent nomination for president, was born into a family of considerable local prestige and political power. Not quite one of Okemah's "best citizens," his father, Charley Guthrie, held the elected position of Okfuskee County Court clerk and had built his wife a six-room house on Okemah's better side at the time of Woody's birth. Bad luck and tragedy, however, marred Charley's political and financial career as well as his personal life. Fire several times caused the family great distress. Their newly built house burned to the ground; Clara, Woody's older sister, was burned to death one day doing chores; and Charley was seriously burned by a kerosene lamp. Woody's mother, Nora Guthrie, suffered from bouts of depression and anger, eventually diagnosed as Huntington's chorea.

Nevertheless, Guthrie grew up happily amid the financial and personal ups and downs and recalled his childhood fondly as a carefree time full of adventure.[1] During his childhood years, Okemah experienced the hustle and excitement of a frontier oil boom town, and he witnessed firsthand the rise and fall of fortunes both within his family and outside it. He was often left to his own devices as his family slowly broke apart. His father recuperated from his burns at his sister's farm in the Texas Panhandle. After recovering, he moved to the nearby town of Pampa, where he ran a seedy lodging house known to locals as "little Juarez." Woody joined his father in 1929 and made his living selling bootleg liquor and painting signs. He most enjoyed those people who were least concerned about money, probably because they had the time to sit and tell him stories, and he never developed a responsible attitude toward money, toward either earning it or keeping it.

Guthrie displayed talent in many areas: telling stories, making up words to old songs his mother had taught him, painting and drawing, absorbing what he read. He read widely in psychology, biology, and law, yet never did well in school. At the age of twenty-one, Guthrie married Mary Jennings, the younger sister of his best friend and sometime singing partner, over the objections of her family. Soon they had a child, Gwendolyn Gail, and Guthrie attempted to be a responsible father. With the help of relatives and friends, he started to focus on music as a way to make a living. At the same time music gave him an outlet for his creative energies and thoughts about the world. He wrote his first truly original songs after the Great Dust Storm of April 14, 1935, which blackened Pampa's skies with dust and topsoil blown by winds racing across the plains. One song recalled not only the dust storm but also Guthrie's own desire to leave Pampa:

So long, it's been good to know you,
So long, it's been good to know you,
So long, it's been good to know you,
This dusty old dust is a-gettin' my home,
And I've got to be drifting along.*

Guthrie would drift away for weeks at a time, sometimes without letting Mary know where he was going or when he would be back. He traveled to the Gulf of Mexico, around the Southwest, and out to California mainly by hitching rides (he hated riding the rails and did so only as a last resort). Along the way he saw hundreds of migrants leaving the Southwest and heading for California. He witnessed the "Bum Blockade" of the Los Angeles police at the California-Arizona border and heard the derogatory label "Okie" applied to himself and people like him. Usually making money by singing in bars, Guthrie discovered that his music sustained him and that migrants in the fields and the unemployed along Los Angeles's skid row identified with the old songs he sang and enjoyed the words he made up, sometimes on the spot. His singing became more than entertainment; it became a link to his people. Even though Guthrie never really experienced the despair of many of the migrants (he never had trouble singing for food or drinks, and did not need much money since he had left his family back in Texas and didn't worry about supporting them), he felt a kinship with them. He had known hard times, and the migrants understood his pain and anger.

In the spring of 1937 Guthrie left Pampa again and headed for California, leaving behind a pregnant wife and child. He moved in with some relatives living

---

*"So Long It's Been Good to Know Yuh (Dusty Old Dust)." Words and music by Woody Guthrie. Copyright 1940 (renewed), 1950 (renewed), and 1963 (renewed) Folkways Music Publishers, Inc., New York, New York. Used by permission.

in Glendale and became the sidekick of his cousin, aspiring singing cowboy Jack "Oklahoma" Guthrie. A number of local gigs led to a daily show on a small Los Angeles radio station, KFVD. On July 19 "The Oklahoma and Woody Show" aired, featuring Jack's Jimmie Rodgers–style cowboy ballads, yodeling, and his hillbilly sidekick Woody. A family friend of Jack's, Maxine Crissman, joined the show in late August and became Woody's singing partner. In mid-September Jack left the show to seek more lucrative prospects, leaving Woody and Maxine (renamed Lefty Lou for the stage) to carry on the show. Woody dropped the slick Hollywood cowboy songs like "Back in the Saddle Again" in favor of more traditional ballads and songs of Appalachia, the South, and the Southwest. He accompanied himself and Lefty Lou with a guitar and sometimes a harmonica. Between songs he told stories and handed out bits of "cornpone philosophy" in a hillbilly accent as much contrived as real. The show found a receptive audience in Los Angeles, a city that absorbed over a third of the southwestern migrants between 1935 and 1940.[2] Letters to the radio station attested to the show's popularity and appeal. One listener wrote: "It floats me away from these hectic days of rush and heartache and jazz into a green valley of rest and peace. I have never heard any program like it—two perfectly blended voices, quiet, restful, unpretentious, singing sweet old melodies of the past, to me alone."[3]

By November "Woody and Lefty Lou" were performing three shows daily. Increasing requests for the lyrics to his songs prompted Guthrie, with the help of station owner Frank Burke, to mimeograph a songbook and to write more original songs. Fan letters arrived by the hundreds each month, and Guthrie felt genuinely loved by his audience. Because of his casual style, many listeners regarded him as an old friend and not as a celebrity. He encouraged listeners to write about anything they had on their minds. Not only his audience but Guthrie himself mistook the intimacy of radio for a direct relationship with these migrants.[4] To be sure, Guthrie was a migrant himself and had experienced rough times in his trek to California; but unlike those from rural areas who ended up as migrant agricultural workers, he settled in Los Angeles and found a steady job with the help of family members already in California. Even though he was often penniless, that was more the result of irresponsibility, lack of career ambition, or just plain choice (he would squander money on drinks for others before he had a chance to send money to Mary and his two children) than a lack of opportunity. The main difference between Guthrie and most dust bowl migrants was the fact that his traveling was a matter of preference, not necessity; and while his audience could identify with his stories of the road, he did not experience the despair created by the migrants' complete lack of options.

In December Guthrie sent for Mary and his children, and they moved in with friends until a place could be found for them to live. A month later Woody and Lefty Lou received an offer from a Mexican border station, XELO in Tijuana, and he moved his family and other assorted relatives and friends, who would be part of the show, to Chula Vista, a suburb of San Diego. Within a month of leaving KFVD, Woody and Lefty Lou were back (the XELO job turning out to be a scam by a shady station owner), and Guthrie became cynical about future job offers and tried to provoke prospective employers and sponsors, which he succeeded in doing more often than not. By the summer of 1938 he had tired of the daily routine of performing and become impatient with his familial responsibilities. In June he left Los Angeles to roam the state and encountered first-hand the conditions of migrant workers. During these travels he wrote many of the songs later included on the album *Dust Bowl Ballads,* such as "Dust Bowl Refugee," "Dust Pneumonia Blues," and "Dust Can't Kill Me." These songs strengthened Guthrie's relationship with the migrants; each was a first-person narrative that described the dust storms and their effects. In "Dust Can't Kill Me" he wrote:

> That old dust storm killed my baby,
> But it can't kill me, Lord, and it can't kill me.
> That old dust storm killed my family,
> But it can't kill me, Lord, and it can't kill me.
>
> That old Landlord, he got my homestead,
> But he can't get me, Lord, and he can't get me.
> That old dry spell killed my crop, boys,
> But it can't kill me, Lord, and it can't kill me.*

Even though Guthrie never lost a homestead or a family member to a dust storm, there were people who did, and this song told their story through him. In addition, Guthrie told their story in their own manner: no fancy guitar playing or even very good singing. Through his songs, many migrants identified Guthrie as one of their own.

Returning to Los Angeles, Guthrie resumed his radio show, this time as "the lone wolf." His shows became more political, more concerned with current events such as the release of Tom Mooney, a labor leader questionably convicted of murder in 1916. His political stance attracted the notice of Ed Robbin, who

---

*"Dust Can't Kill Me." Words and music by Woody Guthrie. Copyright 1960 (renewed), 1963 (renewed) Ludlow Music, Inc., New York, New York. Used by permission.

had a show on KFVD as a correspondent for the West Coast Communist Party paper *People's World.* Through Robbin, Guthrie sang at Communist Party functions and began to tailor his songs to this new audience. He met actor Will Geer, who also performed at most of these functions, and Geer introduced Guthrie to Hollywood's Bohemian and radical community. At these Communist Party fund-raisers Guthrie combined politics with the Okie character he had cultivated for radio. He utilized folk elements (music, language, dress) to present political messages. In his outlaw songs he romanticized the Robin Hood–like actions of people such as the Dalton Gang and Belle Starr.

In March 1939 Guthrie wrote his most famous outlaw song, "Pretty Boy Floyd," in which Floyd becomes the hero of the farmers and unemployed when the authorities wrongly accuse him of "every crime in Oklahoma." Having become an outlaw, Floyd seeks the assistance of farmers to hide him from the lawmen and in return leaves some of his riches with the farmers.

> There's many a starving farmer the same old story told
> How the outlaw paid their mortgage and saved their little home
> Others tell you 'bout a stranger that comes to beg a meal
> And when the meal was finished left a thousand dollar bill.

Not confining his assistance to those who helped him, Floyd becomes a hero to all in need.

> It was in Oklahoma City, it was on a Christmas Day,
> There come a whole carload of groceries with a note to say:
> "You say that I'm an outlaw, you say that I'm a thief.
> Here's a Christmas dinner for the families on relief."

The song is more than a tale about a local legend, someone outwitting authority; it is also an indictment of "respectable" robbery:

> Now as through this world I ramble, I see lots of funny men
> Some will rob you with a Six gun, and some with a fountain pen.
> But as through your life you travel, as through your life you roam
> You won't ever see an outlaw, drive a family from their home.*

With this song Guthrie clearly aligned himself on the side of the outlaw, and the outlaw on the side of poor people. He took a story about authority and extended it into a statement about class.

---

*"Pretty Boy Floyd." Words and music by Woody Guthrie. Copyright 1958 (renewed) by Fall River Music Inc. All rights reserved. Used by permission.

In the fall of 1939, with Mary expecting their third child and close to delivering, Guthrie took off for the cotton fields of California's south-central valley to support the migrant workers in their strike against the growers. Improvising on the picket line, Guthrie realized that his songs were more than a link with the migrants. They could be used by the migrants as weapons in their struggles with the growers and other big-money men. After the strike, Will Geer returned to New York to play the lead in *Tobacco Road* on Broadway; left to his own devices, Guthrie quickly overstayed his welcome among Hollywood's leftists. What had been a novelty (a hillbilly with a political consciousness) was now tiresome. Guthrie's radio show was being attacked and red-baited, moreover, as a result of his staunch support of the Communist Party in the wake of the Hitler-Stalin pact and the invasion of Poland. In November 1939 Guthrie packed up his wife and three children, drove them back to Pampa, sold his car, and headed for New York City.

In New York Guthrie quickly became a part of the radical artistic community. On March 3, 1940, Will Geer organized a "Grapes of Wrath Evening" at the Forrest Theater in support of the John Steinbeck Committee for Agricultural Workers. Guthrie was only one of the many folk singers who performed at the concert, but he stood out in the eyes of a young folklorist named Alan Lomax. Lomax was the son and assistant of John Lomax, director of the Archive of Folk Song at the Library of Congress. The Lomaxes had for years collected "authentic American songs," mainly in southern prisons. It was on one such trip that they discovered Huddie Ledbetter, better known as Leadbelly, and launched him on a career of performances for academic audiences.

The success of *The Grapes of Wrath*, both the novel and the film, along with the general New Deal concern for the common and forgotten man, led to a growing interest in folk music outside of the academic circles of folklorists and musicologists. In addition, the Communist Party's popular front agenda sought a uniquely American expression of radical politics and found it in folk music. Guthrie perfectly fit the image of the poetic proletarian.

Alan Lomax, whose interest in Guthrie was both academic and political, interviewed Guthrie for the folk song archives. For the Library of Congress sessions, Lomax planned a "spontaneous" interview format using alcohol as his main tool. The results of three days of recording illustrate Guthrie's singing and songwriting as well as his storytelling, which is more autobiographically based fiction than truth.[5] In these interviews Guthrie talked about growing up in the Southwest and displayed strong pride in his native state of Oklahoma. He tried to dispel the image of Oklahoma as a wasteland with no resources, full of backward people. He claimed that Oklahoma had the biggest oil fields in the world and that "the second most famous man in the entire world" was Oklahoma-born Will Rogers (Jesus Christ was first). "Everyone in Oklahoma knew Will Rogers," and his reputation as a good-natured, moral, yet common man could be attributed to every resident of Oklahoma.[6]

Guthrie himself was quickly becoming perhaps Oklahoma's second most famous son, as he received national exposure on Norman Corwin's Sunday afternoon variety show *The Pursuit of Happiness*. On April 21, 1940, Burgess Meredith introduced Guthrie as someone who "has really traveled":

> He is Woody Guthrie of Oklahoma, one of those Okies who, dispossessed from their farms, journeyed in jalopies to California. There, Woody, who always had been a great man at playing the guitar and making up songs of his own, managed to get some work performing at a small radio station. He got fan letters, one of which was from John Steinbeck, who wrote the saga of the Okies. Not long ago, he set out for New York and rode the freights to get here . . . and we've asked him to perform one of his own compositions.[7]

Guthrie went on to perform "Do Re Mi," a song about the illegal border blockades set up by the Los Angeles police. What is interesting about this introduction is the way in which Guthrie is made to represent all of the Okies, and all of the Okies are assumed to have come from farms. The ease with which Guthrie found himself on the radio (his cousin Jack initiated the KFVD deal) is ignored in favor of intimations that Guthrie struggled to find work. Guthrie's position is validated, furthermore, not by other migrants but by John Steinbeck. Guthrie, in turn, reinforced Steinbeck's position as the Okie chronicler when he recorded a collection of Dust Bowl songs, including a song called "Tom Joad" based on *The Grapes of Wrath*.

Woody Guthrie was more than a singing and talking illustration of the dust bowl migration. He felt the need to improve the conditions of the migrants in California by publicizing their plight and predicament and becoming the migrants' representative through song and story. This political awakening developed slowly and in tandem with Guthrie's realization that his music could speak so intimately to his people. Guthrie's early travels revealed a California that did not live up to the image he had in his head from stories and songs heard back in Oklahoma and Texas. Famous western singer Jimmie Rodgers sang about how "California's waters taste like cherry wine," and how it would be better to be in California "than to be in Texas, treated like a dirty dog." The song also mentions Oklahoma and Georgia as places better left behind. Guthrie remarked on one recording: "Notice how this song hits all of those southern states, and welcomes them all to come to California." Thousands of families in the South and Southwest listened to this song and said to each other: "Boy, there's a place to go, that old boy's a singin' the truth."[8] Guthrie himself had followed Rodgers's advice but found that California's water had a bitter taste. Guthrie saw the people living under bridges; he saw attempts by police and railroad "bulls" to keep the unemployed out of California's towns and cities; and his experience led him to seek a political solution.

At KFVD Guthrie was fortunate to work for Frank Burke, a left-wing station owner who editorialized daily over the airwaves. Burke allowed Guthrie the freedom to sing and to say what he pleased. One of Guthrie's first political forays was an attack on the landlords of Los Angeles who would not rent to him and his wife because they had children. Guthrie went on to talk about migrant living conditions, the corruption of bankers and lawyers, and even the war between China and Japan. With the help of Ed Robbin, Guthrie started writing a column for *People's World* in May 1939 entitled "Woody Sez." His first column contained this introduction:

Woodrow Guthrie or just plain Woody, as he is known to thousands of radio listeners, will be a daily feature in The People's World from now on.
. . . Woody has gathered a great deal of homely wisdom from his people. Every day he will speak to you on this page in his own way about how he looks at things.[9]

In his columns Guthrie solidified his position as spokesman for the Okies, someone who offered an inside view of the migrant experience or, in his own words, "a Hillbilly's Eye-View of the hole [sic] Migratious Labor movement from the South to the Pacific Coast." He reasoned: "I figgered it wood be helpful to my people, the dustbowl refugees" (9). In these writings Guthrie criticized bankers, politicians, and lobbyists, among others. He framed his attacks within anecdotes without the use of political or ideological jargon. This nonideological approach is best summed up in the line "I aint a communist necessarily, but I have been in the Red all my life" (153).

About bankers Guthrie wrote:

That reminds me of the one about the one eyed banker that spent a young fortune buying himself the best glass eye that could be made. It was finished and he went around betting everybody that you couldn't tell which was the glass eye and which was the real eye. He was dealing with a farmer, buying a load of tomatoes, and the banker bet him $100, and laid it down. The farmer looked at the banker for a minute, and pointed out the glass eye. The banker lost. The farmer won. "Tell me—how did you pick the glass eye?" The banker wanted to know. And the farmer remarked, "Well 'y gad, ye see, I jest went to a lookin' fer th' eye that had a little gleam of life an' friendliness fer us farmers in it—an' I knowed dern well that it would be—th' Glass One." (34–35)

About policemen he wrote: "I SOMETIMES THINK OF A POLICEMAN AS A FELLER that wont let you take back what some guy has just took from you" (58). As for politicians, "The housewives of the country are always afraid at nite, afraid they's a Robber in the House. Nope, Milady most of em is in the Senate" (19).

In addition to attacking the "big-money men" and other authority figures, these writings give a view of Guthrie's feelings toward the use of folk songs in the struggles of poor people:

All you got to do is to set down and write up what's wrong and how to fix it. That's all there is to it. Lord knows there is plenty of matter to work on. All we need is more songwriters. . . . Best part is, you don't even have to be able to write. You don't even have to be able to hum, whistle, or sing. You just got to speak it. That's all. Just whale away and yell it right out. Loud as you can. So somebody else can hear what's haywire and how to fix it. (138–139)

The purpose of folk songs, as Guthrie saw it, was political: to express the demand for rights. In a letter to Alan Lomax he reiterated his belief that "a folk song is whats wrong and how to fix it," adding:

or it could be whose hungry and where their mouth is or whose out of work and where the job is or whose broke and where the money is or whose carrying a gun and where the peace is—thats folk lore and folks made it up because they seen that the politicians couldnt find nothing to fix or nobody to feed or give a job of work. We dont aim to hurt you or scare you when we get to a feeling sorta folksey and make up some folk lore, we're a doing all we can to make it easy on you. I can sing all day and all night sixty days and sixty nights but of course I ain't got enough wind to be in office.[10]

Guthrie believed that the folk song grew organically from the experience of the oppressed, "that song and that tune aint got no end." Every instance of oppression led to "a new verse added to the song." He concluded that "this aint a song you can write down and sell. This song is everywhere at the same time. Have you heard it? I have" (141).

Of course, Guthrie's greatest political statements were not in his writings but in his songs. His most famous song, "This Land Is Your Land," was an attack on the private interests taking the country away from the people. As Guthrie traveled to New York in the fall of 1939, the patriotic ring of Irving Berlin's "God Bless America" pervaded the airwaves. Guthrie disliked the passive optimism of the song and shortly after reaching New York wrote a response called "God Blessed America." It began:

> This land is your land, this land is my land
> From California to the New York Island
> From the redwood forest, to the Gulf Stream waters
> God blessed America for me.[11]

Completing the six verses of the song, Guthrie signed and dated the manuscript and then laid it aside for five years. In 1945 Guthrie returned to his manuscript and changed the last line of each verse from "God blessed America for me" to "This land was made for you and me." The song recalls the beauty of the American landscape in memorable phrases such as "I saw above me that endless skyway, and saw below me that golden valley," and "the sparkling sands of her diamond deserts." But the song also contains two highly political verses:

> Was a big high wall there, that tried to stop me
> A sign was painted said: Private Property.
> But on the back side it didn't say nothing—
> This land was made for you and me.
>
> One bright sunny morning in the shadow of the steeple
> By the Relief office I saw my people—
> As they stood hungry, I stood there wondering if
> This land was made for you and me.[12]

The song illustrates the two major tendencies in Guthrie's work: description and accusation. He described the magnificence of the natural landscape and showed pride in America's democratic origins, but he accused big business, the government, and religion of corrupting the democratic principle.

In one song, "The Jolly Banker (Banker's Lament)," Guthrie combined descriptions of events familiar to the migrants in California with his interpretation of how a banker would react:

When dust storms are sailing
And crops they are failing
I'm a jolly banker, jolly banker am I.
I check up your shortage
And bring down your mortgage
I'm a jolly banker, jolly banker am I.

If you show me you need it
I'll let you have credit
I'm a jolly banker, jolly banker am I.
Just bring me back two
For the one I lend you
I'm a jolly banker, jolly banker am I.*

The song has a playful attitude and melody, which encourage the listener to laugh accusingly at the banker for his smug ways.

Guthrie did more than describe and accuse; he also suggested solutions. In the song "I'm A-Lookin' for That New Deal Now," he likened the world to a poker game in which "Wall Street drawed the aces down" and "the working folks, they lost the pot." He continued:

The workin' folks gotta all pitch in,
And play together if they hope to win.
I'm a-lookin' for that New Deal now.
You gotta play "ball" with F. D. R.
And Mr. Olsen, your governor.
I'm a-lookin' for that New Deal now.**

Guthrie cleverly radicalized the idea of FDR's New Deal by comparing it to the reshuffling of cards, a "New Deal" being not only reform but a redistribution of wealth and power.

Guthrie's ability to inject important elements of the migrants' culture into his political songs made his interpretation accessible to the migrants. This is evident in his songs about outlaws. In one song he combined the outlaw legend with religion (another traditional element in Okie culture):

---

*"Jolly Banker." Words and music by Woody Guthrie. Copyright 1964 (renewed) by WOODY GUTHRIE PUBLICATIONS, INC. All rights reserved. Used by permission.
**"I'm A-Lookin' for That New Deal Now." Words and music by Woody Guthrie. Copyright 1997 by WOODY GUTHRIE PUBLICATIONS, INC. All rights reserved. Used by permission.

Jesus Christ was a man that traveled through the land
A hard workin' man and brave
He said to the rich, "Give your goods to the poor,"
So they laid Jesus Christ in his grave.

    Jesus was a man, a carpenter by hand
    His followers true and brave
    But one dirty coward called Judas Iscariot
    He has laid poor Jesus in his grave.

When Jesus come to town, the workin' folks around
Believed what he did say
But the bankers and the preachers, they nailed him on the cross
And they laid Jesus Christ in the grave.

This song it was wrote in New York City
Of rich man, preacher, and slave
If Jesus was to preach what he preached in Galilee
They would lay poor Jesus in his grave.*

The parallel between Judas Iscariot and modern-day bankers and preachers presented a readily accessible model of the "dirty coward" to a predominantly Baptist audience. Guthrie portrayed a very important person in the lives of most of the migrants—Jesus Christ—as a working man fighting on the behalf of the working poor. As far as Guthrie was concerned, Jesus was an Okie.

Perhaps the best illustration of Guthrie's ability to speak politically in folk terms are the songs he recorded for his first commercially released project, *Dust Bowl Ballads.*

On May 3, 1940, Guthrie recorded thirteen songs about the dust bowl and the Okie migration at the RCA Victor studios in Camden, New Jersey. In the *Daily Worker,* Guthrie wrote about the project: "The songs are liberal as the dickens and as progressive as the angels. . . . They came out of the hearts and mouths of the Okies." He added, "I'm sure Victor never did a more radical album."[13] The album featured songs Guthrie had written over the past five or six years such as "Dust Can't Kill Me," "Dust Pneumonia Blues," "Dusty Old Dust (So Long, It's Been Good to Know You)," and "Pretty Boy

---

*"Jesus Christ." Words and music by Woody Guthrie. Copyright 1961 (renewed), 1963 (renewed) Ludlow Music, Inc., New York, New York. Used by permission.

Floyd." Guthrie wrote a short introduction for the collection in which he proclaimed himself "The Dustiest of the Dust Bowlers." From the start, he insisted on the authenticity of the songs:

> They are "Oakie" songs, "Dust Bowl" songs, "Migratious" songs, about my folks and my relatives, about a jillion of 'em, that got hit by the drouth, the dust, the wind, the banker, and the landlord, and the police, all at the same time . . . and it was these things all added up that caused us to pack our wife and kids into our little rattletrap jallopies, and light out down the Highway—in every direction, mostly west to California.[14]

The rhetorical use of the collective "we" was meant to establish Guthrie as one of the folks forced to migrate in search of work. He subsequently claimed that some people did not even have cars to drive, "lots of us had to walk. Wife and Children had to walk." This implied that his wife and children had walked to California, while in reality they had arrived in California on a passenger train. Yet some folk's wives and children did have to walk along the highways, so Guthrie's statements were true in essence if not in detail.

Guthrie also tried to establish his authority by aligning himself with Steinbeck's vision of the migrant experience:

> There was a feller that knew us Oakies, and he knew what it was like in Oklahoma, and he knew about the dust and the debts that covered us up, and he knew why we blowed out to California, because early in the deal, he throwed a pack on his back and trapsed around amongst us, and lived with us, and talked to us, and et with us, and slept with us, and he felt in his heart and knew in his head that us Oakies was a lookin' for "A Living WITH Labor"—that man was John Steinbeck.[15]

Guthrie not only reinforced the myth of Steinbeck's travels with the Okies but endorsed the reform goals shared by both men. Guthrie called for government camps to house working people and even suggested the establishment of something like an office of labor management, which would direct the employment of migrant labor. At the same time he called for this "living with labor" as the program of a rural proletariat, however, he also reinforced the Jeffersonian ideals of the small farmers:

> They need a piece of land. You need a good house on it, with a coat or two of good paint, and three or four cows, and some chickens, and lots of stuff like that, farm tools, and stuff to eat, and some spendin' money in your pocket

for a little good time once in a while, and a long time to pay your place out, about forty years.[16]

He even reinforced Ford's image of the migrants as independent and persevering: "Them folks are just a lookin' for one thing, and that one thing is what all of the books and bibles call Freedom. . . . We're hard hit, we're hard hitters, but it's a dern cinch, we aint quitters."[17]

The songs in the collection range from the descriptive to the accusatory, and many reinforce traditional values. The simply descriptive songs ("Dust Storm Disaster," "Dust Pneumonia Blues," "Dust Bowl Refugee," and "Dust Bowl Blues") relate the experience of the dust storms and their effects:

> Yes, we wander and we work
> In your crops and in your fruit,
> Like the whirlwinds on the desert,
> That's the dust bowl refugees.*

Some of the songs hint at the political and economic source of the problem. In "Talkin' Dust Bowl Blues" Guthrie describes an insubstantial migrant meal, a stew so thin "you can read a magazine right through it." He relates the ability to see through the stew to politicians' inability to identify problems:

> Always have figured, that if it had been just a little bit thinner
> Some of these here politicians could have seen through it.**

As he sang the last line, Guthrie emphasized and drew out "pol-i-tish-uns." The song "Blowin' Down This Road" (also known as "Goin' Down This Road Feeling Bad" or "I Aint Gonna Be Treated This Way") intimated action on the part of the Okies in its recurring tag line, "And I ain'ta gonna be treated this way." Guthrie sang this song for a production team working on *The Grapes of Wrath*. He later remarked that it was sung in the film "kinda classical," and not in the way real Okies would have sung it. Guthrie sang it slightly up-tempo and with force, while in the film Eddie Quillan sang it slowly and almost passively, more a reaction than a statement of action.

Forceful accusations come out in "I Aint Got No Home," "Vigilante Man,"

---

*"Dust Bowl Refugee." Words and music by Woody Guthrie. Copyright 1960 (renewed), 1963 (renewed) Ludlow Music, Inc., New York, New York. Used by permission.
**"Talkin' Dust Bowl (Talking Dust Blues)." Words and music by Woody Guthrie. Copyright 1960 (renewed), 1963 (renewed) Ludlow Music, Inc., New York, New York. Used by permission.

and "Do Re Mi." Each song describes a social situation pertinent to the migrants, and while causes are not always clear, the person to blame is obvious. In introducing "I Aint Got No Home," Guthrie wrote: "This old song to start out with was a religious piece called 'I Can't Feel at Home in This World Any More.' [also known as 'This World Is Not My Home']. But I seen there was another side to the picture. Reason why you can't feel at home in this world any more is mostly because you aint got no home to feel at."[18] The song blames "the rich man" for the migrants' condition:

> My brothers and my sisters are stranded on this road
> It's a hot and dusty road that a million feet have trod.
>
> Rich man took my home, and he drove me from my door,
> And I ain't got no home in this world any more.

The song questions the acquisition of wealth without labor:

> Now as I look around it's mighty plain to see
> This wide and wicked world is a funny place to be,
> The gambling man is rich and the working man is poor,
> And I ain't got no home in this world any more.*

In this song Guthrie inverts the traditional idea of religion and heaven (passive patience) into an angry statement of a problem (active stance). Rather than saying "This world is not my home, my home is in heaven," the song accuses the rich of stealing the working man's home. Heaven is not in the future, after death, but rather in the past, something to be reclaimed. This idea of tradition, of regaining something lost, is echoed in "Vigilante Man," in which Guthrie questions the morality of paid thugs, railroad bulls, and vigilante groups:

> O, why does a vigilante man?
> O, why does a vigilante man?
> Carry that sawed-off shot-gun in his hand?
> Would he shoot his brother and sister down?

After relating an incident that happened to himself, Guthrie included a verse in which Preacher Casy from *The Grapes of Wrath* is included in those victimized by the vigilante man:

---

*"I Ain't Got No Home." Words and music by Woody Guthrie. Copyright 1961 (renewed), 1964 (renewed) Ludlow Music, Inc., New York, New York. Used by permission.

Preacher Casey was just a working man,
And he said, "Unite all us working men."
They killed him in the river, some strange men
Was that your vigilante man?*

By including the fictional Casy in a song based on actual experiences, Guthrie validated the novel and film for the song's audience. He also reinforced the Okies' view of vigilance as immoral by pitting the vigilante man against workers in general, and in particular, one worker who symbolized (for Guthrie) both the economic and the spritual aspects of Okie culture, Preacher Casy.

In the song "Do Re Mi," Guthrie took an actual event, the blockade of the California-Arizona border by the Los Angeles Police Department, and generalized it to attack the treatment of migrants in California:

If you ain't got the Do Re Mi, folks,
If you ain't got the Do Re Mi,
Why, you better go back to beautiful Texas,
Oklahoma, Kansas, Georgia, Tennessee.

California is a garden of Eden,
A paradise to live in or see.
But believe it or not, you won't find it so hot,
If you ain't got the Do Re Mi.

As he demythologized California as a paradise for all, Guthrie reinforced Jeffersonian notions of the independent yeoman farmer:

If you want to buy you a home or farm,
That can't do nobody harm,
Or take your vacation by the mountains or sea.
Don't swap your old cow for a car,
You'd better stay right where you are.**

Other songs add to the image of the Okie as the bearer of traditional values, such as the persevering tone of "Dust Can't Kill Me" and the down-home morality of "Pretty Boy Floyd."

One song combines description, accusation, and traditional values, while sug-

---

*"Vigilante Man." Words and music by Woody Guthrie. Copyright 1961 (renewed), 1963 (renewed) Ludlow Music, Inc., New York, New York. Used by permission.
**"Do Re Mi." Words and music by Woody Guthrie. Copyright 1961 (renewed), 1963 (renewed) Ludlow Music, Inc., New York, New York. Used by permission.

gesting a solution to the entire problem. The song was requested by the management of Victor Records, which wanted to cash in on the popularity of *The Grapes of Wrath*, and Guthrie wrote it after seeing the film in New York. The song, "Tom Joad," describes the action of the film from Tom's release from prison to his farewell speech to Ma. Sung to the tune of "John Hardy," a traditional outlaw ballad, "Tom Joad" translates Steinbeck's universal concern for the migrants into the story of one man and his fight for justice. It narrows the focus of the film from the Joad family to Tom and Casy. This attention to Tom reinforces Okie traditions of the outlaw; Tom Joad has joined the ranks of Pretty Boy Floyd and Jesse James. We know Tom is a morally good person from the opening verse:

> Tom Joad got out of the old McAlester pen,
> There he got his parole,
> After four long years on a man-killin' charge,
> Tom Joad come a-walking down the road, poor boy,
> Tom Joad come a-walking down the road.

The indication of Tom as a "poor boy" clues the audience that he is one of them. The song continues to describe Tom's homecoming, the Joads' departure, Grandpaw's and Grandmaw's deaths, and the Hooverville camp. The song does not give any indication of the causes of the Joads' situation (gone are the political, economic, and environmental determinants) but accuses authorities (deputy sheriffs and vigilante men) for the brutal treatment of the migrants:

> Now a deputy sheriff fired loose at a man,
> Shot a woman in the back,
> Before he could take his aim again,
> Preacher Casey dropped him in his tracks,
> Preacher Casey dropped him in his tracks.

The deputy shoots at the man for no apparent reason and then does the unforgivable deed (in the code of the West) of shooting a woman, in the back no less.

> They handcuffed Casey and they took him to jail,
> And then he got away,
> And he met Tom Joad by the old river bridge,
> And these few words he did say, poor boy,
> These few words he did say.

Casy is given prestige since he escapes from jail, undoubtedly outwitting authority, and his meeting with Tom seems to be planned, if not by themselves then by destiny. Casy tells Tom:

I preached for the Lord a mighty long time,
Preached about the rich and the poor,
Us working folks is all get together,
'cause we aint got a chance any more,
We aint got a chance any more.

This is the only song in the dust bowl collection that contains a call to action on behalf of the migrants, although Guthrie's ideas about what action is necessary are made clear in the liner notes. The song continues with Tom taking up Casy's mission after Casy is killed by a vigilante man. It ends with Tom's words to Ma:

Everybody might be just One big soul,
Well it looks that-a way to me,
Everywhere that you look in the day or night,
That's where I'm a-gonna be, Ma,
That's where I'm a-gonna be.

Wherever little children are hungry and cry,
Wherever people aint free,
Wherever men are fighting for their rights,
That's where I'm a-gonna be, Ma,
That's where I'm a-gonna be.*

Guthrie takes Tom's final speech and emphasizes the bad conditions—children hungry and crying, and people not free—and ends with the suggestion of fighting for rights. In the novel and film, Tom's speech ends with "the people" living in their own houses and eating their own produce, a dream image; Guthrie ends with an image of action and the idea that just as outlaw Pretty Boy Floyd stood behind the farmers, so Tom Joad will stand behind his folks.

"Tom Joad" illustrates the way in which Guthrie combined the traditional values of morality, family, and religion with the idea of collective action and civil rights. Whereas Steinbeck denounced tradition as a stumbling block to the migrants' inclusion in the proletariat (Steinbeck's Casy was an ex-preacher) and Ford favored tradition as an end in itself ("We'll go on forever, 'cuz we're the people"), Guthrie utilized traditional values in support of change. Guthrie's use of traditional values, reinforced by his inclusion in the Okie folk culture, made

---

*"Tom Joad." Words and music by Woody Guthrie. Copyright 1960 (renewed), 1963 (renewed) Ludlow Music, Inc., New York, New York. Used by permission.

his radical political views accessible to the Okie audience. At the same time he validated his position with the radical elite of Hollywood and New York, in part by reinforcing Steinbeck's position as an Okie expert. With the release of *Dust Bowl Ballads* and its ties to the enormous popularity of *The Grapes of Wrath* (both novel and film), Guthrie built a popular reputation as a wandering minstrel. The mutual authority claimed by Guthrie and Steinbeck, and to a lesser degree Ford (Guthrie claimed the film was an accurate representation), established a highly politicized image of the migrant, an important factor in the class struggle.

By combining the moral fortitude of the Fordian migrant with the demands of Steinbeck's Okie, Guthrie created an image of the Okie migrant as a political threat to those currently in power, and therefore his songs became, in essence, the Okie platform, which consisted of a quest for the goals of the American Dream (landownership, prosperity, independence) by means of reform. In other words, Guthrie utilized the reformist agenda of Steinbeck and the FSA in order to realize, in part, the "plain-folk Americanism" of the migrants. The preservation of values through changes in the political economy is at the heart of Guthrie's work. But as we have seen earlier, the migrants, rather like Ford, sought tradition as an end in itself, a panacea for the ills of modern society. Guthrie offered the Okie migrants the maintenance of their traditional values combined with a change in their political and economic status. He proposed a new image of the democrat (part Jeffersonian and part social democrat) in which the migrant retained familial, religious, and moral values while becoming part of a working class dependent on its solidarity. For Guthrie, rights were defined morally but gained politically. His interests and goals defined politics and economics as separate from the traditional values of the migrants. In other words, he tried to radicalize the political and economic aspects of the migrants' culture while conserving its traditional elements. For the migrants, politics and economics were inexorably a part of their culture, and their traditional values formed the basis for their political and economic conservatism. Guthrie's envisioned democracy discounted the political and economic voice of the migrants in favor of the reformist program developed by experts speaking on behalf of the migrants.[19] Once again, an attempt to generalize the migrant experience (Lange symbolically, Steinbeck philosophically, Ford mythically, and Guthrie economically) resulted in a representation of the migrant experience that was at odds with the migrants' own desires and wishes.

Guthrie's synthetic approach to the dust bowl migration rested on his ideas about the role of the folksinger. More than an agent of folk culture, Guthrie saw the folksinger as an activist, a privileged spokesman in the fight for minority rights. His use of the office of folksinger aligned him with intellectuals and civil servants against the migrants. Academics and government folklorists sought to preserve what they saw as a dying American form, which expressed the radical political potential of workers. On the other hand, the participants in the dust bowl migration looked to the folk song, and its evolution into country music, as a way to define and express themselves against the modern world of California. The folklorists sought to freeze the folk song in order to preserve what they perceived as a dying culture, while the migrants adapted the folk song in order to create an "Okie subculture" in California. Ironically, the folklorists' attempt to preserve folk culture was motivated by a desire to change the Okies into class-conscious workers, while the migrants' attempt to distinguish themselves through country and western music led to their assimilation into California society. As with the migrant camp program, the migrants resisted the designs of outsiders and experts and attempted to forge their own identity.

6

The Okies who spoke and sang into our microphones were the real thing, and certainly they ought to be the final authority on what it's like to be a dust bowl refugee, living in a government tent out in the hot valley of the San Joaquin. Let's get to know some of these people.—Robert Sonkin, "Songs of the Okies"

THE USES OF

AMERICAN CULTURE

Folklorists and

the Migrant

"Songs of the Okies," broadcast on WNYC in New York City over three weeks in three installments, featured the music collected by Robert Sonkin and his partner Charles Todd in the FSA migrant labor camps of California in 1940 and 1941.[1] Todd and Sonkin made over two hundred recordings of folk songs, conversations, and meetings in California for the Library of Congress and the Archive of Folk Song (now Archive of Folk Culture). Todd, a graduate student in English literature at Columbia, and Sonkin, a linguist at the City College of New York, sought to create a cultural record of the Okies' folk life. They documented the traditions and folk songs of the migrants and used this material in order to publicize the migrants' plight.

Todd and Sonkin's work reinforced a strong current in American folklore studies that sought to establish an American folk tradition, which forms the basis of a uniquely American character. This intellectual position was deeply embedded in a democratic ideology that placed greater emphasis on the "natural," and therefore democratic, idiom of American folk narrative than on the highly structured and cultivated style of European literature. Building on the work of folk song collectors John and Alan Lomax, Todd and Sonkin searched the migrant camps for examples of American folk songs to establish the democratic culture of the migrants. By celebrating the traditions evident in the migrants' folk songs, they reinforced notions of "natural" democratic rights and equality. For these folklorists the folk song was more than an expression of tradition tinged by contemporary circumstances; it was a statement by "the people" of their aspirations and dreams. The folk song, since it was democratically produced, expressed more than the concerns of the folksinger; it represented the common man, the noblest of citizens. In essence, folklorists elevated the migrant (and folk like them) into the privileged position of "natural democrat," the reborn American far removed from the corrupting influences of "civil society."

This attempt to integrate the migrants into an American tradition of pioneer balladeers neglected the vital role that folk songs played as an expression of the migrants' distinctive culture. The migrants, coming to California from various parts of the country and various backgrounds, found a common language in folksinging. Not only was folksinging common to the migrants, but it was different from the popular style of music in California. While Todd and Sonkin used folk music to integrate the migrants into an American tradition and thereby render them worthy of the rights and respect of all Americans, the migrants themselves used folk songs (by transforming them into country music) as a way to express their distinctiveness. The traditions and values expressed in these songs were not links between the migrants and modern American society but traits that made them different from modernized society. Ironically, the folklorists' attempts to integrate the migrants into an American tradition led to a politically progressive position that sought to transform the migrants into a rural proletariat (therefore distancing the migrants from contemporary American society), while the migrants' use of country music to establish difference led to mainstream acceptance of many aspects of Okie culture and acceptance of the Okies themselves. The folklorists' desire to preserve traditional culture resulted in attempts to eliminate the central aspects of Okie culture, while the migrants' attempts to create their own identity resulted in the assimilation of their culture by mainstream American culture. The migrants' main concerns, it turns out, were not unique to the migrants but part of a conservative cultural tradition.

The difference in approach between folklorist and migrant depended on the role each accorded to folk songs within migrant culture. For the folklorists, the folk songs of the Okies reinforced theoretical ideas about a distinctive American character. Drawing a close connection between folk songs and the land (physical geography, especially the frontier), folklorists saw the folk song as the ultimate natural democratic expression of Americans and therefore worthy of a significant place in American culture. For the migrants, folk songs provided a language, common to most of the migrants, that made it possible for them to celebrate those characteristics that set them apart from the larger national culture, while at the same time providing a means of adapting to American society.

In collecting dust bowl folk songs, Charles Todd and Robert Sonkin called upon a folk ideology that placed the foundation of a distinctly American culture in the folk, defined as those whose close connection with the land took precedence over considerations of civilization. This definition, derived from the European definition of the folk as peasant, translated the class distinctions of Europe into a distinction between wilderness and civilization. What in Europe was the peasant (low, vulgar, and uncultivated) in America became the rugged individualistic pioneer of the frontier.

In eighteenth-century Germany, Johann Gottfried von Herder developed a counterargument to the pretensions of French civil society over the various economic and political territories making up modern Germany. Herder argued for the importance of the German language in the creation of a German culture distinct from French culture with its Roman and Greek antecedents. He urged Germans to "know your own language . . . and develop it for poetry, philosophy, and prose. For then you are building the foundation which will hold a building."

In using native language, Herder emphasized the use of idioms, since "idioms of every language are the impressions of its country, its nationality, its history."[2]

For Herder, the use of native language, characterized by the linguistic traditions of the *Volk*, provided fruitful ground for German literary growth. "It will remain eternally true that if we have no *Volk*, we shall have no public, no nationality, no literature of our own which shall live and work in us."[3] In claiming the primacy of the *Volk*, Herder reversed the idea that culture originates with elites and filters down to the lower strata of society; for Herder, culture grew from the bottom up. Civil society did not destroy *Volk* culture; rather, the culture of the *Volk* reinvigorated civil society and gave it its national character. In addition, Herder believed that each nation created its own culture in light of its geographical, political, economic, and historical context, resulting in a culture equally valid to any other national culture created from a different context.[4]

Herder's ideas about national cultures translated well into the American setting. As Gene Bluestein has noted, "While Herder's views about the roots of a nation's culture were a shock to the sensibilities of many in his own time, they could be readily adapted to the already existing structure and ideology of a nation conceived (at least in theory) on democratic principles."[5] Influencing writers such as Ralph Waldo Emerson and Walt Whitman, Herder's formulation of the *Volk* as the foundation for a national culture sent American writers in search of the American folk. Emerson, in seeing American culture in his time as a secondhand expression of European experience, called for the development of an American culture based directly on American experience. He wrote in "Nature":

> Our age is retrospective. It builds the sepulchres of the fathers. It writes biographies, histories, and criticism. The foregoing generations beheld God and nature face to face; we, through their eyes. Why should not we also enjoy an original relation to the universe? Why should not we have a poetry and philosophy of insight and not of tradition, and a religion by revelation to us, and not the history of theirs? . . . There are new lands, new men, new thoughts. Let us demand our own works and laws and worship.[6]

For Emerson this culture of insight and revelation depended on a close relationship to nature. In America this direct contact with nature was most evident where "the prevalence of secondary desires—the desire of riches, of pleasure, of power, and of praise," had not tainted the relationship of man to nature.[7] Indeed, civilization in all its forms inhibited the creation of a new culture. "Not out of those on whom systems of education have exhausted their culture, comes the helpful giant to destroy the old or to build the new, but out of unhandselled savage nature; out of terrible Druids and Berserkers come at last Alfred and Shakespeare."[8] This close relationship to nature was made possible by the immense expanses of apparently unsettled land, which Americans felt was there for the taking. In such an environment, a great culture could arise.

Whitman likewise called for the creation of a uniquely American form of literature. Condemning European poetry for expressing systems of caste and class, Whitman asked: "Of the great poems receiv'd from abroad and from the ages, and to-day enveloping and penetrating America, is there one that is consistent with the United States, or essentially applicable to them as they are and are to be? Is there one whose underlying basis is not a denial and insult to democracy?"[9] For Whitman, a native literature not only expressed the uniqueness of its people but also justified their existence. "Above all previous lands, a great original literature is surely to become the justification and reliance (in some respects the sole reliance of American democracy)."[10] But America, according to Whitman, had failed to produce "talented writers or speakers [who] have yet really spoken to this people, created a single image making work for them, or absorb'd the central spirit and the idiosyncrasies which are theirs—and which, thus, in highest ranges, so far remain entirely uncelebrated, unexpress'd."[11]

In failing to create a native, democratic literature, Americans had yet to reach what Whitman saw as the third stage of democratic development, the first being political democracy, the second economic. Whitman's own attempts to write a modern and new form of poetry in *Leaves of Grass* tried to fill the cultural void in American democracy, but he, like Herder, realized "that really great poetry is always (like the Homeric or Biblical canticles) the result of a national spirit, and not the privilege of a polish'd and select few."[12]

For Herder the national spirit rested in the *Volk*. The *volkslied*, or folk song, expressed most immediately the concerns and desires of the *Volk*. "The music of a nation, in its most imperfect form and favorite tunes, displays the internal character of the people."[13] In America, the persistence of English ballads led many folklorists to believe that America had no original folk song, resulting in America having no original culture or the foundation necessary to sustain an original literature. This thought persisted mainly through the dominance of the English ballad tradition in folk song studies. The publication of Francis James Child's five-volume *English and Scottish Popular Ballads* (1882–98) established a literary approach to folk song study, and consequently a focus on the literate ballad. For Child and his followers, the ballad represented the culmination of a particular historical context that had been destroyed by cultivated society. The aim of folklore studies, according to the Child tradition, should be to record and recover traces of the ballad in areas that had not yet succumbed to civilization.[14] Unlike Herder, who thought that the folk reinvigorated civil society, most folklorists believed the folk was a passing phenomenon.

Attacking the Child tradition, John A. Lomax, in an address to the American Folklore Society in 1913, conceded that America did not have original ballads of its own according to the definition widely accepted by folklorists.[15] Yet the United States had produced a remarkable number of folk songs, which—even though they did not fit the accepted definition of a ballad—performed the same function. They provided "a fresh, direct, and simple expression,—not of an individual, but of a people,—upon a subject that has a common interest and a common appeal, because of its common association to all of that people; and the emotions it expresses are the abiding experiences of the human heart."[16] In the process of collecting hundreds of American folk songs, Lomax categorized them into seven groups: songs of miners, lumbermen, inland sailors, soldiers, railroaders, Negroes, and cowboys. He reserved a special group for "songs of the down-and-out classes—the outcast girl, the dope fiend, the convict, the jailbird, and the tramp."[17] Lomax's formulation for American folk song, while not revolutionary, formed the basis for a new folk ideology based on the ideas of Emerson and Whitman. Just as these nineteenth-century writers called for the creation of a uniquely American voice, John Lomax and his son, Alan, sought to find the basis for that voice in the American folk song.

For the Lomaxes the American folk song told the story of the American man of action, the pioneer:

> Frankly, my own interest in American ballads is largely because they are human documents that reveal the mode of thinking, the character of life, and the point of view, of the vigorous, red-blooded, restless, Americans, who could no more live contented shut in by four walls than could Beowulf and his clan, who sailed around the coasts of Norway and Sweden.[18]

In publishing their collections of songs, the Lomaxes sought to give voice to "the people who still sing the work songs, the cowboy songs, the sea songs, the lumberjack songs, the bad-man ballads, and other songs that have no occupation or special group to keep them alive."[19] For the Lomaxes, American folk songs relied on two important traits: individuality and heterogeneity. The songs came from people who had been "wanderers, walking and riding alone into the wilderness, past mountains and the broad rivers, down the railroad lines, down the highways. Like all wanderers, they have been lonely and unencumbered by respect for the conventions of life behind them."[20] Leaving behind the conventions of the East, these pioneers transformed the old songs of Europe into the characteristically American folk songs collected by folklorists. The American folk song was more than just an old ballad in the individualistic context of the frontier; it was an amalgam of styles from Britain, Africa, Spain, France, and Germany. Expressing both the individualism of the American character and the harmonious mixing of styles in a melting pot fashion, American folk songs "reflect the life [of the American people] with more honest observation, with more penetrating wit and humor, with more genuine sentiment, with more true, energetic passion than other forms of American art, cultivated or subsidized."[21] Not only were folk songs the best expression of the American people, but folksingers had "created and preserved for America a heritage of folk song and folk music equal to any in the world." The task of the folklorist was to collect and present these songs in the "hope that the American people will learn from these records to know itself better."[22]

The belief that folk songs best expressed the American character was based in the idea that folk songs were created communally. While the original idea or story for a folk song might be the creation of an individual, the acceptance of the song by a community (regional, occupational, or ethnic), along with changes effected by oral transmission and memory, created a democratic product. "This is a truly democratic art, painting a portrait of the people, unmatched for honesty and validity in any other record."[23] Not only was the folk song democratically created, but it also had as its focus the common man, the central figure in American democracy.

Long before Whitman, American folk singers rhapsodized the common man in all his dazzling variety, putting him first in all the ballads, describing him at work and play, and making his passions and problems their main concern. This is the big theme of American folk song, running through all the songs—the theme stated by Burns' " . . . A man's a man for a' that." and even more powerfully in the Negro ballad, "John Henry." A man ain't nothin' but a man.[24]

In addition to its concern with the common man, the folk song had deep connections to the land. It was in agrarian settings that the folk song flourished in America, especially on the frontier, where man confronted "savage nature" on a daily basis. Not only was frontier man closer to nature, which Emerson declared was necessary for an American culture, but the frontier, according to historian Frederick Jackson Turner, created a more democratic man than could be found in the cities of civil society. In his most famous essay, "The Significance of the Frontier in American History," Turner argued for the importance of the frontier in the creation of a uniquely American individual beyond the grasp of European conventions of civilization and organization. "American social development," he wrote, "has been continually beginning over again on the frontier. This perennial rebirth, this fluidity of American life, this expansion westward with its new opportunities, its continuous touch with the simplicity of primitive society, furnish the forces dominating American character."[25] Turner's frontier thesis built on ideas of American distinctiveness first suggested by Emerson and Whitman. All three men saw the effect of nature and the wilderness on the character of Americans, and each emphasized the need to maintain this close connection to "savage nature." For Turner the result of this close relationship to nature was significant not for the implications it had for a national literature but for the effect it had on the political structure of the United States. "The most important effect of the frontier has been in the promotion of democracy here and in Europe." He emphasized the importance of the individual in the creation of a democracy. "As has been indicated, the frontier is protective of individualism. Complex society is precipitated by the wilderness into a kind of primitive organization based on the family. The tendency is anti-social." Furthermore, for Turner, this "frontier individualism has from the beginning promoted democracy."[26]

> The result is that to the frontier the American intellect owes its striking characteristics. That coarseness and strength combined with acuteness and inquisitiveness; that practical, inventive turn of mind, quick to find expedients; that masterful grasp of material things, lacking in the artistic but powerful to effect great ends; that restless, nervous energy; that dominant individualism, working for good and for evil, and withal that buoyancy and exuberance which comes with freedom—these are traits of the frontier, or traits called out elsewhere because of the existence of the frontier.[27]

This belief in the democratic nature of the frontier experience informed the work of the Lomaxes, who sought out folk songs in rural areas and among those occupations that relied on a close connection to the land. The seven categories of American folk song offered by John Lomax did not include the songs of factory workers or other industrialized laborers. Alan Lomax recounted the effect the frontier had on the formation of American folk songs in the introduction to his collection, *The Folk Songs of North America* (1960):

On the American frontier men worked and sang together on terms of amity and equality impossible in the Old World. A man was judged not by his accent or his origins, but by his character and capacities. A song was treasured for its suitability to frontier life. Inherited regional patterns of speech and song broke down beneath this pragmatic, democratic pressure.[28]

Because of the democratic pressure of the frontier, the American folk song expressed the fundamental and persistent desires of Americans. "They are," wrote Alan Lomax, " 'the stuff that dreams are made on' ":

They murmur of wishes and emotional conflicts too disturbing to be more openly stated by the singer and his community. Because these songs are passively accepted as favored fantasies by whole human families over long periods of time, they can be taken as the signposts of persistent patterns of community feeling and can throw light into many dark corners of our past and our present. An ideal folk-song study could be a history of popular feeling.[29]

Lomax concluded that his collection of folk songs illustrated "the deepest ills that afflict us—the colour bar, our repressed sexuality, our love of violence, and our loneliness."[30] Because they were able to express ideas and feelings that could not be "openly stated," Lomax felt that folk songs were an ideal form of social protest and had performed the function of protest from the beginning of American history:

The mass of the colonists were poor country folk, carriers of traditional melodies. Many were rebels, fleeing from political persecution and longing to express their feelings openly. Thus a note of social protest rang through native American balladry, and the lives and problems of the common people became its main concern.[31]

Alan Lomax's belief in the protest function of folk songs led him to value the protest-oriented songs of Woody Guthrie over the traditional ballads of the Okies as an expression of the migrant experience and the migrants' desires. Lomax's role in "discovering" Guthrie, recording him for the Library of Congress, and helping him gain exposure through concerts and radio shows paralleled Steinbeck's role in publicizing the migrants' plight. Like Steinbeck, Lomax felt the migrants were incapable of speaking for themselves, and therefore he promoted Guthrie as their representative.

In the section on "The West" in *Folk Songs of North America,* a subsection entitled "The Last West" recounts the songs of the Okie migrants, the last in a line of pioneers that included " '49ers, Pikers, cowboys, [and] prairie farmers."[32] The majority of the songs in this section are by Woody Guthrie. Only one song, "The Kickin' Mule," was collected in a California migrant camp and actually sung by a migrant laborer, Henry King, and his family. Lomax supported his belief in "experts" representing the migrants when he wrote: "At the time that Steinbeck was speaking for the Okies in *The Grapes of Wrath,* Woody, the dusty-headed folk-poet, was singing for them over a one-horse radio station in Los Angeles."[33] Discounting his own concern for the democratic creation and acceptance of folk songs, Lomax favored Guthrie's songs since they fit his idea of the folk song as a means of protest. He believed that Guthrie, being an Okie himself, understood the desires of the migrants and through his unique talent expressed their concerns about politics and the economy. As we have seen, Guthrie's closest tie to the migrant population was not in his interpretation of the political economy but in his ability to utilize the folk song form and traditions that were acceptable to the migrants. In taking Guthrie's use of the traditional folk song form as the justification for Guthrie's politics, Lomax failed to see the difference between form and content. Because Lomax characterized the folk as "primitive," or at least preindustrial, he discounted the possibility that the migrants could be deeply conflicted in their interpretations of events and ambiguous about their desires. In trying to reduce the migrant experience to one voice of protest, Lomax excluded the varieties of experience arising out of the dust bowl migration. In much the same vein, collectors Todd and Sonkin also found it difficult to reconcile their own reformist politics with the migrants' conservatism. Their attempts to represent the migrants' culture obscured the most important aspects of that culture.

In 1940 and 1941 Charles Todd and Robert Sonkin, both instructors at the City College of New York at the time, traveled to California with a Presto recording machine and acetate- and glass-based records given to them by Alan Lomax in order to record and interview dust bowl migrants. Focusing their work on the FSA migrant labor camps, they collected the songs of the Okies and used them to illustrate the traditional values and democratic nature of the migrants, thereby justifying relief and reforms on the migrants' behalf.

The original idea for collecting the migrants' songs came from Todd, who became interested in the Okies after reading Steinbeck's journalistic piece "Their Blood Is Strong." Early in 1939, Todd visited his mother in California and wrote to a family friend, Alfred Bingham (editor of *Common Sense*), about the possibility of writing a piece about the migrants from firsthand observations. The resulting article, "Trampling Out the Vintage," clearly aligned Todd with Steinbeck in his support of government-sponsored reforms for the migrants. In his praise for the FSA camps, Todd concluded with a vision of the migrant as the hope of a new American social democracy:

> For many "Okies" this government camp is the first taste of real democracy. Theirs is a collective life, with plenty of outlets for individualism. The camp councils, two men and two women, are solving the little problems of every-day democracy without benefit of police or Vigilantes. Those men at the Arvin Camp to whom the Government has entrusted three-fifths of an acre apiece know the meaning and the necessity of production for use. In short, these lonely, drought-stricken migrants, under the guidance of humane and liberal men and women, are standing on the threshold of a new order, breaking ground for a civilization that nothing can stop.[34]

Todd's support of the FSA camp program led him to call his friend Alan Lomax and to suggest the recording of folk songs in the camps. Lomax and Todd were both a part of the Greenwich Village folk crowd in the late 1930s. Lomax lent Todd and his friend Robert Sonkin a recording machine and gave them instructions on what sort of information they should get from the subjects they recorded. This collection of instructions and questionnaires, written by the Joint Committee on Folk Arts of the WPA, included questions concerning the case history of the informant, the circumstances of the interview, the case history of the song, and twenty-four questions covering the aesthetic and psychological elements of the subject. Though not systematically utilized by Todd and Sonkin, these instructions and questions were their only education in folk song collecting and oral interview techniques; they illustrate the type of information seen as important by the predominant institution of folk song study, the Archive of Folk Song in the Library of Congress. What is striking about the questionnaire and instructions is the central role that the interviewer played in recording a folk song. First, it was suggested that the interviewer "interview himself according to Part I [Case History of the Informant], and that his life history be used as a means of evaluating his material."[35] This approach limited the degree to which the informant could raise topics and issues not covered by the questionnaire or of interest to the interviewer. The recording and interview process, as outlined by the Committee on Folk Arts, placed the interviewer in a position superior to the informant. By specifying the aspects of folksinging most important and therefore worthy of attention, the folklorists became, in effect, not observer/recorders of folksinging and folklore but creators of folklore data, who removed folksinging from the contexts in which it was used.

Todd and Sonkin collected most of their material at events specifically arranged for the recording of folk songs. Mainly through the services of the camp manager, the folklorists arranged to meet migrants who had reputations as good singers, musicians, or sources of a lot of folk material. In one of their first attempts to record the migrants, Todd and Sonkin had trouble getting people to sing for the recording machine. Most of the migrants played down any ability to perform and, when finally persuaded, would sing a recent song heard over the radio. After a day of explaining why they were there, Todd and Sonkin got a few of the people to sing "old songs" learned back home. After recording Nathan and Lura Judd singing "Maple on the Hill," Todd and Sonkin played another version they had recorded and talked with the Judds about the differences in the songs. Lura's mother, Rosetta Spainhard, revealed that the Judds' version was a late version. This type of concern for detailing the origins of a song seems to have been uppermost in the folklorists' minds. Whenever possible, Todd and Sonkin made reference to the migrants' songs as probable versions of English or Scottish ballads. In so doing, the folklorists were trying to establish a connection between the migrants and other rural folk, both contemporary and past, and in particular to other white migrants and immigrants such as the original colonists and frontier settlers.

This attempt to characterize the migrants within a rural ballad tradition led Todd and Sonkin to a selection process that favored what they saw as authentic over what seemed professional. One singer introduced himself as "Homer Pierce, the singin' cowboy from way down in Missouri, and I'd like to do a couple of my own tunes for you." The field notes do not indicate what songs Pierce sang except for the comment: "Pierce turned out to be more or less the professional cowboy type, but his own songs were good."[36] Another example of Todd and Sonkin's selectivity is the description of one couple who sang for the folklorists:

Mr. and Mrs. Trueman of Texas came in and announced that they were the "Texas Gospel Singers," and would like to hear themselves because they were "goin on the air soon." Both Migrants, but a little better dressed. Fake piousness, and somehow a little unwholesome. Mrs. Trueman played the guitar. Very fat. Probably had done a bit of street singing. "Firebrands for Jesus" etc. The other people seemed to resent them a little. One or two women walked out in noticeable anger. A confident pair, with a semi-professional touch.[37]

Todd and Sonkin made no mention of where the Truemans learned the songs they sang, why they came to California, what kind of work they had done since leaving their Texas home, or how long they had been traveling. These questions were put only to "authentic" migrant folksingers.

Todd and Sonkin attempted to get the migrants to talk and sing about the migrant experience. Their first attempts resulted in Fred Ross, the Arvin Camp manager, reading a poem "by an anonymous camper" entitled "Cotton Fever," which recounted the struggles of trying to earn a living on the low wages of a cotton picker. Reciting the poem to a square dance accompaniment, Ross fumbled with the words and pace, and several attempts were made to secure a good, clean recording. Ross later admitted, off the record, that he had written the poem himself and placed it in the camp newsletter, as he had done on other occasions. Instead of discrediting this recording, Ross's admission of authorship made Todd and Sonkin admire the song. They made another attempt at recording the poem with a musical accompaniment and succeeded with a version in which the music slowly faded at the end, giving the recording a professional quality. Upon arriving at the Shafter Camp, Todd and Sonkin played some of the records made at the Arvin Camp in order to illustrate what they were after. One of the records they played was Ross's recording of "Cotton Fever." Sonkin noted in his journal that Dewey Rogers, assistant camp manager at Shafter, especially liked "Cotton Fever"—unaware that it was written by Ross—and remarked, that "there's plenty of truth in that."[38] After returning to the East Coast, Todd and Sonkin submitted several original poems and lyrics to the journal *The American Poet*. The May 1941 issue contained three of these submissions, one of which is "The Least 'Un" by Fred Ross. An editorial note says: "Fred Ross is, strictly speaking, not an Okie; he lives in California, writing what he calls 'Cotton Ballads,' but the collectors [Todd and Sonkin] say, 'He has the Okie lingo.' "[39] The poem "The Least 'Un" recounts the trials of a man's children as they confront the children of "the boss man." Written in the first person, Ross's poem takes the ideal of Okie landownership and emphasizes the negative aspects of being a small farmer, instead of idealizing the individual autonomy the migrants sought. While most Okie poets were extolling the virtues of a farm, family, and God, Ross was more intent on condemning the large landholder:

Now my lan' lies just a right smart piece
From the lan' where the Big House joins my lease.
An' the Boss Man never has much to say; . . .
Still, I can't holp wishin' we was further away.[40]

In their notes and actions, Todd and Sonkin clearly aligned themselves with the reformist program of the camp managers.

Todd and Sonkin reinforced their commitment to the camp program by publicizing the FSA's efforts to assist the migrants. This publicity centered around the idea that the migrants were a special group of people who had not lost the folk traditions of the past and therefore deserved the attention and respect of modern society. By emphasizing the need to document the lives of these people, Todd and Sonkin placed the dust bowl migrant on a kind of cultural "endangered species" list. They played some of the songs they had collected for Eleanor Roosevelt, gaining her enthusiastic support. Todd became so involved with the camp program that he eventually became an assistant manager of the Visalia Camp. He recalled how much he enjoyed helping the Okies and how they affectionately called him "the boss man."[41] In retrospect, Todd wrote of those years as his idealistic period from a "distant planet called YOUTH."[42] He regretted having exploited the plight of the migrants. "It was somehow a bit obscene to exploit the misery of those bedraggled Okies and Arkies."[43] At the time, however, Todd and Sonkin did not hesitate to use the material they collected to publicize the migrants' plight.

A series of radio programs capped their efforts. Broadcast over three weeks on WNYC in New York City, "Songs of the Okies" brought the work of Todd and Sonkin to the public.[44] In "Songs of the Okies" they created a picture of the migrants aligned with their reformist goals. The first program focused on the migration and the songs resulting from the migrant experience. Todd introduced the first song—"Goin' Down the Road Feeling Bad"—as being *the* song of the Okies. This song, featured on Woody Guthrie's *Dust Bowl Ballads* and in the film *The Grapes of Wrath*, emphasized the hard luck of the migrants and their disposition to resist unfair treatment and injustice. The recurring line—"And I ain't a-gonna be treated this a-way"—is more than a statement of discontent; it is a warning, a threat from the oppressed to the oppressors. From the outset, Todd and Sonkin placed the migrant in a position of victim and fighter and reinforced this dual image throughout the first program by mixing original songs of hardship with traditional songs of strength and perseverance. One original song called "Arizona," by Jack Bryant of the Firebaugh Camp, warned the folks back home about the perils of heading West:

> You people in Oklahoma
> If you ever come out west
> Have your pockets full of money
> And you better be well dressed
>
> If you wind up in the desert
> You're gonna wish that you were dead
> You'll be longing for Oklahoma
> And your good old feather bed.[45]

This song is followed by a discussion of the migrants' love of outlaw songs in which the moral outlaw is pitted against men of corruption—songs such as "Bold Jack Donahue," "Dewey Lee," "Jesse James," "Pistol Pete," "John Dillinger," and "Pretty Boy Floyd." Todd played one outlaw song, "John Hardy," as sung by four-year-old Jack Bryant Jr. This traditional song about "a desperate little man" hunted, caught, and hung by a sheriff, lent its melody, and therefore some of its meaning, to "Tom Joad," Woody Guthrie's version of *The Grapes of Wrath*. The emphasis Todd and Sonkin placed on the outlaw song in the migrant tradition strengthened the image of the migrants as people willing to use violence to maintain their way of life, especially when pushed by circumstance or authority. But it was also necessary for Todd and Sonkin to argue the validity of the migrants' position in terms acceptable to contemporary Americans. Describing the migrants as victims with violent tendencies would not have gained acceptance for the migrants or support for reforms on their behalf. Todd and Sonkin, therefore, focused attention on the traditional elements of the migrants' culture by assimilating them to the traditions of all Americans. In describing the situation in California, Todd remarked how on the west side of the coast mountain range there is the "shiney [sic] civilization of the new west"; but on the other side "the picture changes," and there you will find a people not modern, not civilized, but "their ways are the ways of our grandfathers and grandmothers." Todd closed the first program with several traditional ballads and emphasized the perseverance of the Okies, quoting an editorial from the *New York Times:* "But men who make songs, good or bad, for the fun of it, or because they can't help it, are not cowed by fate or hopelessness."[46]

The second program further emphasized traditional elements in the migrants' culture by featuring many traditional ballads that Todd and Sonkin collected in California. Sonkin thought these songs were as "much a part of the cultural baggage the Okies brought with them to California as are beds and mattresses they piled on top of the rattling jalopy—and when the migrants think about life back home—especially the older folks—the old songs are inextricably associated with their dearest memories."[47] In addition to placing the migrants in an American folk tradition of English ballads, along with the colonists and pioneers, Todd and Sonkin reinforced the pioneer drive of the migrants. Sonkin recounted the story of one migrant, Jim Hurlburt of the Visalia Camp:

> He was planning to go to Oregon and get himself a little piece of land, some land of his own. He wasn't quite sure how he would be able to work it—but that was the dream that had drawn him out west, as it drew young men nearly a hundred years ago. Small matter that the frontier was gone—that land could no longer be had for the asking. Jim hadn't even thought of that. He said he only knew one thing—that if a man wasn't afraid of work, hard work with his hands and on his own land, he'd get by.[48]

Sonkin continued by playing several traditional songs sung by children. This cleverly supported the idea of the persistence of tradition in Okie culture by showing a new generation hanging on to old songs and, by extension, old values and desires.

The second program concluded with a square dance tune, "Sally Goodin," and a statement of the migrants' prominent position in American culture: "The men and women out there, are no longer Okies in a California Migratory Labor Camp. They are just plain ordinary folks from Oklahoma and Arkansas having the time of their lives in a dance that is as American as the mountains from which they came."[49]

In the third program Todd and Sonkin reiterated the themes of the previous shows and culminated in an assessment of the migrants' future. Sonkin noted that most of the migrants had come to California to stay and start a new life. "And in these camps [the FSA camps], they are beginning to shape the outlines of that new life." Sonkin then played a recording of a camp council meeting and remarked that the "Okies solve their own problems in a democratic way . . . problems of making a home out of the temporary state in a government camp. Problems of cooperating with one another and governing themselves so they can live together decently." The excerpt of the council meeting featured a speech by Mr. Sailor of the Viasalia Camp Council: "The council is not going to tell you what to do, you are going to tell the council what you want. . . . All of you are equal there."[50] Taken out of context, the remark seems to emphasize the migrants' concern for self-determination, yet this was not a speech from a council meeting, as Sonkin implied, but an announcement from the weekly literary program (talent show) in which Mr. Sailor pointed out the necessity of participation in the council proceedings. This announcement was most likely prompted by a lack of support for and interest in the workings of the council.

What Todd and Sonkin saw as they collected songs in the migrant camps, as well as what they presented to the public as a result of their collecting, was a picture of the migrant as a victim of modern society holding on to the best of traditional American society. They characterized the migrants as traditional Americans and as uniquely American in the sense that they possessed the most fundamental American characteristic of all, an inherent democratic nature. Sonkin closed "Songs of the Okies" by saying:

> Yes, there's hope among these people, and it's a hope that we can share for it seems to be based on a faith in the democratic way. Well, you've met the Okies and you have heard their stories and songs. You've been in their camps and you've seen something of the life they're leading and the life they are trying to create. But before you leave the Okies, you ought to meet one more couple, Nathan and Lura Judd. It would be easy to sentimentalize about them, but we'll just say we have faith in Nathan and Lura Judd and in their ability to work out their own destiny. And that destiny will probably be something as American as the traditional style in which they sang for us the popular hillbilly tune "The Maple on the Hill."[51]

Behind this nicely edited and produced series of broadcasts, Todd and Sonkin obscured aspects of Okie culture that did not conform to the image in their minds. Comments quite prominent in their field notes regarding the professional air of migrants such as Mr. and Mrs. Trueman and Homer Pierce were absent from the radio broadcasts, even though recordings of both were presented. Both the Truemans and Pierce were introduced by the stage names they had given themselves: the Texas Gospel Singers and the Singing Cowboy. Todd and Sonkin characterized them in a way that was strikingly different from the description in the field notes. Instead of the "fake piousness" recorded in the field notes, Sonkin remarked on the Truemans' singing by saying: "Yes, you need plenty of faith and courage to live the life these folks lead." Instead of the "professional type," Sonkin characterized Homer Pierce as reminiscent of the "old balladeers." It is interesting to note that two of the recordings to which Todd and Sonkin clearly gave lower authenticity in the field notes were both used in the radio programs selected out of over two hundred songs that had been collected. One possible reason for this is the "professional" quality of the recordings, which was more acceptable to the radio listening audience than the raspy, nasal whine of many dust bowl folk singers.

In characterizing both the Truemans and Pierce as inauthentic, Todd and Sonkin revealed a basic misunderstanding of the role of music in the migrants' culture, at least for the Truemans and Pierce, for whom music was a way out of their economic situation. These singers utilized the growing southwestern migrant population in California as an audience for their music. In order to be successful, migrant singers needed to satisfy both segments of the migrant population, rural and urban. As James Gregory has noted, a vast number of migrants from the Southwest relocated to the cities of California, especially Los Angeles. In the cities the migrants assimilated much more quickly into the dominant California culture than those who remained in rural areas. Yet the assimilated population remained loyal to their native states and to their native folk and country music (stylized to fit accepted standards of music in California). The "professional" air of the Truemans and Pierce was an aspect of this style produced from a mixing of rural folk music with the Hollywood and Tin Pan Alley styles accepted in California. Successful examples of this mixture of styles can be found principally in the singing cowboys such as Gene Autry and Roy Rogers. Woody Guthrie was one of the few singers who insisted on sticking to the traditional form of folk music, and his songs did not really gain national popularity until they were sung by other people in a more "professional" style. Yet country music, which this blending of folk and Hollywood came to be called, was more than a way out for a few selected migrants. It was, as James Gregory puts it, "the language of a sub-culture."[52]

While a few migrants found in music an economic escape from migrant farm labor, most found an emotional escape there. Robert Sonkin observed the emotional transformation that took place in the migrants as they sang: "When they start to sing, you know they haven't a care in the world no matter how much their shoes need mending."[53] What the migrants liked to listen to, however, was not the traditional ballads Todd and Sonkin collected or the protest-oriented music of Woody Guthrie but an emerging genre that combined rural folk music (such as hillbilly music from the southeastern states, southern blues, and southwestern cowboy ballads) with urban production techniques and values mainly derived from Hollywood.

Country music developed out of two basic regional musical styles that gained popularity in the 1920s and 1930s: hillbilly music and cowboy songs. Due mainly to the success of the Carter Family, hillbilly music (multiple-voiced melodies accompanied by the string bands predominant in the mountain Southeast) became a national phenomenon. This music's appeal had little to do with the music itself but rested on hillbilly humor. This cartoon humor, as seen in comic strips like "Li'l Abner," often overshadowed the musical portions of hillbilly radio shows, the appeal being more novelty than an appreciation of the music. The second strain of rural music eventually became the more popular and ascendant feature of country music and is exemplified by the cowboy ballads and blues of Jimmie Rodgers. Accompanied by guitar instead of fiddle, and singing solo instead of in groups, the singing cowboy dropped many of the regional characteristics of southern and southwestern rural singing, mainly the pinched, nasal singing style and farmer attire. Rodgers and other cowboy singers favored Hollywood cowboy attire over the overalls of hillbilly singers and rural folk generally. The singing cowboy reached his peak with Gene Autry. Born in Texas and raised in Oklahoma, Autry embodied the most accessible aspects of Okie culture and presented it to mainstream American society, first over the nationally broadcast radio show *National Barn Dance* and then in Western films, starting with *In Old Santa Fe* in 1934. Autry's theme song, "Back in the Saddle Again," expressed the traditional values essential to country music: "I'm back in the saddle again, out where a friend is a friend."[54] James Gregory concludes that country music made a choice between traditional values and modern life: "Rejecting the postures and preoccupations of modern urban existence, country music chose the cleansing open spaces, the dignity of 'real' work, the genuineness of friendship and family, and the democracy of rural life."[55]

This emerging country music was not designed exclusively for a migrant audience. It provided the link between the Okie subculture and mainstream American culture, while providing a means of distinguishing the Okie subculture from the mainstream. Gregory, in his discussion of the role of country music in Okie culture, writes:

> Southwesterners became its primary agents of dispersion, dominating it as performers and claiming it as consumers. And through this participation the music helped to shape their adjustment to California, conveying some of the political and social values and regional symbols that sharpened their sense of special identity.[56]

It is important to note that while many of the elements of country music are drawn from traditional sources, it is the loss of specifically regional elements, such as the unique singing style of the South and Southwest, that makes country music accessible to a larger audience. Migrants combined the old with the new in an attempt to adapt their "old" ways to the "new" ways of California. The traditional values expressed in country music found an empathetic ear among the migrants, while regional heroes sharing the migrants' background who became successful in the new form represented to many migrants the possibility of succeeding in modern America without sacrificing traditional values. For the migrants, country singing stars such as Gene Autry represented the triumph of their way of life over the corrupt ways of urban America.

Like the folklorists, the migrants used the symbols of country music to defend their culture. Relying heavily on images of "back home" and of cowboy individualism, country music expressed the "plain-folk Americanism" of the migrants. In both cases, traditional elements of the folk song became the basis for a claim of Americanness. The folklorists, however, focused mainly on the way folk songs were democratically produced—on the frontier, in occupational or regional groups, in traditional styles of balladry—while the migrants focused more on content than form. This difference in emphasis led the folklorists to favor the folk style and its practitioners, such as Woody Guthrie, over migrant favorites such as Gene Autry, who sang of traditional values in a modern style. Guthrie's songs expressed a politically progressive position, while Autry and country music expressed a political conservatism.

Attempts to publicize the migrant experience in the name of social reform were based on an ideology that favored expressions of the "common man" as more democratic, and therefore more American, than commercially produced leisure commodities. This folk ideology, combined with a radical critique of the capitalist economy, led Todd and Sonkin to characterize the migrants as victims of modernity—a modernity brought about by capitalist expansion and dominated by corporate hegemony. In seeing the migrants as victims of external circumstances, Todd and Sonkin (along with such government workers as the FSA camp managers) neglected the migrants' responses to their problems such as the continuation of Okie culture through commercial country music. For the folklorists and reformers, the migrants illustrated the injustice of American political economy. Unconcerned with, or at least unaware of, the unique aspects of the migrants' culture, these "experts" sought to eliminate the most important aspects of Okie culture in the name of preserving that culture. Folklorists and reformers saw traditional elements of Okie culture—pioneer spirit, individualism, and opposition to authority—as expressions of class struggle and a call for progressive or radical politics. For the migrants, these elements of Okie culture formed the basis of a populist politics defending the Jeffersonian ideals of the yeoman farmer, or at least a landowner independent of others. Country music reaffirmed this position by celebrating traditional values of independence, family, and the land, by means of a lucrative medium that rewarded personal talent and initiative.

Todd and Sonkin failed to see the role music played in the migrants' transition from a nineteenth-century agrarian society to a twentieth-century industrial economy. Their focus on folk song form, the ballad tradition, and the political aspects of folksinging obscured the conservative nature of the emerging country music. The disdain Todd and Sonkin showed for the slick cowboy manner of Homer Pierce (and their characterization of him as a ballad troubadour) illustrates their misunderstanding of the role of music in the migrant experience. The folklorists were concerned with a folk population and the role of music in a folk community. The migration to California, however, removed the migrants from the folk community. The migrants responded to this relocation by transforming their folk music into country music. The only changes in the migrants' music that Todd and Sonkin would accept were the original migration songs created from the migration experience. Todd and Sonkin saw the migrants as model American workers worthy of and fighting for the rights of all workers. For Todd and Sonkin, the migrants were worthy of attention because they illustrated the inequities of capitalism, which the folklorists placed highest on their list of social concerns. Any attempts by the migrants to adapt their culture to mainstream American society were seen by the folklorists as a loss, and attempts by migrants to commercialize their music were looked upon negatively.

The failure of the folklorists to understand the role of music in the migrant experience and the failure of the FSA to produce "contented, clean, and willing workers" out of the migrants both illustrate a basic misunderstanding of the migrants' culture, their beliefs and aspirations, and their political and economic conservatism. Both the government reformers and folklorists paternally viewed the migrants as ill equipped for modern society while, in fact, the migrants adapted their traditional values to their immediate circumstances. The way in which the migrants adapted their values conflicted with the vision the folklorists and reformers sought to create.

While Paul Taylor, Tom Collins, Charles Todd, and Robert Sonkin failed to create the rural proletariat they envisioned, they did influence the representations of the migrant experience created by Lange, Steinbeck, Ford, and Guthrie. This misrepresentation of the migrant as a class-conscious laborer and victim of circumstances was echoed throughout their works. Differences between these representations, and between the representations and migrant expressions, can best be understood in terms of differing conceptions of a democratic America and the migrants' place within this democracy. The various representations of the migrants' place in a democratic America relied on the attitude each producer had toward the migrants' culture and their understanding of it. Appropriation of the migrant experience resulted in an image of the migrant quite separate from expressions of the migrant experience by the migrants' themselves, and these representations have had a more lasting impression on the American imagination than the migrants' own expressions. What remains are many voices speaking for the migrants, and one of those voices is our own.

It is 1988. We could see the face on the Six O'clock News. It could be a Walker Evans or Dorothea Lange shot, but that's fifty years off. It is a face of despair, of an Iowa farmer, fourth generation, facing foreclosure. I've seen this face before. It is the face of Pa Joad, Muley Graves, and all their lost neighbors, tractored out by the cats.

In the eyes of Carroll Nearmyer, the farmer, is more than despair; there is a hardly concealed wrath: as there was in the eyes of his Okie antecedents.

—Studs Terkel

THE GHOST OF TOM JOAD

The Persistence of

Dust Bowl Representations

Upon the fiftieth anniversary of the publication of *The Grapes of Wrath,* Studs Terkel wrote: "This anniversary edition is more than a golden anniversary celebration of an enduring book. It is as contemporary as the 1988 drought, astonishingly so."[1] Terkel's introduction, which stresses the relevance of Steinbeck's book to the ruthless corporate world of the 1980s, illustrates the enduring nature of representations of the migrant experience. It is no longer the historical dust bowl that is compared to contemporary experience but rather the dust bowl of John Steinbeck.

Woody Guthrie has been admired and celebrated by such contemporary performers as Bruce Springsteen, U2, Bob Dylan, and John Cougar Mellencamp in *A Vision Shared: A Tribute to Woody Guthrie and Leadbelly* (1988), a record album and documentary describing the contributions of these men to contemporary music and featuring new interpretations of songs by Guthrie and Leadbelly. In the documentary Harold Leventhal describes why Guthrie's music remains important:

I think the important thing is the fact that Woody's music, written forty years ago or more, is relevant today. Take the song "I Ain't Got No Home." When Woody wrote this he dealt about the people who were homeless during the depression, we're talking quite some time ago. Yet today in the '80s, we have a gigantic homeless problem in this country and this song is as valid today as when Woody wrote it."[2]

Singer Bono, from the Irish rock band U2, went even farther in his assessment of Guthrie's importance today: " 'Jesus Christ' is a song that has to be sung. Its not a question of U2 wanting to sing it, we have to sing that song because its more relevant today then it was even when he wrote it."[3] Bruce Springsteen acknowledged Guthrie's relevance to contemporary America but saw Guthrie's music as a universal statement that would always be relevant:

> I think that the heart of the song, it cries out for some sort of belief and reckoning with the idea of universal family, which is something that people long for, everybody longs for that. And that is why it is so resonant and will always be resonant. It reaches down and pulls out that part of you that thinks of the next guy. And I think that's embedded in every song he wrote, every story he told, every song he wrote."[4]

Dorothea Lange's *Migrant Mother* continues to serve as the model for hundreds of images, from political posters to rock videos.[5] But perhaps the 1990 stage version of *The Grapes of Wrath* best illustrates the continued representational potential of the dust bowl migration, for in this production the problems of contemporary racism and homelessness are recast into the tale of the Joads. Updating the story of the Joads is at the heart of the 1990 stage version of *The Grapes of Wrath.* Produced by the Chicago-based Steppenwolf Theater Company and adapted and directed by Frank Galati, the play closely follows the form and narrative of the novel. Interchapters from the novel are presented as either narration (by a minor character) or a song. The music, a collection of old songs and originals written by Michael Smith, draws heavily on the Woody Guthrie interpretation of the dust bowl migration. One song relates the singer's attempt to revive his girlfriend by throwing a bucket of dust on her, a joke Guthrie tells in the Library of Congress recordings. Images from the film are echoed in the framing of characters in the truck as the Joads travel west, and in the use of natural lighting from campfires and lamps rather than the expressionistic lighting of most stage productions. The stark sets and placement of characters echo many of the FSA photographs of the migrants. By combining elements from the novel, the film, Lange's photographs, and Guthrie's *Dust Bowl Ballads,* the stage version of *The Grapes of Wrath* draws much of its historical meaning from these representations rather than from the actual migrant experience. Indeed, the expressed purpose of the Steppenwolf Theater Company was to remain faithful to Steinbeck's vision of the dust bowl migrants and not to present a new interpretation of the migration. Frank Galati claimed that the story of the Joads "needs to be told again for our time," since we are, he said, "on the threshold of a new world, at the end of a catastrophic century. This story comes back to us from a dark time to invite us to reflect on what we really value."[6] What "we" really value, it seems, is not the same as what the migrants valued, but what Steinbeck valued. Galati's audience, like Steinbeck's, consists of educated elites who attend the theater and read novels. For such an audience, the Joads represent the ills of American society and provoke contemplation of the American scene. It is in this sense that the stage version of *The Grapes of Wrath* recreates Steinbeck's novel. Yet in many ways the stage version does present a new interpretation, one that consists of elements from its predecessors.

The play is most closely aligned with the interpretation presented by Steinbeck, with some important alterations. The theme of people being forced out of their homes is emphasized, as are the similarities between the white dust bowl migrants and blacks. At a roadside camp, Pa Joad talks about the land the family used to work. A black man sitting nearby asks Pa if they were sharecroppers, and to Pa's reply of "yes" the man adds, "same as us." In the play's final scene, a childless Rose-of-Sharon gives her maternal breast to a dying black man. The image is more than Steinbeck's picture of realization that the bonds of family reach beyond the blood lines of kin and encircle all of humanity; it focuses attention specifically on the need to see different races as part of the family of man.

The main difference between the novel and the play is in the way the interchapters are presented onstage. Whereas Steinbeck's interchapters were the author's direct contact with his audience, informing the audience of trends and situations unknown to the migrants themselves, the staged interludes—many taken directly from the interchapters—are presented by the migrants themselves. These narrators, even though they are not characters in the play's action, are attired in Okie costume yet do not speak in the language or dialect of the Okies. The play opens with a narrator quoting and paraphrasing Steinbeck's opening chapter, which describes an anonymous migrant family and not the Joads. The narrator says:

The dawn came, but no day. In the morning the dust hung like fog. Men stood by their fences and looked at the ruined corn, drying fast now, only a little green showing through the thin film of dust. And the women came out of their houses to stand beside their men, to feel whether this time the men would break. The women studied the men's faces, secretly; for the corn could go, as long as something else remained.[7]

The effect of having Steinbeck's words coming from the mouth of an Okie character presents the migrants as being more conscious of their situation than Steinbeck had intended. One of the songs, which accompanies Tom as he searches outside the peach ranch, even takes Steinbeck's words and presents them as coming from a migrant, in this case a singer who, dressed as an Okie, wanders around the action and acts both as narrator and as one of the migrants who happens to sing. In this song—a sad, mournful tune not really in the folk song style—he describes poetically the growing anger in Tom:

> In the soul of the people
> The grapes of wrath are filling
> And growing heavy, growing heavy
> For the vintage.

In this instance the distinction between authorship and character is blurred, leaving one with the feeling that what is being presented is not a representation of the migrant experience by John Steinbeck but the migrants telling us their own story.

Not only do we feel we are seeing the migrants' story as they would present it but we also get the false impression that the migrants were concerned about racial unity. This goes beyond Steinbeck's representation of the migrants as protoproletarians and casts them as liberal humanitarians as well. The Joads represent both a reaction to a specific historical circumstance, the dust bowl migration, and a reaction to a current political issue, race. *The Grapes of Wrath* onstage presents a voice that blurs both the distinction between past and present and the specific concerns of the dust bowl with the concerns of contemporary America. The voices of the migrants have become the voice of America. Indeed, Alan Brinkley, in reviewing the play, noted that what makes Steinbeck's narrative relevant to the present day is that it evokes "one of America's most powerful and cherished images of itself. It suggests that running like a river beneath the surface of the nation's cold, hard, individualistic culture lies the spirit of Ma Joad, a spirit of "fambly" and community that, once tapped, might redeem us all."[8]

Representations of the dust bowl migration have come to represent our deepest fears and most closely held hopes of life in America. Most recently, Bruce Springsteen has utilized Tom Joad, the central character of these dust bowl representations, as the focus for a collection of songs depicting the harsh realities of racism, illegal immigration, discrimination, and economic turmoil in the American Southwest. In *The Ghost of Tom Joad* (1995) Springsteen sets the tone of the album with the title song, in which the spirit of Tom Joad provides the only ray of hope in an otherwise dismal existence characterized by unemployment and homelessness:

> Shelter line stretchin' 'round the corner
> Welcome to the new world order
> Families sleepin' in their cars in the southwest
> No home no job no peace no rest
>
> The highway is alive tonight
> But nobody's kiddin' nobody about where it goes
> I'm sittin' down here in the campfire light
> Searchin' for the ghost of Tom Joad

Springsteen includes several reasons why there are still have-nots in America, reasons culled from *The Grapes of Wrath*.[9] Like Steinbeck, Springsteen sees the problems of the downtrodden as the partial result of a religious belief in equality at the Judgment Day. As long as poor people believe that eventually they will be given justice, then they will not work for it.

> Waitin' for when the last shall be first and the first shall be last
> In a cardboard box 'neath the underpass

The song then presents Tom Joad as the prophet of the underclass by presenting a modified version of Tom's final conversation with his mother:

> Now Tom said, "Mom, wherever there's a cop beatin' a guy
> Wherever a hungry newborn baby cries
> Where there a fight 'gainst blood and hatred in the air
> Look for me Mom I'll be there
> Wherever there's somebody fightin' for a place to stand
> Or decent job or helpin' hand
> Wherever somebody's strugglin' to be free
> Look in their eyes Mom you'll see me."

The song ends with the joining of the contemporary oppressed and the ghost of oppression past, Tom Joad:

Well the highway is alive tonight
But nobody's kiddin' nobody about where it goes
I'm sittin' down here in the campfire light
With the ghost of old Tom Joad.[10]

With *The Ghost of Tom Joad,* the role of the dust bowl migrant as the representative American victim has completely displaced the dust bowl migrant of historical circumstances. The artistic and reformist elements of Lange's, Steinbeck's, Ford's, and Guthrie's work have persisted, become universal, and claimed authority as the voice of the migrants.

Even though the voices we hear from the past are not those of the migrants themselves, neither are they the individual and distinctive voices of Dorothea Lange, John Steinbeck, John Ford, or Woody Guthrie. A variety of voices, shaped by historical circumstance, artistic creativity, and culture, combined to create the voice we hear today. What that voice says depends on how we listen. Ultimately, the voice we hear is our own. In the words of folk singer Peter Rowan, "we are all Dust Bowl children, singing a Dust Bowl song."[11]

APPENDIX

A Note on Method

"It is not going to be easy to look into their eyes."[1] These are James Agee's thoughts upon the return of the Gudger family after he described for display the stuff and substance of the Gudgers' house in his study of southern tenant farming, *Let Us Now Praise Famous Men* (1941). Knowing their ignorance of his dealings, Agee was stricken with guilt at his subterfuge. "In some bewilderment," he wrote, "they yet love me, and I, how dearly, them; and trust me, despite hurt and mystery, deep beyond making of such a word as trust."[2] Agee realized that his intentions, however noble, were far outside the realm of the Gudgers' everyday, or even occasional, experience. The gap between subject and writer faced Agee like a dark abyss as he desperately attempted to build a bridge across it. It is this torment, central to Agee and Walker Evans's *Let Us Now Praise Famous Men* and absent from the dust bowl work of Lange, Steinbeck, Ford, and Guthrie, that led to this study, to show, in Agee's words "the cruel radiance of what is."[3] I seek not to uncover the "truth" but rather to develop a more complete understanding of the complex relationship between artists, reformers, and dust bowl migrants.

As William Stott argues in *Documentary Expression and Thirties America* (first published in 1973), artists of the 1930s were caught up in the need to authenticate their authority to do their work. They related their work—be it photographs, novels, films, or songs—to lived experience, not only their own experience but the experience of each other as well. According to Stott, "Experience per se became a good."[4] Stott, and others, however, have noted in Agee's writing the exact opposite tendency to deny authority: "Agee's text repeatedly and obsessively undermined its author's authority to write the very text we read, rejecting therefore one of the era's most valued documentary conventions."[5] It has been my goal not to credit or discredit authorial authority but to try to understand how that authority, cultivated by each artist, affected the art created. For this understanding, Agee's text proves most useful, since it serves as an exception to the norm. The message of *Let Us Now Praise Famous Men* is quite different than the impact of *Migrant Mother*, either version of *The Grapes of Wrath*, or the *Dust Bowl Ballads*. That difference informs this study.

My interpretation relies on my authority as a historian since this study crosses the boundaries of disciplines and methods. Having trained neither as a photographer, a novelist, a filmmaker, a folksinger, nor a scholar of any one of these specific fields but as a cultural historian, I need to explain the validity of cultural history as a means to argue my main thesis: that representations of the dust bowl migrants provide a greater understanding of the artists and reformers who created and informed them—their aspirations and democratic ambitions—than of the migrants themselves and their aspirations and vision of American democracy. To argue the necessity of cultural history as a method for understanding dust bowl representations, *Let Us Now Praise Famous Men* again proves useful. Agee and Evans raised the issues of art versus reality, the ability to represent reality, and the object of the endeavor itself. They questioned the ability to justly represent another's reality, given the tools and techniques available to them, and to others such as Lange, Steinbeck, Ford, Guthrie, and the government reformers. In addition, Agee questioned the usefulness of representation, for both the subject and the audience. Agee's words are most apt for this discussion since he wrote within the same historical circumstances in which the other artists and reformers worked—historical circumstances that were formed prior to the widespread intellectual development of narrow specializations, which includes the development of specialized and highly theoretical language that more often than not obfuscates rather than facilitates understanding.

AGEE REGARDED his study of southern tenant farmers as more than a view into certain aspects of tenant life; he also used the task of documenting the lives of these people as an illustration of the difficulties and issues involved in trying to represent the reality of another person. He wrote, "Actually, the effort is to recognize the stature of a portion of unimagined existence, and to contrive techniques proper to its recording, communication, analysis, and defense."[6] This task necessitated the development of techniques equal to it. In other words, Agee felt a new method of documentation needed to replace the older documentary tradition, to which Lange, Steinbeck, Ford, and Guthrie belonged. The documentary tradition, which relied on the authority of the author, was inadequate to fully describe and capture the lives of the three southern tenant farmer families represented in *Let Us Now Praise Famous Men*. Agee believed that other attempts at documenting the lives of poor people failed to take their subjects seriously; that is, they tended to treat their subjects as just another persuasive element in their arguments. Agee warned his readers that it would "be wise to bear the nominal subject, and his expectation of its proper treatment, steadily in mind. For that is the subject with which the authors are dealing, throughout."[7]

The same holds true for my study, in which the subject is not the migrants who were the subjects of the artistic representations but rather the artists creating the representations. The expected treatment of these artists has been to reinforce the authority that they sought by viewing their work as direct expressions of the migrant condition either directly from a migrant, in the case of Woody Guthrie, or directly from a participant observer, in the case of Lange, Steinbeck, and Ford. Calling into question the authority of artists to represent the migrants relies on the ability to interpret the actions and creations of artists, and to do so persuasively. Cultural history provides the tools for this interpretation.

Cultural history aims for an understanding of a person, people, society, institution, and/or nation by examining the products of those agents. These products include material artifacts utilized by the subject, as well as the intellectual and artistic creations of the subject. These artifacts and creations, when examined within their various contexts, reveal information about the values held by the subject. These values could be held individually (that is, representative of only one person) or by a society as a whole. Determining the depth and breadth of the values evident in cultural artifacts and creations requires an understanding of the various contexts within which the creations operate. The contextual understanding goes beyond the textual analysis of current visual, literary, film, and musicological studies and involves a historical understanding of change over time. The contextual aspect of change over time differentiates the work of historians from other disciplines whose search for understanding is most often limited in time. Agee continues his warning to his readers by adding, "If complications arise, that is because they [the authors, Agee and Evans] are trying to deal with it not as journalists, sociologists, politicians, entertainers, humanitarians, priests, or artists, but seriously."[8] Which is to say, the goals of these fields are not necessarily to provide as complete an understanding as is humanly possible but to serve some other agenda. Likewise, the goal of history is to seek as complete an understanding as possible, given the available sources, which means not only comprehending the text (its form, content, creation, function, and effect) but understanding the context in which the artist created the text and into which the text was presented.

AGEE'S CONCERN for an understanding, complete as humanly possible, led him to question the validity of describing the real world in the make-believe world of language: "If I could do it, I'd do no writing at all here. It would be photographs; the rest would be fragments of cloth, bits of cotton, lumps of earth, records of speech, pieces of wood and iron, phials of odors, plates of food and of excrement."[9] For Agee, words were a poor substitute for reality, and the only way that words could compensate for their shortcomings was if a writer used them in overwhelming numbers. That is why Agee spent page after page of his text describing the smallest of details and the most remote of objects. A concern for language is also one of the major interests of this study since the languages created to describe each of the cultural documents analyzed here are often not applicable to all the documents without substantial redefinition and translations, which would confuse rather than clarify the intended goal. The academic discourses surrounding visual studies, literary studies, film studies, and ethnomusicological folklore studies may provide a greater understanding of their correlative documents, but only within the narrow limits of textual (form and content) analysis, and not historical context.

Solving the problems created by the desire to analyze various forms of media without resorting to the specific languages of each narrow discipline requires language that adapts to the unique circumstances of each medium and provides understanding across disciplines as opposed to the exclusion of other disciplines. The use of such language has the benefit of fitting comfortably with descriptions of historical context and maintaining continuity within the larger narrative, a continuity necessary to complete the fullest possible understanding sought in this study.

The use of such language has placed, however, an added emphasis and importance on structure as a means of subtly adapting language to the differing demands of this study. Therefore, the work has a patterned format in which each chapter deals with the general context of its subject before focusing more closely on the central document under consideration. The various contexts form the basis from which a closer analysis of each artist or reformer is examined. In the first chapter, the history of California agriculture and relief efforts for farm laborers provides the context for the individual efforts of Paul Taylor, Carey McWilliams, and the migrant camp program. The development of a documentary style in Lange's photography resulted in Lange's involvement with government reformers, in particular Paul Taylor, while Steinbeck's relationship with Tom Collins is best understood within the context of the philosophical intentions of Steinbeck's use of literature. Likewise, John Ford's interpretation of American history grew out of the development of his filmic technique and the Hollywood studio system. The intellectual acceptance of politically charged folk music as representative of "the people" coincided with Guthrie's growing political awareness and radicalism, while the development of a uniquely American interpretation of the folk song tradition led to the preservation attempts of Todd and Sonkin. From these analyses, each chapter focuses on the representations created by the artists and reformers: the reports of camp managers and migrant newsletters, Lange and Taylor's *American Exodus* and Lange's *Migrant Mother,*

Steinbeck's and Ford's versions of *The Grapes of Wrath,* Guthrie's *Dust Bowl Ballads,* and Todd and Sonkin's "Songs of the Okies." The structure of each chapter reinforces the idea that even though each of these artists and reformers dealt in different contexts and created different forms of documents, each followed a similar pattern of development in which the ultimate creation resulted in the pervasive image of the migrant that persists to this day.

AGEE WROTE of the photographs in *Let Us Now Praise Famous Men:*

> The photographs are not illustrative. They, and the text, are coequal, mutually independent, and fully collaborative. By their fewness, and by the impotence of the reader's eye, this will be misunderstood by most of that minority which does not wholly ignore it. In the interests, however, of the history and future of photography, that risk seems irrelevant, and this flat statement necessary.[10]

While I make no such grand claims for the use of photographs, Agee's statement does illuminate the photographic essay contained in this work. The text describes and analyzes the various forms under consideration with the goal of adequately presenting each of the various media in words, while the photographs relate another form of the same argument, presented in images and words, the combination of which hopefully embodies meaning more than they describe action. The photographic essay, since it relies on structure to convey meaning—the juxtaposition of words and images—provides a somewhat different interpretation of the argument, resulting in the same conclusion.

The separation of the photographic essay from the text of the work reinforces the goal of describing and analyzing the various media under consideration in coherent and cohesive language without relying on the presentation of the photographs, or the novel, film, or folk songs. I hope that the text and the photographs speak for themselves as distinct narratives and reinforcing arguments.

AGEE UNDERSTOOD the value of representing reality as accurately as possible:

> But art and the imagination are capable of being harmful, and it is probably neither healthy for them nor, which is more to the point, anywhere near true even to the plainest facts, to rate them so singly high. It seems to me there is quite as considerable value (to say nothing of joy) in the attempt to see or to convey even some single thing as nearly as possible as that thing is.[11]

For Agee the task of representing reality was a significant human endeavor, surpassing artistic creations in importance. This stems from Agee's belief that the noblest endeavor is not only based on the fact of existence, especially the existence of a person unique from all others, but centered on the recognition of beauty in that person. The beauty inherent in the existence of a person also resides, for Agee, in objects as well. Therefore, the objects that made up the Gudgers' household were, in Agee's mind and prose, as beautiful and essential as any work of art. Agee appreciated everyday objects aesthetically and also believed that people should keep this idea in mind and thereby appreciate the significance and importance of trying to represent reality as closely as possible. "I would further insist," Agee wrote, "that it would do human beings, including artists, no harm to recognize this fact, and to bear it in mind in their seining of experience, and to come as closely as they may be able, to recording and reproducing it for its own, not for art's sake."[12] This is not to say that this task of representing reality as closely as possible should obliterate art, but rather that artistic renderings of reality should be seen for the fictions they are and reality appreciated for what it is.

It is this split between art and reality that plays a central role in this study. The difference between the goals of art, even socially aware art such as that discussed here, is markedly different from the goals of representing reality. Art seeks to present a point of view, while the point of representing reality is the fact of reality's existence. These distinct goals lead to discrete products. Once again, I do not prefer one over the other but simply illuminate the difference. In the case of dust bowl art, the blurred line between art and reality is the result of the attention and authority granted to Lange, Steinbeck, Ford, and Guthrie (mainly from such government reformers as Paul Taylor, Carey McWilliams, Charles Todd, and Robert Sonkin) and of the persistence of the images and descriptions created by them and reinforced by one another.

In order to see the beauty in both the art and the reality of the dust bowl migration, it is necessary to understand how each came into being, which includes understanding artistic creation and intention (form and content analysis) and the historical developments leading to both the subject of the art and the creation of the art (the study of change over time). This combination of historical and cultural analysis could not be fully understood by examining "texts" alone but only by employing the methods of cultural history. Overall, this work attempts to illustrate the usefulness of cultural history in its most synthetic of applications.

NOTES

The Migrants as American Victims

1. Walter J. Stein, *California and the Dust Bowl Migration* (Westport, Conn.: Greenwood Press), p. xi.

2. Ibid., pp. ix–xi.

3. "I Wonder Where We Can Go Now," *Fortune*, April 1939.

4. James N. Gregory, *American Exodus: The Dust Bowl Migration and Okie Culture in California* (New York: Oxford University Press, 1989), p. 142.

5. Ibid., p. 243.

6. Dan Morgan, *Rising in the West: The True Story of an "Okie" Family from the Great Depression through the Reagan Years* (New York: Alfred A. Knopf, 1992), pp. 111–12.

7. Gregory, *American Exodus*, p. xvi.

Chapter 1. New Deal Reformers

1. M. P. Bruick, "History of the Farm Workers' Community," *The Hub*, Tulare Farm Workers' Community, May 16, 1941; S. K. Blackmon, "The Twilight of Democracy," *The Hub*, Tulare Farm Workers' Community, May 23, 1941.

2. Carey McWilliams, *Factories in the Field* (Boston: Little, Brown, 1939), p. 300.

3. Cletus E. Daniel, *Bitter Harvest: A History of California Farmworkers, 1870–1941* (Ithaca, N.Y.: Cornell University Press, 1981), p. 18. Most histories of California agriculture focus on its divergence from the development of agriculture in other western states and in the United States as a whole. Other general histories of California agriculture are Claude B. Hutchison, ed., *California Agriculture* (Berkeley: University of California Press, 1946), and Lawrence J. Jelinek, *Harvest Empire: A History of California Agriculture*, 2d ed. (San Francisco: Boyd and Fraser, 1982).

4. McWilliams, *Factories in the Field*, p. 15.

5. Ibid.

6. Henry George, as quoted in ibid., p. 24.

7. Frank Adams, "The Historical Background of California Agriculture," in Claude B. Hutchison, ed., *California Agriculture* (Berkeley: University of California Press, 1946), p. 35.

8. Ibid., p. 40.

9. Alan L. Olmstead and Paul Rhode, "An Overview of California Agricultural Mechanization, 1870–1930," *Agricultural History* 62, no. 3 (1988): 89.

10. *Migratory Labor in California* (1936), as quoted in McWilliams, *Factories in the Field*, p. 10.

11. McWilliams, *Factories in the Field*, p. 124.

12. Linda C. Majka and Theo J. Majka, *Farm Workers, Agribusiness and the State* (Philadelphia: Temple University Press, 1982), p. 67.

13. Ibid., pp. 69–70.

14. James N. Gregory, *American Exodus: The Dust Bowl Migration and Okie Culture in California* (New York: Oxford University Press, 1989), p. 7.

15. For a detailed study of the conditions and reasons of migration from the Southwest, Gregory's *American Exodus* provides the best brief summary of this phenomenon; see especially chapter 1, "Out of the Heartland." See also Donald Worster, *Dust Bowl: The Southern Plains in the 1930's* (New York: Oxford University Press, 1979); Paul Bonnifield, *The Dust Bowl: Men, Dirt, and Depression* (Albuquerque: University of New Mexico Press, 1979), and R. Douglas Hurt, *The Dust Bowl: An Agricultural and Social History* (Chicago: Nelson-Hall, 1981).

16. Unnamed migrant to Dorothea Lange, as quoted in Lange, "Interview of Dorothea Lange," conducted by Richard K. Doud, May 22, 1964, Archive of American Art, Smithsonian Institution, Washington, D.C., p. 11.

17. Gregory, *American Exodus,* p. 11.

18. Ibid., pp. 17–19.

19. Ibid., p. 28.

20. Ibid., pp. 39–41.

21. Walter J. Stein, *California and the Dust Bowl Migration* (Westport, Conn.: Greenwood Press, 1973), p. x.

22. Ibid., p. xi.

23. Dorothea Lange and Paul S. Taylor, *An American Exodus: A Record of Human Erosion* (New York: Reynal and Hitchcock, 1939). Much of Taylor's most important work on the migrant labor situation of the 1930s has been collected in *On the Ground in the Thirties* (Salt Lake City: Peregrine Smith Books, 1983). Other notable works include Paul S. Taylor and Tom Vasey, "Drought Refugee and Labor Migration to California, June–December 1935," *Monthly Labor Review,* 42, no. 2 (February 1936): 312–18; Paul S. Taylor, "Migratory Farm Labor in the United States," *Monthly Labor Review* 44, no. 3 (March 1937): 537–49; and Paul S. Taylor and Edward J. Rowell, "Patterns of Agricultural Labor Migration within California," *Monthly Labor Review* 47, no. 5 (November 1938): 980–90.

24. Paul S. Taylor, "The Migrants and California's Future: The Trek to California, and the Trek in California" (speech delivered before the Commonwealth Club of California, San Francisco, September 13, 1935); manuscript copy in the Harry Everett Drobish Collection, Bancroft Library, University of California, Berkeley; reprinted in *On the Ground in the Thirties,* pp. 175–76.

25. Lillian Creisler, " 'Little Oklahoma' or the Airport Community: A Study of the Social and Economic Adjustment of Self-Settled Agricultural Drought and Depression Refugees" (master's thesis, University of California, Berkeley, 1940), p. 11.

26. Wiley Cuddard Sr., quoted in James Bright Wilson, "Social Attitudes of Certain Migratory Agricultural Workers in Kern County, California" (master's thesis, University of Southern California, 1942), p. 307.

27. John Bailey, quoted in Wilson, "Social Attitudes of Certain Migratory Workers," p. 316.

28. Homer Towney, quoted in Wilson, "Social Attitudes of Certain Migratory Workers," p. 388.

29. Roy Turner, "With the Poets," *The Hub,* Tulare Farm Workers' Community, February 21, 1942.

30. L. Thrasher, "America Today," *The Woodville Community News,* Woodville Farm Workers' Community, August 13, 1941.

31. Creisler, " 'Little Oklahoma,' " p. 26.

32. Charles Robinson, quoted in Wilson, "Social Attitudes of Certain Migratory Workers," p. 388.

33. A Camper, "The Whys of the Migrant," *Voice of the Migrant,* Marysville Migratory Labor Camp, December 8, 1939.

34. McWilliams, *Factories in the Field,* pp. 92–96.

35. Ibid., p. 206.

36. *Final Report Division of Land Settlement,* June 30, 1931, as quoted in ibid., p. 207.

37. Harry Drobish to Robert Clarckson, October 6, 1934, Harry Everett Drobish Papers, Bancroft Library, University of California, Berkeley.

38. Ibid.

39. Harry Drobish to Mr. Roy W. Pilling, acting administrator, SERA, February 5, 1935, Drobish Papers.

40. Harry Drobish, "Camp Program for Migrants," Drobish Papers.

41. Harry Drobish to Frank Y. McLaughlin, administrator, SERA, March 15, 1935, Drobish Papers.

42. Sidney Baldwin, *Poverty and Politics: The Rise and Decline of the Farm Security Administration* (Chapel Hill: University of North Carolina Press, 1968), pp. 18–19.

43. Ibid., p. 4.

44. Ibid., p. 65.

45. Harry Drobish to Frank Y. McLaughlin, March 15, 1935, Drobish Papers.

46. Harry Drobish, "A Review of the Steps Taken in the Development of the Program for Farm Laborers," Drobish Papers.

47. Lee A. Stone, "A Discussion of the Advisability of the Resettlement Administration of the U.S. Government Building Camp Sites for the Housing of Migratory Labor," Drobish Papers.

48. Irving Wood, "Instructions to Camp Managers," Irving William Wood Papers, Bancroft Library, University of California, Berkeley.

49. Ibid.

50. Irving Wood, "State of Regional Office of Resettlement Administration on Possible Establishment of Migrant Camps," Wood Papers.

51. "Constitution for Migratory Labor Camps," Farm Security Administration Collection, Bancroft Library, University of California, Berkeley.

52. Thomas Collins, "The Human Side in the Operation of a Migrants Camp," Wood Papers.

53. Ibid. (emphasis mine).

54. Ibid.

55. Ibid.

56. Margaret Sloan, "Letter to the Editor," *Camp Echo,* Brawley Migratory Labor Camp, Brawley, California, March 31, 1939. The parenthetical phrases are those of the

paper's editor, who is not credited in this issue, unlike in previous and subsequent issues. My guess is that the camp manager edited this issue but did not credit himself since the publication was supposed to be run by the migrants and free of the manager's influence.

57. Thomas Collins, "General Comments," *Weekly Report of the Arvin Migratory Labor Camp,* week ending February 8, 1936, Wood Papers.

58. Gregory, *American Exodus,* p. 53.

59. Garin Burbank, *When Farmers Voted Red: The Gospel of Socialism in the Oklahoma Countryside, 1910–1924* (Westport, Conn.: Greenwood Press, 1976), p. 45. See also James R. Green, *Grass-Roots Socialism: Radical Movements in the Southwest, 1895–1943* (Baton Rouge: Louisiana State University Press, 1978).

60. A Camper, "The Whys of the Migrant," *Voice of the Migrant,* Marysville Migratory Labor Camp, Marysville, California, December 8, 1939.

61. "As Others See Us: Lee Side of L. A.," *The Hub,* Tulare Migrant Workers' Camp, Visalia, California, October 11, 1941.

62. Ray C. Mork, "Weekly Letter from Your Manager on the State of the Camp," *The Covered Wagon,* Indio Farm Laborers Camp, Indio, California, February 4, 1939.

63. Ray C. Mork, untitled article, *The Covered Wagon,* Indio Farm Laborers Camp, Indio, California, December 31, 1938.

64. Reginald A. F. Loftus, "Manager's Message," Calipatria Mobile Unit Number 1 Newsletter, January 24, 1941.

65. Editorial, *The Camp Herald,* Firebaugh Migratory Labor Camp, Firebaugh, California, October 10, 1941.

66. Conrad C. Reibold, "Monthly Narrative Report, Firebaugh Farm Workers Community for October 1941," Farm Security Administration Records, RR-CF-37-918-02, National Archives and Record Administration, San Bruno, California.

67. John Spencer, "Weekly Letter from Your Camp Manager," *Covered Wagon News,* Shafter Migrant Labor Camp, Shafter, California, January 11, 1941.

68. UCAPAWA handbill, FSA Records, RR-CF-31-163-01, National Archives and Record Administration, San Bruno, California.

69. Gregory, *American Exodus,* pp. 142, 144, 154, 164.

Chapter 2. Dorothea Lange and Migrant Mother

1. Dorothea Lange, *The Making of a Documentary Photographer,* an oral history conducted 1968, Regional Oral History Office, University of California, Berkeley, 1968, p. 27. Courtesy of The Bancroft Library. Much of the biographical information on Dorothea Lange comes from Milton Meltzer's *Dorothea Lange: A Photographer's Life* (New York: Farrar, Straus and Giroux, 1978).

2. Ibid., p. 16.

3. Ibid., p. 17.

4. Dorothea Lange, as quoted in Meltzer, *Dorothea Lange,* p. 24.

5. Beaumont Newhall and Nancy Newhall, *Masters of Photography* (New York: Braziller, 1958), p. 10.

6. Meltzer, *Dorothea Lange,* p. 31.

7. Lange, *Making of a Documentary Photographer,* p. 90.

8. Ibid., p. 144.

9. Ibid., pp. 144–45.

10. Dorothea Lange, "Interview of Dorothea Lange," conducted by Richard K. Doud, May 22, 1964, Archive of American Art, Smithsonian Institution, Washington, D.C., p. 5.

11. Dorothea Lange, quoted in Daniel Dixon, "Dorothea Lange," *Modern Photography* 16, no. 12 (December 1952): 75.

12. Lange, "Interview of Dorothea Lange," p. 6.

13. Lange, *Making of a Documentary Photographer,* p. 154.

14. Ibid., pp. 205–6. In this interview Lange gives an example of a good descriptive caption. "A caption such as 'Winter in New England' only tells you that it's New England. The picture should indicate that it's winter. That caption shouldn't be necessary. But you could say: 'This part of the country is, contrary to the rest of the country, losing its population.' You could say: 'People are leaving this part of the United States which was really the cradle of democratic principles bred there in the very early days of our country.' Such things could give you a different look into winter in New England. They need not be your own ideas."

15. Ibid., p. 166.

16. Ibid., pp. 174–75.

17. Lange, with Daniel Dixon, "Photographing the Familiar," *Aperture* 1, no. 2; reprinted in Nathan Lyons, ed., *Photographers on Photography* (Englewood Cliffs, N.J.: Prentice-Hall in collaboration with the George Eastman House, Rochester, New York, 1966), p. 72.

18. Paul S. Taylor, *Paul Schuster Taylor: California Social Scientist,* an oral history conducted in 1973, Regional Oral History Office, University of California, Berkeley, 1973, vol. 1, p. 138. Courtesy of The Bancroft Library. The two reports used to advocate the migrant camp program are located in the FSA files, Prints and Photographic Division of the Library of Congress, Washington D.C.; see Paul S. Taylor and Dorothea Lange, "Establishment of Rural Rehabilitation Camps for Migrants in California," March 15, 1935, Lot 898, and Paul S. Taylor and Dorothea Lange, "Migration of Drought Refugees to California," April 17, 1935, Lot 897.

19. Dorothea Lange to Roy Emerson Stryker, October 6, 1937, Roy Emerson Stryker Collection, University of Louisville Photographic Archives, University of Louisville, Louisville, Kentucky.

20. Zoe Brown, "Dorothea Lange: Field Notes and Photographs, 1935–1940" (master's thesis, John F. Kennedy University, 1979), p. 26.

21. Ibid., pp. 64–65. Brown transcribed and analyzed Lange's field notes and came to the conclusion that, "as is true of most of Lange's papers in the Oakland Museum, the field notes comprise a throughly extroverted document" (p. 66).

22. Dorothea Lange, "Field Notes and Photographs," transcribed by Zoe Brown, vol. 2, p. 69. Zoe Brown's two-volume master's thesis contains an analysis of the field notes (vol. 1) and a transcription of the field notes (vol. 2).

23. Lange, "Field Notes and Photographs," caption to photograph RA 2464E, following page 84.

24. Dorothea Lange to Roy Emerson Stryker, January 18, 1939, Stryker Collection.

25. Dorothea Lange to M. E. Gilfond, October 19, 1936, Stryker Collection.

26. Lange, "Field Notes and Photographs," p. 255.

27. Ibid., p. 311.

28. Ibid., p. 369.

29. Dorothea Lange to Roy Emerson Stryker, June 14, 1937, Stryker Collection.

30. Lange, "Field Notes and Photographs," p. 379.

31. Ibid., p. 387.

32. Lange, "Interview of Dorothea Lange," p. 8.

33. Ibid., p. 11.

34. Ibid., p. 11.

35. Dorothea Lange and Paul S. Taylor, *An American Exodus: A Record of Human Erosion* (New York: Reynal and Hitchcock, 1939), p. 5.

36. Ibid., p. 102.

37. Ibid., p. 6.

38. Ibid., p. 145.

39. Ibid., pp. 5–6.

40. Taylor, *Paul Schuster Taylor,* vol. 1, p. 219.

41. Dorothea Lange, "The Assignment I'll Never Forget," *Popular Photography* 46, no. 2 (February 1960): 42.

42. Ibid., p. 128.

43. Since Dorothea Lange did not ask the name of the "migrant mother," the photograph remained an unidentified symbol of the depression until 1983 when the children of Florence Thompson used the photograph to publicize their mother's illness. The publicity generated by the photograph resulted in $30,000 worth of contributions to help defray Thompson's medical expenses. For a full description and analysis of the photographs and their creation, see James C. Curtis, "Dorothea Lange, Migrant Mother, and the Culture of the Great Depression," *Winterthur Portfolio* 21, no. 1 (1986): 1–20.

44. Lange, "The Assignment," p. 128.

45. Ibid.

46. *San Francisco News,* March 10, 1936.

47. *Survey Graphic* 25, no. 9 (March 1936): 524.

48. Paul S. Taylor, "From the Ground Up," *Survey Graphic* 25, no. 9 (March 1936): 526–29, 537–38. Reprinted in Taylor, *On the Ground in the Thirties* (Salt Lake City: Peregrine Smith Books, 1983), pp. 185–93.

49. "Look in Her Eyes," *Midweek Pictorial,* October 1936.

Chapter 3. John Steinbeck and The Grapes of Wrath

1. Early in his career critics labeled Steinbeck as a teller of stories and local chronicler of California and not a serious author. The superficial nature of his nonfictional writing has haunted serious students of Steinbeck's work into dogmatic defenses of Steinbeck's literary genius against his popularity—drawing a negative correlation between popular success and literary achievement. With the publication of Peter Lisca's study *The Wide*

World of John Steinbeck (New Brunswick: N.J.: Rutgers University Press, 1958), Steinbeck criticism arrived at a sophistication necessary to deal with his work in its appropriate social, historical, and artistic contexts. Major works on Steinbeck include Robert DeMott, *Steinbeck's Reading: A Catalog of Books Owned and Borrowed* (New York: Garland, 1984); Richard Astro, *John Steinbeck and Edward F. Ricketts: The Shaping of a Novelist* (Minneapolis: University of Minnesota Press, 1973); Joseph Fontenrose, *John Steinbeck: An Introduction and Interpretation* (New York: Barnes and Noble, 1963); Warren French, *John Steinbeck* (Boston: Twayne, 1975); and Peter Lisca, *John Steinbeck: Nature and Myth* (New York: Thomas Y. Crowell, 1978).

2. Biographical information is derived mainly from Jackson J. Benson, *The True Adventures of John Steinbeck, Writer* (New York: Viking, 1984). Benson's biography is generally held to be the standard and most comprehensive work on the life of Steinbeck. Other less useful sources include Brian St. Pierre, *John Steinbeck: The California Years* (San Francisco: Chronicle Books, 1983); Thomas Kiernan, *The Intricate Music: A Biography of John Steinbeck* (Boston: Little, Brown, 1979); and Nelson Valjean, *John Steinbeck, The Errant Knight: An Intimate Biography of His California Years* (San Francisco: Chronicle Books, 1975).

3. John Steinbeck, "One Day," manuscript at the Humanities Research Center, University of Texas. Also published as part of the preface to Steinbeck's *Acts of Arthur and His Noble Knights* (New York: Farrar, Straus and Giroux, 1976), p. xi.

4. Benson, *True Adventures of John Steinbeck*, p. 53.

5. A large portion of these letters are edited into the book *Steinbeck: A Life in Letters,* ed. Elaine Steinbeck and Robert Wallsten (New York: Viking, 1975). Benson's *True Adventures of John Steinbeck* relies quite heavily on these letters as the major source of information on the writer. Steinbeck firmly believed in an author's need to remain anonymous since he felt notoriety tarnished the purity of literature.

6. William Emerson Ritter and Edna W. Bailey, "The Organismal Conception: Its Place in Science and Its Bearing on Philosophy," *University of California Publications in Zoology* 31 (1931): 307, as quoted in Astro, *Steinbeck and Ricketts*, pp. 44–45.

7. William Emerson Ritter, *The Natural History of Our Conduct* (New York: Harcourt, Brace, 1927), p. 4.

8. Astro, *Steinbeck and Ricketts*, pp. 48–49.

9. This view of Steinbeck as a pragmatic philosopher rather than a detached scientist is best expressed in Richard Astro's *Steinbeck and Ricketts*, in which Astro argues against the direct connection most Steinbeck scholars make between Steinbeck and the marine biologist Ed Ricketts. Ricketts's belief in a nonteleological view of the world has often led Steinbeck's critics to an interpretation of Steinbeck's work as animalistic and detached from his characters. In addition, by looking at the work of Smuts, Briffault, and Boodin, Astro eliminates the debates over the influence of thinkers such as Ralph Waldo Emerson, Thomas Jefferson, Henry David Thoreau, Walt Whitman, and William James on Steinbeck by placing Steinbeck in a scientific context rather than in the naturalist/humanistic context in which he is often placed.

10. John Steinbeck, *To a God Unknown* (New York: Penguin, 1976), p. 261; originally published by Robert O. Ballou, 1933. I will be using the Penguin editions of Steinbeck's works for citations since they are the most accessible.

11. John Steinbeck, *In Dubious Battle* (New York: Penguin, 1988), p. 60; originally published by Covici, Friede, 1936.

12. Most of the information on Steinbeck's access to materials and information on the Okies is taken from Benson's *True Adventures of John Steinbeck* and his article, " 'To Tom Who Lived It': John Steinbeck and the Man from Weedpatch," *Journal of Modern Literature* 5 (April 1976): 151–224.

13. John Steinbeck, "Dubious Battle in California," *The Nation*, September 12, 1936, pp. 302–4.

14. Benson, " 'To Tom Who Lived It,' " pp. 180–81.

15. Citations to these articles are from John Steinbeck, *The Harvest Gypsies: On the Road to the Grapes of Wrath* (Berkeley: Heyday Books, 1988). This edition is the latest reprint of the articles, the first being the Simon J. Lubin Society pamphlet "Their Blood Is Strong," published in 1938. Here Steinbeck's concern for the downtrodden is distinctly discriminatory in a section recounting the history of California farm labor in which the treatment of former agricultural minority groups, such as the Chinese, Japanese, Mexicans, and Filipinos, is deemed unsuitable for white American labor. "Foreign labor is on the wane in California, and the future farm workers are to be white and American. This fact must be recognized and a rearrangement of the attitude toward and treatment of migrant labor must be achieved." Steinbeck, *Harvest Gypsies*, p. 57.

16. The subsistence farms program, as suggested by Harry Drobish and publicized by Steinbeck, proposed to create small farm plots for agricultural workers. This was an attempt not to make small farmers independent on their own farms but to give workers a "subsistence" plot on which to raise produce and livestock for personal consumption. Drobish also believed that these farms would give temporarily unemployed workers something to do.

17. Benson, " 'To Tom Who Lived It,' " p. 190.

18. Thomas Collins, "Report for week ending February 29, 1936," Wood Papers, Bancroft Library, University of California, Berkeley.

19. Benson, " 'To Tom Who Lived It,' " p. 191. Benson's article recounts the similarities in Collins's reports and Steinbeck's novel in abundant detail. I agree with Benson that the effect of Collins on Steinbeck was one of reinforcement and not direct influence. My argument rests on the ideas that were reinforced by Collins and are expressed in *The Grapes of Wrath*.

20. John Steinbeck to Mavis McIntosh, quoted in Benson, *True Adventures of John Steinbeck*, p. 315.

21. These trips that Steinbeck and Collins made were mistaken by some of Steinbeck's friends as a trip to Oklahoma and back with a migrant family. Steinbeck did nothing to discourage this notion and in later years spoke as if that trip actually occurred. For further detail see Benson, " 'To Tom Who Lived It.' "

22. In his journal Steinbeck often mentioned the importance of the book and his need for it to "be far and away the best thing I have ever attempted." John Steinbeck, *Working Days: The Journals of The Grapes of Wrath*, ed. Robert DeMott (New York: Viking, 1989), p. 25.

23. Ibid., p. 36.

24. Ibid., pp. 39, 25.

25. John Steinbeck, *The Grapes of Wrath* (New York: Viking, 1989), p. 50; citations refer to the 1989 reissue of the original 1939 printing.

Photo Essay: The Image of the Migrants

1. Roy Emerson Stryker, "The FSA Collection of Photographs," in Roy Emerson Stryker and Nancy Wood, eds., *In This Proud Land* (New York: Galahad, 1973), pp. 8–9.

2. Dorothea Lange, quoted in Daniel Dixon, "Dorothea Lange," *Modern Photography* 16, no. 12 (December 1952): 75.

3. John Steinbeck, *The Grapes of Wrath* (New York: Viking, 1989), pp. 46–47.

4. Seema Weatherwax, as quoted in Dave Marsh, ed., *Pastures of Plenty* (New York: HarperCollins, 1990), p. 261.

Chapter 4. John Ford and The Grapes of Wrath

1. John Ford, "Veteran Producer Muses," *New York Times,* June 10, 1928; reprinted in Richard Koszarski, *Hollywood Directors, 1914–1940* (New York: Oxford University Press, 1976), pp. 199–204.

2. An example of this criticism is found in Michael Dempsey, "John Ford: A Reassessment," *Film Quarterly* 29 (Summer 1975): 2–15. He says: "Ford the contemporary of Dreiser and Dos Passos and even Steinbeck gives us, in *The Grapes of Wrath* (1940), a hollow celebration of that emptiest abstraction, The People, along with a cop-out analysis which avoids blaming any individual or interest for the plight of the Okies" (p. 5).

3. As a case in point, film scholar Lindsay Anderson places Ford's birth on February 1, 1895, in Port Elizabeth, Maine, and his name as Sean Aloysius O'Feeney (*About John Ford* [London: Plexus, 1981], p. 9). Biographer Andrew Sinclair agrees on the date and place but notes Ford's given name as John Augustine Feeney (*John Ford* [New York: The Dial Press/James Wade, 1979], p. 9). French critic Jean Mitry claims that February 1, 1895, was probably the date Ford's parents were naturalized and that Ford's birth took place "four or five years before in Ireland" ("Interview with John Ford," *Cahiers du Cinema,* no. 45 [March 1955]; translated by and reprinted in Andrew Sarris, ed., *Interviews with Film Directors* [New York: Bobbs-Merrill, 1967]) p. 162). Even Ford's grandson Dan Ford claims John Feeney Jr. was born at Cape Elizabeth, Maine, on February 1, 1895 (*Pappy: The Life of John Ford* [Englewood Cliffs, N.J.: Prentice-Hall, 1979], p. 5). However, Tag Gallagher has found that the town records of Port Elizabeth list the birth of John Martin Feeney on February 1, 1894. Further evidence of this is found in baptismal records and on Ford's tombstone. Aloysius was Ford's confirmation name (*John Ford: The Man and His Films* [Berkeley: University of California Press, 1986], p. 2).

4. Gallagher, *John Ford,* p. 1.

5. Kevin Starr writes: "With *The Birth of a Nation,* the movies came permanently to Los Angeles." *Inventing the Dream: California Through the Progressive Era* (New York: Oxford University Press, 1985), p. 303.

6. John Ford, quoted in Richard Schickel, "Good Days, Good Years," *Harper's*, October 1970, p. 46; and in Gallagher, *John Ford*, p. 15.

7. Baker also recalled an incident in which a down-and-out actor from Ford's old Universal days approached Ford in front of a crowd of people and nervously asked for two hundred dollars as a hospital deposit for his wife, who desperately needed an operation. As a quiet crowd gathered, Ford backed away from the man and then suddenly attacked him shouting, "How dare you come here like this. Who do you think you are to talk to me this way?" Ford then walked away. An indignant crowd watched the beaten man leave the room, but Baker followed the man unnoticed and witnessed Ford's business manager catching up to the man with a thousand-dollar check from Ford. Ford also supplied an ambulance to drive the wife to the hospital, where a specialist from San Francisco, also supplied by Ford, was flown in to perform the procedure. Eventually, Ford purchased a house for the couple and pensioned them for life. Gallagher, *John Ford*, pp. 40–41.

8. Douglas Gomery, *The Hollywood Studio System* (New York: St. Martin's, 1986), p. 76.

9. Gallagher, *John Ford*, p. 46.

10. John Ford, as quoted in Sarris, *Interviews with Film Directors*, p. 160.

11. Films from the 1930s include *Men without Women, Born Reckless, Up the River* (1930); *Seas Beneath, The Brat, Arrowsmith* (1931); *Air Mail, Flesh* (1932); *Pilgrimage* (1933); *The Lost Patrol, The World Moves On* (1934); *The Whole Town Is Talking* (1935); *The Prisoner of Shark Island, Mary of Scotland, The Plough and the Stars* (1936); *The Hurricane* (1937); *Four Men and a Prayer,* and *Submarine Patrol* (1938).

12. While *Wee Willie Winkie* is not a musical, its use of music as a statement of emotion is clearly evident in the scene in which Winkie sings "Auld Lang Syne" to her dying friend, Sargeant McDuff.

13. For the best summary of Ford and American myth see Peter Stowell, *John Ford* (Boston: Twayne, 1986), in which Stowell divides American myths into five catagories: the American Adam, the American frontier, American agrarianism, American individualism, and American civilization.

14. Ibid., p. xiv.

15. Nunnally Johnson, "Will 'The Grapes of Wrath' Be Shelved?" *Photoplay* (November 1939); reprinted in Richard Griffith, ed., *The Talkies: Articles and Illustrations from a Great Fan Magazine, 1928–1940* (New York: Dover, 1971), pp. 260–61, 320.

16. John Baxter, *The Cinema of John Ford* (New York: A. S. Barnes, 1971), p. 87.

17. Johnson, "Will 'Grapes' Be Shelved?" p. 320.

18. Richard Fine, *Hollywood and the Profession of Authorship, 1928–1940* (Ann Arbor, Mich.: UMI Research Press, 1985), p. 156.

19. It is possible that Steinbeck helped Collins in this matter since an earlier attempt by Steinbeck to help Collins publish his camp reports failed to gain results. Collins's contribution probably extends no further than the design of the government camp sets.

20. John Ford, as quoted in Peter Bogdanovich, *John Ford* (Berkeley: University of California Press, 1968), p. 76. Interestingly, in a different interview with George Bluestone, Ford recounts that he never read Steinbeck's novel. George Bluestone, *Novels into Film* (Berkeley: University of California Press, 1971), p. 169.

21. John Ford, speaking at a film seminar at UCLA, as reported by George J. Mitchell, "Ford on Ford," *Films in Review* 15 (June–July 1964), pp. 321–32.

22. Bogdanovich, *John Ford*, p. 78.

23. See Gallagher, *John Ford*, p. 179, and footnote, pp. 179–80. It is not clear exactly how the film came to have the ending it has. Ford has been characteristically vague about the entire matter, and any kind of documentation concerning the original script is scarce, if existing at all. Ford claims to have agreed to the ending and asked Zanuck to direct it, while in other instances he recalls being present while Johnson wrote the final scene on the set. Johnson claims that he wrote the scene in his original draft but that neither Ford or Zanuck was set on it as filming started. Zanuck's concern for secrecy during the filming resulted in only three full copies of the screenplay existing, and the collection of partial copies made for actors and the crew each night during production. Warren French, *Filmguide to The Grapes of Wrath* (Bloomington: Indiana University Press, 1973), p. 18; see also Mel Gussow, *Don't Say Yes Until I Finish Talking: A Biography of Darryl F. Zanuck* (Garden City, N.Y.: Doubleday, 1971). French critic Jean Mitry claims to have seen a version of the film in Switzerland in which Rose-of-Sharon breast-feeds a dying man—the novel's ending—but it is doubtful that this version ever existed.

24. Nunnally Johnson, "The Grapes of Wrath" (screenplay), reprinted in *Twenty Best Film Plays*, ed. John Gasser and Dudley Nichols (New York: Crown, 1943), p. 377.

25. Ibid.

26. One would expect to find Bowdon in Ford's next film as a mother, but she seems not to have made any more films with Ford.

Chapter 5. Woody Guthrie and the Dust Bowl Ballads

1. Biographical background is derived mainly from Joe Klein, *Woody Guthrie: A Life* (New York: Alfred A. Knopf, 1980). Woody's own reminiscences about his childhood can be found in his autobiography: *Bound for Glory* (New York: Dutton, 1943); and in several short autobiographical sketches written for various publications such as Alan Lomax, Woody Guthrie, and Pete Seeger, eds., *Hard Hitting Songs for Hard-Hit People* (New York: Oak Publications, 1967); *American Folksong: Woody Guthrie*, ed. Moses Asch (New York: Oak Publications, 1947); and Woody Guthrie, *Pastures of Plenty: A Self-Portrait*, ed. Dave Marsh and Harold Leventhal (New York: HarperCollins, 1990).

2. Gregory, *American Exodus*, p. 41.

3. As quoted in Klein, *Woody Guthrie*, p. 92.

4. During the 1920s and 1930s, radio personalities were often accepted by audiences as acquaintances and friends rather than celebrities. FDR exploited this tendency in his fireside chats, and figures such as Aimee Semple McPherson, Huey Long, and Father Coughlin built their careers on the radio.

5. The recordings took place on March 21, 22, and 27, 1940, at the Department of the Interior studios in Washington, D.C. The majority of these sessions were released in a three-record set in 1965. See *Woody Guthrie: The Library of Congress Recordings* (reissued on Rounder Records). The complete recordings are available at the Archive of Folk Culture in the Library of Congress. Quotes from these recordings are my own transcriptions.

6. Woody Guthrie, *Library of Congress Recordings* (Cambridge, Mass.: Rounder Records, 1988).

7. As quoted in Klein, *Woody Guthrie*, p. 160.

8. Guthrie, *Library of Congress Recordings*.

9. Reprinted in Woody Guthrie, *Woody Sez*, ed. Marjorie Guthrie, Harold Leventhal, Terry Sullivan, and Sheldon Patinkin (New York: Grosset and Dunlap, 1975), p. xix.

10. Woody Guthrie to Alan Lomax, September 19, 1940, Woody Guthrie Manuscript Collection, Archive of Folk Culture, Library of Congress, Washington, D.C.

11. Woody Guthrie, "This Land Is Your Land," original manuscript, Guthrie Manuscript Collection. Reprinted in Guthrie, *Pastures of Plenty*, p. xxiv.

12. These verses appear here as they do in the original manuscript and not as they appear in later printed versions of the song. For the published version of these verses see *Woody Guthrie Songs*, ed. Judy Bell and Nora Guthrie (TRO-Ludlow Music, Inc., 1992), p. 5.

13. Woody Guthrie, reprinted in Klein, *Woody Guthrie*, p. 164.

14. Woody Guthrie, *Dust Bowl Ballads*, liner notes (RCA Victor, 1940), reissued on Rounder Records. Liner notes from the Guthrie Manuscript Collection.

15. Ibid.

16. Ibid.

17. Ibid.

18. Guthrie, *Hard Hitting Songs*, p. 64.

19. Even though Guthrie's ultimate goals envisioned a more radical solution to the migrant problem (landownership as a means of workers' control of production), he supported the FSA's migrant camp program as a first step toward worker control.

Chapter 6. Folklorists and the Migrant

1. Robert Sonkin, "Songs of the Okies," radio broadcast, WNYC, New York, undated, recorded by the Archive of Folk Culture, Library of Congress, Washington, D.C. (my transcription).

2. Johann Gottfried von Herder, *Herder and the Foundations of German Nationalism,* as quoted in Gene Bluestein, *The Voice of the Folk: Folklore and American Literary Theory* (Amherst: University of Massachusetts Press, 1972), p. 6.

3. Ibid., p. 6.

4. Much of this international aspect of Herder's thought has been overlooked in light of the extreme uses of his nationalist ideas in the late nineteenth and early twentieth centuries. The point here is not to establish the credibility of Herder's ideas but to explicate the way in which they formed the basis of a folk ideology in America. Gene Bluestein, in *The Voice of the Folk*, describes this chain of influence from Herder to Emerson and Whitman and argues for the primacy of this folk ideology in American literary theory.

5. Bluestein, *The Voice of the Folk*, p. 10.

6. Ralph Waldo Emerson, "Nature," in *Selections from Ralph Waldo Emerson,* ed. Stephen E. Whicher (Boston: Houghton Mifflin, 1957), pp. 21–22.

7. Ibid., p. 33.

8. Ralph Waldo Emerson, "The American Scholar," in *Selections*, p. 72.

9. Walt Whitman, "A Backward Glance O'er Travel'd Roads" (1888), in *Leaves of Grass and Selected Prose,*, ed. Scully Bradley (New York: Holt, Reinhart and Winston, 1949), p. 479.

10. Walt Whitman, "Democratic Vistas" (1871), in *Leaves of Grass*, p. 491.

11. Ibid., p. 511.

12. Whitman, "A Backward Glance O'er Travel'd Roads," *Leaves of Grass*, p. 487.

13. Herder, as quoted in Bluestein, *The Voice of the Folk*, p. 8.

14. For a clear expression of the Child tradition see the introduction to the one-volume edition of Child's work *The English and Scottish Popular Ballads,* edited and with an introduction by George Lyman Kittredge (Boston, 1904).

15. Lomax specified this definition as "a story in a song, written no one knows when, no one knows where, no one knows by whom, and perhaps, some may think, no one knows 'for why.' " John A. Lomax, "Some Types of American Folk-Song," *Journal of American Folklore* 23 (January–March 1915): 1. The emphasis of this definition is on narrative and communal composition and based on the definition provided by Kittredge.

16. Ibid., p. 2.

17. Ibid., p. 3.

18. Ibid.

19. John A. Lomax and Alan Lomax, *Our Singing Country: A Second Volume of American Ballads and Folk Songs* (New York: Macmillan, 1941), p. ix.

20. Ibid., p. x.

21. Ibid.

22. Ibid., pp. xi, xv.

23. John A. Lomax and Alan Lomax, *Folk Song U.S.A.: The 111 Best American Ballads* (New York: Meredith Press, 1947), p. viii.

24. Ibid.

25. Frederick Jackson Turner, "The Significance of the Frontier in American History," in *The Early Writings of Frederick Jackson Turner* (Madison: University of Wisconsin Press, 1938), p. 187.

26. Ibid., pp. 219–20.

27. Ibid., pp. 227–28.

28. Alan Lomax, *The Folk Songs of North America in the English Language* (Garden City, N.Y.: Doubleday, 1960), p. xvi.

29. Ibid., p. xxi.

30. Ibid., p. xxviii.

31. Ibid., p. xvi.

32. Ibid., p. 428.

33. Ibid., p. 430.

34. Charles L. Todd, "Trampling Out the Vintage," *Common Sense* 8 (July 1939), p. 30. The reference to "those men at the Arvin Camp" refers to the garden homes project of the FSA that supplied small plots of land for migrant workers to grow food for their own consumption in periods of unemployment. These subsistence farms were nothing more than plots to occupy the hands of the laborers whose services were not required year-

round. The title of Todd's article, he claimed, was not a reference to Steinbeck's *Grapes of Wrath* but a mere coincidence. Todd also claimed that as he talked to Okies in the Arvin Camp, Steinbeck was in the camp library researching *The Grapes of Wrath*. Chronologically, this was impossible, and Todd's claims must be considered in the context of oral history, with allowances for memory and elaboration. These assertions were made in an interview Todd gave to archivist Gerald Parsons at the Archive of Folk Culture on August 16, 1985. A tape of this interview is held by the Recorded Sound Division of the Library of Congress, Washington, D.C.

35. Joint Committee on Folk Arts, WPA, "General Instructions," *Folksong Questionnaire* (March 15, 1939), Charles L. Todd/California Migrant Labor Collection, Archive of Folk Culture, Library of Congress, Washington, D.C.

36. Robert Sonkin and Charles L. Todd "Todd-Sonkin Migrant Camp Recordings: Field Notes," Field recordings and notes, Archive of Folk Culture, Library of Congress, Washington, D.C.

37. Ibid.

38. Ibid.

39. "Among Our Contributors," *The American Poet* 1, no. 2 (May 1941): inside cover.

40. Fred W. Ross, "The Least 'Un," *The American Poet* 1, no. 2 (May 1941): 18.

41. Charles L. Todd, interview for the Archive of Folk Culture, Library of Congress, recorded by Margaret Parsons and Gerald Parsons, August 16, 1985. In this interview Todd recounts the time he spent working in the Visalia Camp and recalls an incident in which local authorities were trying to disrupt the camp by causing trouble at the camp dances, so he organized the Okies to surround mischief makers and escort them out of the camp without hurting them. This story, familiar as a scene from Steinbeck's *Grapes of Wrath* and a prominent scene in the film, may have happened to Todd, but other details of those years recounted in the interview contain wrong dates and other misinformation. Nevertheless, the paternalistic attitude of Todd is evident.

42. Charles L. Todd to Gerald Parsons, September 10, 1985, Todd/Migrant Labor Collection.

43. Charles L. Todd to Gerald Parsons, October 16, 1985, Todd/Migrant Labor Collection.

44. No date is given for these broadcasts either on the remaining script for program two or on the tape recording of programs one and three. Quotations from programs one and three are my own transcriptions from recordings held at the Archive of Folk Culture, Library of Congress. Quotations from program two are from the program script in the Todd-Sonkin Manuscript folder accompanying the Todd-Sonkin field recordings.

45. Jack Bryant, "Arizona," recorded by Todd and Sonkin, Firebaugh Camp, Firebaugh, California, August 17, 1940. From the Todd-Sonkin Collection; reprinted in *The American Poet* 1, no. 2 (May 1941): 16–17.

46. "Songs of the Okies," *New York Times,* quoted in "Songs of the Okies," program tape, Todd-Sonkin Collection.

47. Robert Sonkin, "Songs of the Okies," program script, Todd-Sonkin Collection.

48. Ibid.

49. Ibid.

50. Sonkin, "Songs of the Okies," program tape, Todd-Sonkin Collection.

51. Ibid.

52. James N. Gregory, *American Exodus: The Dust Bowl Migration and Okie Culture in California* (New York: Oxford University Press, 1989), p. 233.

53. Sonkin, "Songs of the Okies," program tape, Todd-Sonkin Collection.

54. "Back in the Saddle Again" by Gene Autry and Ray Whitley. Copyright 1939 Western Music Publishing Company; 1964, renewed Gene Autry Publishing Company. Used by permission.

55. Gregory, *American Exodus*, p. 236.

56. Ibid., p. 223.

The Persistence of Dust Bowl Representations

1. Studs Terkel, "We Still See Their Faces," introduction to the fiftieth anniversary edition of John Steinbeck, *The Grapes of Wrath* (New York: Viking, 1989), pp. v, ix.

2. Harold Leventhal, interview included in *A Vision Shared: A Tribute to Woody Guthrie and Leadbelly* (Washington, D.C.: Folkways Records, 1988).

3. Bono, interview in *A Vision Shared*.

4. Bruce Springsteen, interview in *A Vision Shared*.

5. The 1989 video by the rock band Poison for their song "Something to Believe In" contains an image of a homeless mother sitting on the back of a flatbed truck surrounded by her children with a sign that reads: "Will work for food." Her pose and expression are almost identical to those of Lange's *Migrant Mother*, as is the sense of despair.

6. Frank Galati, as quoted in Alan Brinkley, "Why Steinbeck's Okies Speak to Us Today," *New York Times*, March 18, 1990, p. 12.

7. *The Grapes of Wrath*, a new play based on the novel by John Steinbeck, adapted and directed by Frank Galati, produced by the Steppenwolf Theater Company (New York: Cort Theater, 1990); presented by *American Playhouse* (PBS), March 22, 1991.

8. Brinkley, "Why Steinbeck's Okies Speak to Us Today."

9. In the liner notes Springsteen credits John Ford's *Grapes of Wrath* as one of the main sources behind the album's songs.

10. Bruce Springsteen, "The Ghost of Tom Joad," from the compact disc *The Ghost of Tom Joad* (New York: Columbia Records, 1995).

11. Peter Rowan, "Dust Bowl Children," *Dust Bowl Children* (Durham, N.C.: Sugar Hill Records, 1990).

Appendix: A Note on Method

1. James Agee and Walker Evans, *Let Us Now Praise Famous Men*, rev. ed. (Boston: Houghton Mifflin, 1960), p. 189.

2. Ibid., p. 189.

3. Ibid., p. 11.

4. William Stott, *Documentary Expression and Thirties America* (Chicago: University of Chicago Press, 1986), p. 38.

5. Michael E. Staub, *Voices of Persuasion: Politics of Representation in 1930s America* (New York: Cambridge University Press, 1994), p. 34.

6. Agee and Evans, *Let Us Now Praise Famous Men*, p. xiv.

7. Ibid., p. xv.

8. Ibid.

9. Ibid., p. 13.

10. Ibid., p. xv.

11. Ibid., p. 232.

12. Ibid., pp. 233–34.

BIBLIOGRAPHY

Unpublished Primary Sources: Manuscripts and Recordings

Drobish, Harry Everett. Harry Everett Drobish papers (BANC MSS C-B 529).
Bancroft Library, University of California, Berkeley.
Guthrie, Woody. Woody Guthrie Manuscript Collection. Archive of Folk Culture,
Library of Congress, Washington, D.C.
Lange, Dorothea. "Dorothea Lange Interview, May 22, 1964." Conducted by
Richard K. Doud. Archive of American Art, Smithsonian Institution,
Washington, D.C.
———. Dorothea Lange Photograph Collection. Oakland Museum, Oakland,
California.
Records of the Farm Security Administration, Record Group 96. Federal Archives
and Records Administration, San Bruno, California.
Sonkin, Robert. Radio program tapes and scripts. Archive of Folk Culture, Library of
Congress, Washington, D.C.
Sonkin, Robert, and Charles L. Todd. Field recordings and notes. Archive of Folk
Culture, Library of Congress, Washington, D.C.
Stryker, Roy Emerson. Roy Emerson Stryker Manuscript Collection. University of
Louisville Photographic Archives, University of Louisville, Louisville, Kentucky.
Todd, Charles L. Charles L. Todd/California Migrant Labor Collection. Archive of
Folk Culture, Library of Congress, Washington, D.C.
United States Farm Security Administration. Regional Office IX, San Francisco
records, 1936–46 (BANC MSS C-R 1). Bancroft Library, University of
California, Berkeley.
Wood, Irving William. Irving William Wood papers (BANC MSS 77/111c). Bancroft
Library, University of California, Berkeley.

Published Primary Sources: Written, Filmed, and Recorded

Ford, John. *Drums Along the Mohawk.* 20th Century–Fox, 1939.
———. *The Grapes of Wrath.* 20th Century–Fox, 1940.
———. *The Informer.* RKO Radio, 1935.
———. *The Iron Horse.* William Fox, 1924.
———. *Judge Priest.* Fox Film, 1934.
———. *Stagecoach.* Walter Wanger–United Artist, 1939.
———. *Wee Willie Winkie.* 20th Century–Fox, 1937.
———. *Young Mr. Lincoln.* Cosmopolitan/20th Century–Fox, 1939.
Guthrie, Woody. *American Folksong,* ed. Moses Asch. New York: Oak Publications,
1947.

————. *Ballads of Sacco and Vanzetti.* New York: Oak Publications, 1960.

————. *Bound for Glory.* New York: Dutton, 1943.

————. *Born to Win,* ed. Robert Shelton. New York: Collier Books, 1965.

————. *Dust Bowl Ballads.* Cambridge, Mass.: Rounder Records, 1988.

————. *From California to the New York Islands.* New York: The Guthrie Children's Trust Fund, 1958.

————. *The Library of Congress Recordings.* Cambridge, Mass.: Rounder Records, 1988.

————. *Pastures of Plenty: A Self-Portrait,* ed. Dave Marsh and Harold Leventhal. New York: HarperCollins, 1990.

————. *Seeds of Man.* New York: Dutton, 1976.

————. *Woody Sez,* ed. Marjorie Guthrie, Harold Leventhal, Terry Sullivan, and Sheldon Patinkin. New York: Grosset and Dunlap, 1975.

Lange, Dorothea. "The Assignment I'll Never Forget." *Popular Photography* 46, no. 2 (February 1960): 42, 128.

————. "Documentary Photography." In *Photographers on Photography,* ed. Nathan Lyons. Englewood Cliffs, N.J.: Prentice-Hall in collaboration with the George Eastman House, Rochester, New York, 1966, pp. 67–68.

————. *Dorothea Lange: Farm Security Administration Photographs, 1935–1939,* 2 vols. Glencoe, Ill.: Text-Fiche Press, 1980.

————. *Dorothea Lange: The Making of a Documentary Photographer,* an interview conducted in 1968 by Suzanne Riess, Regional Oral History Office, The Bancroft Library, University of California, Berkeley, 1968. Courtesy of the Bancroft Library.

————. "Draggin' around People." *Survey Graphic* 25, no. 9 (March 1936): 524–25.

————. "Pea-Pickers' Child," written under pseudonym "Lucretia Penny." *Survey Graphic* 24, no. 7 (July 1935): 352–53.

————. *Photographs of a Lifetime.* New York: Aperture, 1982.

Lange, Dorothea, and Daniel Dixon. "Photographing the Familiar." *Aperture* 1, no. 2 (1950): 4–15, reprinted in *Photographers on Photography,* ed. Nathan Lyons. Englewood Cliffs, N.J.: Prentice-Hall in collaboration with the George Eastman House, Rochester, New York, 1966, pp. 68–72.

Lange, Dorothea, and Paul Taylor. *An American Exodus: A Record of Human Erosion.* New York: Reynal and Hitchcock, 1939. Reprint, New Haven: Yale University Press, 1969.

Steinbeck, John. "Dubious Battle in California." *The Nation,* September 12, 1936, pp. 302–4.

————. *The Grapes of Wrath.* New York: Viking, 1939, 1989.

————. *The Harvest Gypsies: On the Road to the Grapes of Wrath.* Berkeley: Heyday Books, 1936.

————. *In Dubious Battle.* New York: Covici, Friede, 1936.

————. *The Log from the Sea of Cortez.* New York: Viking, 1941.

————. *The Long Valley.* New York: Viking, 1938.

————. *Of Mice and Men.* New York: Covici, Friede, 1937.

————. *The Pastures of Heaven.* New York: Viking, 1932.

———. *To a God Unknown.* New York: Robert O. Ballou, 1933.

———. *Tortilla Flat.* New York: Covici, Friede, 1935.

———. *Working Days: The Journals of The Grapes of Wrath.* Edited by Robert DeMott. New York: Viking, 1989.

Secondary Literature

Adamic, Louis. "Twentieth Century Troubadour." *Saturday Review of Literature,* April 17, 1943, p. 14.

Agee, James, and Evans, Walker. *Let Us Now Praise Famous Men.* Rev. ed. Boston: Houghton Mifflin, 1960.

Anderson, Lindsay. *About John Ford.* London: Plexus, 1981.

Astro, Richard. *John Steinbeck and Edward F. Ricketts: The Shaping of a Novelist.* Minneapolis: University of Minnesota Press, 1973.

Baldwin, Sidney. *Poverty and Politics: The Rise and Decline of the Farm Security Administration.* Chapel Hill: University of North Carolina Press, 1968.

Baxter, John. *The Cinema of John Ford.* New York: A. S. Barnes, 1971.

Beja, Morris. *Film and Literature.* New York: Longman, 1979.

Benson, Jackson J. " 'To Tom Who Lived It': John Steinbeck and the Man from Weedpatch." *Journal of Modern Literature* 5 (April 1976): 151–224.

———. *The True Adventures of John Steinbeck, Writer.* New York: Viking, 1984.

Blackford, Mansel G. *The Politics of Business in California, 1890–1920.* Columbus: Ohio State University Press, 1977.

Bluestein, Gene. *The Voice of the Folk: Folklore and American Literary Theory.* Amherst: University of Massachusetts Press, 1972.

Bluestone, George. *Novels into Film.* Berkeley: University of California Press, 1971.

Bogdanovich, Peter. *John Ford.* Berkeley: University of California Press, 1968.

Bohlman, Philip V. *The Study of Folk Music in the Modern World.* Bloomington: University of Indiana Press, 1988.

Bonnifield, Paul. *The Dust Bowl: Men, Dirt, and Depression.* Albuquerque: University of New Mexico Press, 1979.

Burbank, Garin. *When Farmers Voted Red: The Gospel of Socialism in the Oklahoma Countryside, 1910–1924.* Westport, Conn.: Greenwood Press, 1976.

Caughie, John, ed. *Theories of Authorship.* Boston: Routledge and Kegan Paul, 1981.

Collins, Thomas A. "From Bringing in the Sheaves by 'Windsor Drake.' " *Journal of Modern Literature* 5 (April 1976): 225–30.

Creisler, Lillian. " 'Little Oklahoma' or the Airport Community: A Study of the Social and Economic Adjustment of Self-Settled Agricultural Drought and Depression Refugees." Master's thesis, University of California, Berkeley, 1940.

Curtis, James C. "Dorthea Lange, Migrant Mother, and the Culture of the Great Depression." *Winterthur Portfolio* 21, no. 1 (1986): 1–20.

———. *Mind's Eye, Mind's Truth: FSA Photography Reconsidered.* Philadelphia: Temple University Press, 1989.

Daniel, Cletus E. *Bitter Harvest: A History of California Farmworkers, 1870–1941.* Ithaca, N.Y.: Cornell University Press, 1981.

Davis, Robert. *Steinbeck: A Collection of Critical Essays.* Englewood Cliffs, N.J.: Prentice-Hall, 1972.

DeMott, Robert. *Steinbeck's Reading: A Catalog of Books Owned and Borrowed.* New York: Garland, 1984.

Dempsey, Michael. "John Ford: A Reassessment." *Film Quarterly* 29 (Summer 1975): 2–15.

DeTurk, David A., and A. Poulin, eds. *The American Folk Scene: Dimensions of the Folksong Revival.* New York: Dell, 1967.

Dubofsky, Melvin, and Stephen Burwood, eds. *Agriculture during the Great Depression.* New York: Garland, 1990.

Emerson, Ralph Waldo. "Nature" and "The American Scholar." In *Selections from Ralph Waldo Emerson: An Organic Anthology,* edited by Stephen E. Whicher. Boston: Houghton Mifflin, 1957.

Fensch, Thomas, ed. *Conversations with John Steinbeck.* Jackson: University of Mississippi Press, 1988.

Fine, Richard. *Hollywood and the Profession of Authorship, 1928–1940.* Ann Arbor, Mich.: UMI Research Press, 1985.

Fleischhauer, Carl, and Beverly W. Brannan, eds. *Documenting America: 1935–1943.* Berkeley: University of California Press, 1988.

Fontenrose, Joseph. *John Steinbeck: An Introduction and Interpretation.* New York: Barnes and Noble, 1963.

Ford, Dan. *Pappy: The Life of John Ford.* Englewood Cliffs, N.J.: Prentice-Hall, 1979.

Ford, John. "Veteran Producer Muses." In *Hollywood Directors, 1914–1940,* edited by Richard Koszarski, pp. 199–204. New York: Oxford University Press, 1976.

French, Warren, ed. *A Companion to The Grapes of Wrath.* New York: Penguin, 1963.

———. *Filmguide to The Grapes of Wrath.* Bloomington: Indiana University Press, 1973.

———. *John Steinbeck.* Boston: Twayne, 1975.

Gallagher, Tag. *John Ford: The Man and His Films.* Berkeley: University of California Press, 1986.

Gomery, Douglas. *The Hollywood Studio System.* New York: St. Martin's, 1986.

Green, James R. *Grass-Roots Socialism: Radical Movements in the Southwest, 1895–1943.* Baton Rouge: Louisiana State University Press, 1978.

Greenway, John. *American Folksongs of Protest.* New York: A. S. Barnes, 1953.

———. "Woodrow Wilson Guthrie (1912–1967)." *Journal of American Folklore* 81 (1968): 62–64.

———. "Woody Guthrie: The Man, the Land, the Understanding." *American West* 3, no. 4 (Fall 1966): 25–30, 74–78.

Gregory, James Noble. *American Exodus: The Dust Bowl Migration and Okie Culture in California.* New York: Oxford University Press, 1989.

Guimond, James. *American Photography and the American Dream.* Chapel Hill: University of North Carolina Press, 1991.

Gussow, Mel. *Don't Say Yes Until I Finish Talking: A Biography of Darryl F. Zanuck.* Garden City, N.Y.: Doubleday, 1971.

Guthrie, Majorie, and Harold Leventhal. eds. *The Woody Guthrie Songbook.* New York: Grosset and Dunlap, 1976.

Hampton, Wayne. *Guerrilla Minstrels: John Lennon, Joe Hill, Woody Guthrie, Bob Dylan.* Knoxville: University of Tennessee Press, 1986.

Havens, A. Eugene, with Gregory Hooks, Patrick H. Mooney, and Max J. Pfeffer, eds. *Studies in the Transformation of U.S. Agriculture.* Boulder, Colo.: Westview Press, 1986.

Hurley, F. Jack. *Portrait of a Decade: Roy Stryker and the Development of Documentary Photography in the Thirties.* Baton Rouge: Louisiana State University Press, 1972.

Hurt, R. Douglas. *The Dust Bowl: An Agricultural and Social History.* Chicago: Nelson-Hall, 1981.

Hutchison, Claude B., ed. *California Agriculture.* Berkeley: University of California Press, 1946.

Jackson, Bruce, ed. *Folklore and Society.* Hatburo, Penn.: Folklore Associates, 1966.

Jelinek, Laurence J. *Harvest Empire: A History of California Agriculture.* 2d ed. San Francisco: Boyd and Fraser, 1982.

Johnson, Nunnally. "The Grapes of Wrath" (screenplay). In *Twenty Best Film Plays,* edited by John Gasser and Dudley Nichols. New York: Crown, 1943.

———. "Will 'The Grapes of Wrath' Be Shelved?" *Photoplay* (November 1939), reprinted in *The Talkies: Articles and Illustrations from a Great Fan Magazine, 1928–1940,* edited by Richard Griffith, pp. 260–61, 320. New York: Dover, 1971.

Kiernan, Thomas. *The Intricate Music: A Biography of John Steinbeck.* Boston: Little, Brown, 1979.

Klein, Joe. *Woody Guthrie: A Life.* New York: Alfred A. Knopf, 1980.

Koszarski, Richard. "John Ford (1985–1973)." In *Hollywood Directors, 1914–1940.* New York: Oxford University Press, 1976.

Kozol, Wendy. "Madonnas of the Fields: Photography, Gender, and 1930s Farm Relief." *Genders,* no. 2 (Summer 1988): 1–23.

Lampell, Millard, ed. *A Tribute to Woody Guthrie.* New York: Woody Guthrie Publications, 1972.

Lisca, Peter. *The Wide World of John Steinbeck.* New Brunswick, N.J.: Rutgers University Press, 1958.

———. *John Steinbeck: Nature and Myth.* New York: Thomas Y. Crowell, 1978.

———, ed. *The Grapes of Wrath: Text and Criticism.* New York: Viking, 1972.

Lofaro, Michael A., ed. *James Agee: Reconsiderations.* Knoxville: University of Tennessee Press, 1992.

Lomax, Alan. *The Folk Songs of North America in the English Language.* Garden City, N.Y.: Doubleday, 1960.

Lomax, Alan, Woody Guthrie, and Pete Seeger. eds. *Hard Hitting Songs for Hard-Hit People.* New York: Oak Publications, 1967.

Lomax, John A. "Some Types of American Folk-Song." *Journal of American Folklore* 23 (January–March 1915): 1–17.

Lomax, John A., and Alan Lomax. *Folk Song U.S.A.: The 111 Best American Ballads.* New York: Meredith Press, 1947.

———. *Our Singing Country: A Second Volume of American Ballads and Folk Songs.* New York: Macmillan, 1941.

Majka, Linda C., and Theo J. Majka. *Farm Workers, Agribusiness, and the State.* Philadelphia: Temple University Press, 1982.

May, Lary. *Screening Out the Past: The Birth of Mass Culture and the Motion Picture Industry.* Chicago: University of Chicago Press, 1980.

McBride, Joseph, and Michael Wilmington. *John Ford.* New York: De Capo Press, 1975.

McWilliams, Carey. *Factories in the Field.* Boston: Little, Brown, 1939.

———. *Ill Fares the Land: Migrants and Migratory Labor in the U.S.* Boston: Little, Brown, 1942.

Meltzer, Milton. *Dorothea Lange: A Photographer's Life.* New York: Farrar, Straus and Giroux, 1978.

Miller, Terry E. *Folk Music in America: A Reference Guide.* New York: Garland, 1986.

Millichap, Joseph. *Steinbeck and Film.* New York: Frederick Unger, 1983.

Mitchell, George J. "Ford on Ford." *Films in Review,* 15 (June–July 1964): 321–32.

Morgan, Dan. *Rising in the West: The True Story of an "Okie" Family from the Great Depression through the Reagan Years.* New York: Alfred A. Knopf, 1992.

Ohrn, Karin Becker. *Dorothea Lange and the Documentary Tradition.* Baton Rouge: Louisiana State University Press, 1980.

Olmstead, Alan L., and Paul Rhode. "An Overview of California Agricultural Mechanization, 1870–1930." *Agricultural History* 62, no. 3 (1988): 86–112.

Owens, Louis. *The Grapes of Wrath: Trouble in the Promised Land.* Boston: Twayne, 1989.

Place, J. A. *The Non-Western Films of John Ford.* New York: Citadel, 1979.

Puckett, John Rogers. *Five Photo-Textual Documentaries from the Great Depression.* Ann Arbor, Mich.: UMI Research Press, 1984.

Putnam, Jackson K. *Modern California Politics.* 2d ed. San Francisco: Boyd and Fraser, 1984.

Reed, Joseph W. *Three American Originals: John Ford, William Faulkner, and Charles Ives.* Middletown, Conn.: Wesleyan University Press, 1984.

Reuss, Richard A. *A Woody Guthrie Bibliography 1912–1967.* New York: The Guthrie Children's Trust Fund, 1968.

———. "Woody Guthrie and His Folk Tradition." *Journal of American Folklore* 83, no. 329 (July–September 1970): 273–303.

Robbin, Edward. *Woody Guthrie and Me: An Intimate Reminiscence.* Berkeley, Calif.: Lancaster-Miller, 1979.

Rodnitzky, J. L. "The Mythology of Woody Guthrie." *Popular Music and Society* 2–3 (Spring 1973): 227–43.

Rowell, Edward J. "Drought Refugee and Labor Migration to California in 1936." *Monthly Labor Review* 43, no. 6 (December 1936): 1355–63.

Sarris, Andrew. "John Ford." In *The American Cinema.* New York: Dutton, 1968.

———. *The John Ford Movie Mystery.* Bloomington: Indiana University Press, 1975.

————, ed. *Interviews with Film Directors.* New York: Bobbs-Merrill, 1967.

Seeger, Pete, ed. *Woody Guthrie Folk Songs.* New York: Ludlow Music, 1963.

Sinclair, Andrew. *John Ford.* New York: Dial Press/James Wade, 1979.

Siska, William. "Realism and Romance in the Films of John Ford." *Wide Angle,* no. 4 (1978): 8–13.

St. Pierre, Brian. *John Steinbeck: The California Years.* San Fransisco: Chronicle Books, 1983.

Stanley, Jerry. "Children of the Grapes of Wrath." *American West* 23 (March/April 1986): 22–28.

Starr, Kevin. *Americans and the California Dream, 1850–1915.* New York: Oxford University Press, 1973.

————. *Endangered Dreams: The Great Depression in California.* New York: Oxford University Press, 1996.

————. *Inventing the Dream: California Through the Progressive Era.* New York: Oxford University Press, 1985.

————. *Material Dreams: Southern California Through the 1920s.* New York: Oxford University Press, 1990.

Staub, Michael E. *Voices of Persuasion: Politics of Representation in 1930s America.* New York: Cambridge University Press, 1994.

Stein, Walter J. *California and the Dust Bowl Migration.* Westport, Conn.: Greenwood Press, 1973.

Steinbeck, Elaine, and Robert Wallsten. *Steinbeck: A Life in Letters.* New York: Viking, 1975.

Stock, Catherine McNicol. *Main Street in Crisis: The Great Depression and the Old Middle Class on the Northern Plains.* Chapel Hill: University of North Carolina Press, 1992.

Stott, William. *Documentary Expression and Thirties America.* Chicago: University of Chicago Press, 1986.

Stowell, Peter. *John Ford.* Boston: Twayne, 1986.

Taylor, Paul S. "Foundations of California Rural Society." *California Historical Society Quarterly* 24 (September 1945): 193–228.

————. "Migrant Mother: 1936." *American West* 7 (May 1970): 41–47.

————. "Migratory Farm Labor in the United States." *Monthly Labor Review* 44, no. 3 (March 1937): 537–49.

————. *On the Ground in the Thirties.* Salt Lake City: Peregrine Smith Books, 1983.

Taylor, Paul S., and Edward J. Rowell. "Patterns of Agricultural Labor Migration within California." *Monthly Labor Review* 47, no. 5 (November 1938): 980–90.

————. "Refugee Labor Migration to California, 1937." *Monthly Labor Review* 47, no. 2 (August 1938): 240–50.

Taylor, Paul S., and Tom Vasey. "Drought Refugee and Labor Migration to California, June–December 1935." *Monthly Labor Review* 42, no. 2 (February 1936): 312–18.

————. "Historical Background of California Farm Labor." *Rural Sociology* 1 (September 1936): 281–95.

Thomas, Bob, ed. *Directors in Action.* New York: Bobbs-Merrill, 1973.

Todd, Charles L. "Trampling Out the Vintage." *Common Sense* 8 (July 1939): 7–8, 30.

Tolles, N. A. "A Survey of Labor Migration between States." *Monthly Labor Review* 45, no. 1 (July 1937): 3–16.

Valjean, Nelson. *John Steinbeck, The Errant Knight: An Intimate Biography of His California Years.* San Francisco: Chronicle Books, 1975.

Vassel, Jacques. *Electric Children: Roots and Branches of Modern Folkrock.* New York: Taplinger, 1976.

Weber, Devra. *Dark Sweat, White Gold: California Farm Workers, Cotton, and the New Deal.* Berkeley: University of California Press, 1994.

Weiss, Margaret R. "Recording Life-in-Process." *Saturday Review,* March 5, 1966, pp. 50–51.

Whitman, Walt. "A Backward Glance O'er Travel'd Roads," and "Democratic Vistas." From *Leaves of Grass and Selected Prose.* New York: Holt, Rinehart and Winston, 1949.

Wilson, James Bright. "Social Attitudes of Certain Migratory Agricultural Workers in Kern County, California." Master's thesis, University of Southern California, 1942.

Worster, Donald. *Dust Bowl: The Southern Plains in the 1930's.* New York: Oxford University Press, 1979.

Wyatt, David, ed. *New Essays on The Grapes of Wrath.* New York: Cambridge University Press, 1990.

Yurchenco, Henrietta. *A Mighty Hard Road.* New York: McGraw-Hill, 1970.

INDEX